The Nature Gardens of
SEBASTIAN KNEIPP

Hans Horst Fröhlich

Sterling Publishing Co., Inc.
New York

In memory of Senator H. C. Luitpold Leusser

Library of Congress Cataloging-in-Publication Data Available

10 9 8 7 6 5 4 3 2 1

Published by Sterling Publishing Company, Inc.
387 Park Avenue South, New York, N.Y. 10016
First published in Germany and © 1997 by Heirich Hugendubel Verlag, Munich
under the title *Der Naturgarten des Sebastian Kneipp*
English translation © 2000 by Sterling Publishing Co., Inc.
Distributed in Canada by Sterling Publishing
C/o Canadian Manda Group, One Atlantic Avenue, Suite 105
Toronto, Ontario, Canada M6K 3E7
Distributed in Great Britain and Europe by Cassell PLC
Wellington House, 125 Strand, London WC2R 0BB, England
Distributed in Australia by Capricorn Link (Australia) Pty Ltd.
P.O. Box 6651, Baulkham Hills, Business Centre, NSW 2153, Australia
Printed in Hong Kong
All rights reserved

Sterling ISBN 0-8069-5797-2

Self-treatment must always be performed responsibly:
❖ Anyone under medical treatment must first speak with his or her physician before initiating a supportive therapy using medicinal herbs. In no case should a medication prescribed by a physician be discontinued without first receiving a physician's authorization.
❖ A physician should by all means be contacted in cases where new symptoms develop or where symptoms of long duration are noted. Self-treatment with medicinal herbs is not suitable for acute or emergency medicine or for the treatment of chronic illnesses.
❖ In using medicinal herbs, the accompanying information on the label must always be regarded carefully. The warning to contact your physician or a pharmacist should any adverse symptoms be observed is also applicable when it comes to natural remedies.

CONTENTS

SEBASTIAN KNEIPP'S NATURAL GARDEN FOR
HARMONY OF BODY, MIND, AND SOUL 5

SEBASTIAN KNEIPP'S TREASURY OF PLANTS
AND HERBS
Color Photographs, Text, and Tables......................9

MEDICINAL TEAS
Composition, Preparation, and Applications 165

PURIFYING THE BODY AND REVIVING
THE SPIRIT
Medicinal Herbs for a "Spring Cure"...................168

WHEN COLD SEASON HITS
*Medicinal Herbs for Head Colds, Coughs, and
Hoarseness* 170

WHEN INFLUENZA IS RAMPANT!
*Medicinal Herbs for the Flu and as a
Prophylactic Measure*....................................173

JOINT OR MUSCLE PAIN?
*Medicinal Herbs for the Relief of Rheumatic
Complaints*.......................................176

OH, MY ACHING STOMACH!
Medicinal Herbs for Acute Stomach Problems.......179

WHEN HEARTBURN IS A WAY OF LIFE
Medicinal Herbs for Chronic Gastric Disorders 180

FOR THAT UNCOMFORTABLE BLOATED FEELING
*Medicinal Herbs to Reduce Flatulence and a
Feeling of Fullness* 183

ALTERNATIVES TO TRADITIONAL LAXATIVES
*Medicinal Herbs for Constipation and
Sluggishness of the Bowels*...............................185

NATURAL BINDING AGENTS
Medicinal Herbs for Mild Cases of Diarrhea 187

WHEN PAINFUL COLICS THREATEN
*Medicinal Herbs for Gallbladder and Liver
Conditions*..189

STRENGTHENING YOUR HEART
Medicinal Herbs for Cardiovascular Disorders.....192

INSTEAD OF SLEEPING PILLS AND
TRANQUILIZERS
*Medicinal Herbs for Insomnia, Nervousness,
and Depression* 95

BENEFICIAL "BLADDER AND KIDNEY TEAS"
*Medicinal Herbs for Bladder Disorders and
Kidney Ailments* 198

TROUBLED BY FREQUENT URINATION?
*Medicinal Herbs for a Nervous Bladder
and Prostate Problems* 200

SELF-TREATMENT FOR "TIRED LEGS"
Medicinal Herbs for Venous Disorders.................202

IMPROVING THE QUALITY OF YOUR
"SUNSET YEARS"
Medicinal Herbs for Geriatric Complaints............204

CHILDREN ARE NOT "LITTLE ADULTS"
Medicinal Herbs for Babies and Children 207

BATHE YOURSELF TO HEALTH
Medicinal Herbs as Bath Additives 209

GUIDE TO APPROXIMATE EQUIVALENTS 212

Tabular Information for the Plants in "Sebastian Kneipp's Treasury of Plants and Herbs"

1. Common name(s) of the plant
2. Name of the plant in Latin (genus and species names)
3. Family
4. Blossom time (months specified with Roman numerals)
5. Part of the plant used medicinally
6. Mode of administration
7. Contents (active components)
8. Therapeutic effects (indications)
    (M) = according to the monographs on the plant
    (F) = in folk medicine
9. Special information

Warning!

Poisonous plants are also covered in this book and should never be employed for self-treatment. Collect plants yourself only if you are certain that you can classify them correctly. Should you have any doubts about particular plants, no matter how slight, do not use them!

SEBASTIAN KNEIPP'S NATURAL GARDEN
FOR HARMONY OF BODY, MIND, AND SOUL

From food to fibers, there seems to be a trend today toward everything "natural." This is especially true when it comes to our health, making people more curious than ever about natural remedies. Therefore, it's not surprising to see a resurgence of interest in the science of health derived from the Bavarian parish priest Sebastian Kneipp (1821–1897) as a component of holistic natural medicine.

As a young man, Sebastian Kneipp suffered from pulmonary tuberculosis, a disease that during the nineteenth century was treated inadequately with only fresh air. In his search for a more effective therapy, Kneipp, in the midst of his studies, discovered a book by Johann Siegmund Hahn (1696–1773) entitled *Instructions on the Wonderful Curative Powers of Fresh Water,* published in 1737. This book would eventually prove to save his life.

Brief immersions in the cold waters of the Danube during the winter stimulated the self-healing powers of Kneipp's body to such an extent that he was able to overcome the illness threatening his life. As a result of his own experience, Kneipp developed a number of applications for water in the form of baths, ablutions, wraps, and affusions based on the belief that alternating warm and cold water creates a physical stimulus with powerful effects.

In 1855, Kneipp was appointed priest of the Dominican monastery in Bad Wörishofen, then a small town at the foot of the Bavarian Alps. There, he refined his hydrotherapy treatments and soon became world-renowned as a "water doctor." Kneipp's reputation brought numerous visitors and patients—the rich, the poor, rulers and aristocrats, farmers and workers—to the health resort in Bad Wörishofen. He was able to help many people, and as a result the town grew and became famous.

In 1886, Kneipp published his experiences in a book titled *My Water Cure.* This book, whose intention was to discourage patients from streaming to Bad Wörishofen, resulted in exactly the opposite. With sixty-six different editions from 1886 to 1997, *My Water Cure* has been translated into many languages (in 1890, the English version appeared in

London) and even became a best-seller. The book includes successful natural procedures with practical instructions for remaining healthy and preventing illnesses. Kneipp divided the book into three sections: First he described numerous types of hydrotherapy, next he recommended the contents of the household medicine cabinet, and finally he listed disorders that could be treated successfully using his methods.

In the section dealing with the household medicine cabinet, Kneipp described more than sixty different herbs, as well as animal and mineral agents, with their preparations, effects, and types of application. The benefits and lack of adverse effects of many of these medicinal herbs have been verified by modern scientists, and most are still used successfully today.

Herbal Traditions

Sebastian Kneipp's knowledge of plants is based on ancient traditions. Throughout history, people have collected and tested herbs and then employed them effectively in the treatment of specific illnesses. As early as 3000 B.C. in Egypt, there were already schools of herbal lore. The papyrus of Ebers (2000 B.C.) described the symptoms of various illnesses and their treatment using agents derived from eighty-five different plants, including mint, gentian, and poppy. Around 2800 B.C., Pen Tsao of Shan Xian listed the plant remedies that were used at that time in China. Ayurvedic

5

medicine, founded more than 5,000 years ago in India, combines science, religion, and philosophy, and its aim has to do with increasing well-being for health and longevity. After purifying the body from poisonous substances, plant and mineral agents are prescribed and recommendations are made for the individual's diet and way of life. In traditional Chinese medicine, which dates back to as early as 2000 B.C., the body is viewed as a microcosm within a macrocosm. The continuous interplay in the body can be balanced through a combination of nutrition, herbal medicine, acupuncture, and acupressure. The herbal therapies of the indigenous peoples of North and South America have their roots in shamanic traditions. Plants were indeed used because of their healing properties against physical illnesses. But they were valued primarily for their curative powers in the event of an imbalance in the mind, the senses, or the soul.

In Europe, the origin of phytotherapy (the use of vegetable drugs in medicine) can be traced back to the physicians of ancient Greece. Hippocrates (468–377 B.C.), considered the father of Western medicine, made use of 400 herbs and stressed the importance of fresh air, movement, and balanced nutrition for good health. Theophrastus (372–286 B.C.) and Galen (A.D. 131–201) wrote books on herbs, making use of the Greek knowledge of herbal therapies and the herbal traditions of the Egyptians. The famous treatise compiled by Dioscorides (first century A.D.), *De Materia Medica,* represented the most important source of herbal knowledge for more than 1,500 years. The Roman armies, who used aromatic herbs in their bathing rituals, ensured that many plants, as well as knowledge about their effects, were spread throughout Europe.

Later, during the Middle Ages, this knowledge was upheld and passed on to posterity through Christian monasteries that grew herb and flower gardens. With the beginning of the Renaissance, the era of herbal books began. As with the *New Book of Herbs* by Leonard Fuchs (a renowned physician and botanist, 1501–1566), these books were decorated with ornate botanical figures. More and more herbs and spices from Asia and America were included as well.

But then the general picture began to change. Aside from vegetable drugs, the *Pharmacopoeia* of Paracelsus (1493–1541) contained animal and mineral medicines.

Through his teaching, Paracelsus also initiated an abandonment of the holistic approach in the treatment of illness. His new approach was supported by the earlier discovery that synthetic agents could be used to influence and control illnesses and epidemics. Thus, phytotherapy became less important.

Sebastian Kneipp is credited with rediscovering medicinal herbs and bringing the era of time-tested plants from European herbal traditions into restored favor. In his view, "The Lord did not let herbs grow without a purpose. He wanted us to learn to use them in order to impede, alleviate, and heal the ills and diseases that are rampant during our existence." Sebastian Kneipp's mother had handed down to him traditional means of self-treatment with medicinal herbs and household remedies. He later expanded his knowledge of plants through his observations of nature and by studying the older herb books and herbariums.

The Kneipp System

Especially important during this time were Kneipp's meetings with the Würzburger pharmacist Leonhard Oberhäußer, who later founded with him the Kneipp-Werke. Together, they continued investigating traditional and folk medicine, testing, improving, and refining the applications. Their findings would be the basis for Kneipp bath additives, plant juices, teas, tonics, coated vegetable tablets, and ointments. Oberhäußer agreed to put his friend's name and picture on the medication that they had developed together, and the brand name Kneipp subsequently came into being. Today, in its modern manufacturing plants with production in accord with the latest scientific standards, the fourth generation of Kneipp-Werke is now producing bath additives, natural remedies, and supplements.

Many of the medicinal herbs that Kneipp himself discovered—anti-inflammatory arnica, gastric tonic centaury, curative chamomile, cardiotonic hawthorn, disinfectant sage, and nerve-strengthening common Saint-John's-wort, for example—still grow today in Europe's alpine regions. In Bavaria, such agents undergo a controlled cultivation as phytotherapeutics. Following stringent quality-control standards, they are then manufactured as Kneipp products.

The town of Bad Wörishofen, which was already famous during the nineteenth century, has now become a world-renowned health resort with more than 200 spas, private hotels, sanitariums, and health centers. There each year, as many as 80,000 guests take advantage of the pleasant preventive and curative effects of Kneipp's hygienics. And in more than 660 clubs of the Kneipp Society, the 160,000 Kneipp supporters represent the largest group of individuals active in the European health movement.

Today, "Kneippism" has become a way of life for many people. This healthful lifestyle makes use of warm and cold water, fresh air, sunlight, and herbs, along with diet and exercise, to nurture and strengthen the mind, soul, and body. Kneipp believed that if our mode of life can have a detrimental effect on our health, then a change in this mode of life can restore it.

Kneipp's holistic science of health is based on five elements:

Comforting and strengthening hydrotherapies. With these therapies, water serves as a mediator for temperature stimuli, which cause reactions in the blood vessels, the metabolic system, and the musculature. As a consequence, circulation improves, blood is "purified," and an overall feeling of relaxation is experienced. There is also a toughening up of the body. We develop stronger powers of resistance, reducing our susceptibility to infection. The most simple forms of hydrotherapy involve walking barefoot in the early-morning dew, treading water in a brook, stream, or bathtub, jogging in the snow, taking immersion baths after a sauna, and washing ourselves following athletic activities. In "Kneippism," these simple applications that everyone can perform at home are refined to include more than a hundred variations in the form of baths, affusions, ablutions, wraps, and packs.

Medicinal herbs. Medicinal herbs used in bath additives, teas, plant juices, herbal tablets, and ointments offer a broad spectrum of effects. Because they are tolerated well and generally free of adverse effects, they are especially suitable for long-term use. Herbs are employed to build up the defense mechanisms of the body, diminish risk factors, strengthen organ functions, treat certain disorders and feelings of ill-health, and alleviate many geriatric complaints. We are familiar with their use from our knowledge of traditional and folk medicine of various peoples, and evidence of their efficacy has been demonstrated through modern scientific research. For example, it has been proven that essential oils added to bathwater penetrate through the skin, where they enter the bloodstream and can unfold their calming or stimulating effects on the body.

Movement that is fun. A combination of exertion and rest is essential for well-being. It's up to each of us to decide whether a regular routine of fitness training or some type of sport best suits our physical constitution, age, and condition. Activities like swimming, fast walking, bicycling, tennis, and golf train the heart and circulatory system as well as normalize the body's metabolism. Physical activity also increases mental efficiency, while promoting mental and psychological relaxation. Supportive measures include different forms of massage, gymnastics, and stretching.

Healthful nutrients that taste good. A well-balanced and varied diet should meet all of our calorie and nutrition needs. The best choices are fresh, natural, high-quality foods that are rich in vitamins and low in fat and sugar. It's best to avoid coffee, tea, alcohol, and tobacco—or to use them only in moderation—and stay away from short-term, unbalanced, or fad diets. Regularly eating food that tastes good and supplies the body with vital vitamins, minerals, trace elements, and dietary fibers is the key to health.

Lifestyle—the harmony of body, mind, and soul. As a priest, Sebastian Kneipp was already aware that equanimity of the soul is a prerequisite for physical well-being. The body-mind balance is a central element in his health system. Kneipp believed that an active way of life leads to harmony of body, mind, and soul. But it was also his view that what constitutes an active way of life is up to the individual. In this personal approach to health, reading, painting, music, writing, and hobbies are just as important as physical exercise, and meditation, prayer, relaxation exercises, yoga, qigong, and tai chi are equally valid.

≥∙ ≥∙ ≥∙ ≥∙ ≥∙

With this book, I invite you to participate in an exciting journey through nature, as I present Sebastian Kneipp's treasury of plants and herbs. In putting together the book, my equipment basically consisted of a bicycle and a camera. A basis for my many excursions through Kneipp's native Bavaria was the flora described by the frequent resort visitor Julius Rosenberg, who named more than 350 flowers, herbs, trees, and bushes in and around Bad Wörishofen in 1929. Over the course of one year, I explored the fields and pastures around Kneipp's hometown on my bicycle and collected more than a thousand slides of the flora growing there as captured with my camera. In this way, a "photographic herbarium" came into being, with which I have been able to prove that there are just as many types of plant in Kneipp's area now as there were during his day, contrary to popular belief.

Because I never picked the plants in these meadows, pastures, forests, and clearings, but merely shot them with my camera, nature lovers and hunters were willing to provide me with numerous tips for locating certain sites. That is how I found the magnificent Turk's-cap lily (Martagon lily), the mysterious columbines, the splendid pasque flower, and a colorful collection of different types of foxglove. I spotted a number of flowers that were presumed to be extinct, like the Venus's looking-glass. A newly sown field of spelt proved to be the ideal ecological environment for many plants. The flowers there seemed to be especially healthy, blossoming anew.

I urge you to open your eyes and your soul to the curative powers of nature. Never neglect to see the beauty of nature and of the flowers and plants growing around you. As a Finnish saying goes, "Every weed is a flower for the cheerful, and every flower a weed for the sorrowful."

This book is an homage to Sebastian Kneipp, who encouraged the spontaneous healing powers that are found in each of us. As the founder of a scientifically recognized naturopathic method during the nineteenth century, he was well before his time and ever open to new knowledge and plants from all parts of the world. "With every step we make in God's glorious nature," he affirmed, "we encounter new plants again and again that prove to be highly useful and healthy for us."

Nowadays, treatments such as phytotherapy are an integral part of scientific medicine, and many traditional medicinal herbs are scientifically recognized as medicinal plants. The teas and other natural remedies recommended in this book have been verified through experience and scientific studies. They are highly effective as preventive measures and helpful for the self-treatment of many disorders if used carefully and responsibly.

Dr. Hans Horst Fröhlich

Spring

After the short but often lovely days of winter in the Algau region, the warming rays of the spring sun are welcomed by all. In March, among the first harbingers of spring is the **spring snowflake** (*Leucojum vernum*). This fragrant relative of the snowdrop is also known as the **daffodil.** As a bulb, it has a short, erect stem with leaf bases that serve to store food between each growing season. The bulb is pungent in taste and causes nausea and vomiting.

Native to Asia, the **saffron crocus** (*Crocus sativus*) brings color to the spring flower beds in many front yards. It is from this plant that we get the coveted saffron powder, a popular spice and coloring agent, especially in the Mediterranean region. The saffron crocus is a perennial plant with an onionlike corm that gives rise to basal, linear leaves surrounded at the bottom by cylindrical sheaths, and funnel-shaped flowers. The flowers of cultivated saffron crocuses are picked shortly after they bloom. The stigmas and styles of these flowers are then removed. The styles, which are only slightly colored, are eliminated, and the remainder is then dried. Because of this painstaking process, it can take nearly 200,000 flowers to yield 1 kilogram (2.2 pounds) of saffron powder. This could explain the high price of saffron powder and the frequent use of counterfeit—and less costly—herbs such as field marigolds and ligulate. Saffron is a remedy for menstrual disorders in folk medicine, but today it is employed mainly in the kitchen as a coloring agent. Only a small amount is used, however, as too much of the vibrant, slightly bitter powder can lead to cramping or intestinal colic.

A member of the buttercup, or crowfoot, family, the **winter aconite** (*Eranthis hyemalis*) blooms at the end of winter. The lemon-yellow flowers develop above the hand-shaped, pinnate leaves. Winter aconite contains cardioactive substances that are toxic when consumed in large quantities.

The bulbs of the **bluebell** (*Scilla bifolia*) also contain cardioactive substances and are poisonous in high doses. Excessive amounts have an adverse effect on the gastrointestinal tract, the kidneys, and the bronchial tubes. However, at therapeutic concentrations, physicians use the active components of the different *scilla* species to treat cardiac insufficiency and cardiac irregularity. The best-known medicinal plant related to this species is the sea onion, which is found in the Mediterranean region. The bulbs can easily be separated into cloves, or bulblets; thus, they were classified in the genus *Scilla,* from the Greek word for "split" or "divide." Wild bluebells can be spotted growing in warm beech forests.

1
Spring snowflake, or **daffodil**
(*Leucojum vernum* L.)
Daffodil, or amaryllis, family
(Amaryllidaceae)
III
Pungent-tasting bulb that induces vomiting
2
Saffron crocus (*Crocus sativus* L.)
Iris family (Iridaceae)
III–IV (cultivated)
Yellowish stigmatic cord
Herb, coloring agent, additive to teas
Essential oil, glycosidic coloring agents
(F) Menstrual disorders
3
Winter aconite (*Eranthis hyemalis*)
Buttercup, or crowfoot, family
(Ranunculaceae)
III (cultivated)
Poisonous plant!
Cardioactive glycosides
4
Bluebell (*Scilla bifolia*)
Lily family (Liliaceae)
Poisonous plant!
Cardioactive glycosides

1 Spring snowflake, daffodil
3 Winter aconite

2 Saffron crocus
4 Bluebell

Often when the ground is still carpeted in snow, the bulb of the **snowdrop, or common snowdrop** (*Galanthus nivalis*), emerges, growing into a single- or two-stemmed stalk. After withering, the plant retracts into its bulb. The snowdrop was initially cultivated in gardens, but it has now run to seed in forests and groves. Blossoming outside the normal growth period, it is also known as "the meadow saffron" and "spinster in a shirt." This plant tastes bitter and may cause vomiting.

Unlike the **bird's-eye speedwell,** or **brookline** (*Veronica persica*), which has no significance as a medicinal plant, the roots, and to a lesser extent the flowers, of the **cowslip, primrose,** or **oxlip** (*Primula elatior*), can be applied medicinally. This brilliant-yellow, full-blossoming plant is found on the banks of brooks and in moist meadows and forests. The Latin name of the species, *Primula veris,* praises "those that have blossomed first in the spring." Its flowers have an inflorescence that tilts sideways and looks like a bunch of keys. For this reason, in many fairy tales and legends this plant is considered to be protected by water nymphs and fairies for their keys that could open the gates of heaven. In contrast to the roots of the cowslip plant, which should be preserved, collecting their flowers represents no danger to their extinction. The green sepals should be picked as well, because the soaplike, foamy saponins accumulate there. A plant with a long medicinal tradition, cowslip can be found in herb books dating back to the sixteenth century. According to these texts, the roots were added to pectoral and bronchial teas as a mucolytic (expectorant) component. Cowslip has proven to be especially effective for the treatment of chronic bronchitis and coughs in the elderly, because the saponins increase and liquefy viscous bronchial mucus. A sneezing powder can also be made from the roots of the plant.

The **cornellian cherry** (*Cornus mascula*) is fond of dry forests and fields. The yellow flowers, which have four petals in the form of umbels, provide an adornment to this shrub far above the level of the leaves (this plant reaches a height of up to 5 meters, or more than 16 feet). The red, cherrylike fruit ripen during July. Although the fruit are edible, they taste somewhat tart. This plant is not known for its medicinal uses but rather for its hard wood, called yellow cornus, which is valued highly for wood turning. According to legend, Odysseus and Romulus even brandished lances made of cornellian cherry wood.

5
Snowdrop, or **common snowdrop** (*Galanthus nivalis* L.)
Daffodil, or amaryllis, family (Amaryllidaceae)
III–IV
Sharp bitter principles
Induces vomiting
6
Cowslip, primrose, or **oxlip** (*Primula veris* L., *Primula elatior* L.)
Primrose family (Primulaceae)
III–IV (protected roots)
Roots and flowers
Pectoral and bronchial teas, cough syrups and cough drops
Saponins, flavone, essential oils
(M) Acute and chronic bronchitis, mucolytic and soothing in the event of catarrhs
7
Bird's-eye speedwell, or **brookline** (*Veronica persica* L.)
Figwort, or snapdragon, family (Scrophulariaceae)
V–VI
Tannins, bitter principles, flavonoids
8
Cornellian cherry (*Cornus mascula* L.)
Dogwood family (Cornaceae)
III–V
Tannins

5 Snowdrop, common snowdrop
7 Bird's-eye speedwell, brookline

6 Cowslip, primrose, oxlip
8 Cornellian cherry

The numerous anemone species grow wild or can be cultivated easily from seeds. The anemone gets its name from the Greek word *anemos,* meaning "wind," because in the past it was assumed that the flowers required the wind in order to open. In the spring, the forest floor is covered with **European thimbleweed, or fairy's wind-flowers** (*Anemone nemorosa*). Unfortunately, its blossoms wither very rapidly. These plants "migrate" slowly, as the back end of the rootstock (the rhizome), which is found underground, dies off while the front end continues to grow.

Aside from the rose, the violet is the flower most associated with romance and poetry. Whereas the Greeks decorated their coffins with violets and thus linked them with death, we consider these flowers to be among the first signs of spring, heralding new life. As violets grow inconspicuously in hidden areas, they are regarded as a symbol for modesty. Giving a voice to the violet, Goethe said, "I am hidden and stooped and don't like to speak." In contrast to the fragrant sweet violet and wood violet, the **heath dog-violet** (*Viola canina*) has no scent. This plant creeps further with the aid of offshoots, which first bloom after a period of two years. Capsules develop only from the "useful" summer flowers, not from the spring flowers, and are frequently carried off by ants. The roots and the rootstocks induce vomiting and are effective as expectorants. Candied petals from the flowers are used as sweet ornaments for cakes.

A protected member of the buttercup, or crowfoot, family, the **round-lobed hepatica, liverwort, herb trinity, or kidneywort** (*Anemone hepatica*), is also known as the "early anemone," because of its early blooming period. The name liverwort is derived from its liver-shaped leaves. In the evening, the plant "goes to sleep" by closing its small head and letting it hang. In folk medicine, *Anemone hepatica* is used for disturbances of the liver and biliary tract, but you are advised to consult your physician before using it yourself.

Its yolk-yellow flowers and preferred habitat in swampy marshlands have given the **yellow marsh-marigold, or water cowslip** (*Caltha palustris*), its name. This plant has long-stemmed, dark-green, heart-shaped leaves with a shiny, almost greasy surface. Its propagation occurs by way of seeds that float on water. In the past, butter that turned out to be too pale was dyed with the yellow coloring derived from the petals of this plant. And at one time the flower buds were preserved in vinegar and eaten as a substitute for capers. However, consuming more than five buds of this slightly poisonous plant could be toxic, so its ingestion is discouraged today.

9
European thimbleweed, or **fairy's wind-flower** (*Anemone nemorosa* L.)
Buttercup, or crowfoot, family (Ranunculaceae)
III–IV
10
Heath dog-violet (*Viola canina* L.)
Violet, or pansy, family (Violaceae)
III–IV
Roots and rootstocks, herbage (the leaves, stems, and other parts that are rich in moisture) from the fragrant violets
Tea
Sore throat, bronchitis, "blood purification"
11
Round-lobed hepatica, liverwort, herb trinity, or **kidneywort** (*Anemone hepatica* L.)
Buttercup, or crowfoot, family (Ranunculaceae)
III–IV (Endangered and therefore protected)
Herbage without roots
Tea
Anemonin, anthocyanins, flavonoids, glycosides
(F) Disturbances of the liver and biliary tract
Do not use fresh herbage; consult your physician before using.
12
Yellow marsh-marigold, or **water cowslip** (*Caltha palustris* L.)
Buttercup, or crowfoot, family (Ranunculaceae)
III–IV
Saponins, flavonoids, anemonin, choline
Do not use because of possible toxicity!

9 European thimbleweed, fairy's wind-flower
11 Round-lobed hepatica, liverwort, herb trinity,
kidneywort

10 Heath dog-violet
12 Yellow marsh-marigold, water cowslip

efore the meadows of Bad Wörishofen are splashed with the bright yellow of blooming dandelions, they are dotted with the pale purple of the **cuckoo flower** (*Cardamine pratensis*), also called **lady's smock** and **apple pie.** In some places, the plant is also known as "Jacob's little ladder," as the pinnate hemi-petals look like the rungs of a ladder. A member of the mustard, or cabbage, family, it has flowers with four petals. The spittle bug lays its eggs on the cuckoo flower with its "cuckoo spit," making the plant look as if someone had spit on it. The leaves are used in teas and salads, and have been thought to "purify the blood"; however, large quantities may irritate the stomach.

The **tuberous corydalis,** or **hollow root** (*Corydalis cava*), is a perennial plant frequently found in deciduous forests. One meaning of the Greek term *korydallis* is "tufted swift," and the plant gets it genus name because of its purplish, dirty-looking flowers that have a tuft like the tufted swift. The flowers, which bloom in April and May, are arched like a cornucopia. Because of the plant's high alkaloid content, it has been used to reduce palsy, trembling, and overall excitement.

Sebastian Kneipp produced a breakfast tea with a pleasant flavor thanks to the leaves from the **woodland strawberry,** or **common strawberry** (*Fragaria vesca*). This perennial plant grows wild in forests and clearings and along shady roadsides. Similar to the garden strawberry, it multiplies by way of offshoots above the ground. The fleshy receptacle of the false berry is covered with seeds distributed in the form of "small dots." The leaves and roots of this plant can be used for gastric and intestinal disorders, whereas the fruit is used to treat liver dysfunctions. But use caution, as allergies to the fruit are fairly common.

Often encountered in damper areas, the **fig buttercup, pilewort,** or **lesser celandine** (*Ranunculus ficaria*), presents a glistening presence long before winter is over. The flower is similar to the buttercup, and the leaf axils usually have small bulblets. Because of its form, this plant was believed to be effective against hemorrhoids and skin diseases. For this reason and due to the plant's high concentration of tannins, you will find the same indications in many folk remedies. The grainlike tubercles are frequently washed off during strong rain showers, so they are known in some places as "grain rain" and "bread from heaven." Another name for this plant, "fig root," has to do with its fig-shaped root tuber. The plant's sharp, slightly poisonous sap is said to prevent scurvy. Flower buds soaked in saltwater for one day, and then preserved in tarragon vinegar for another day, can be eaten as capers. However, large quantities of this plant can irritate the stomach.

13
Cuckoo flower, lady's smock, or **apple pie** (*Cardamine pratensis* L.)
Mustard, or cabbage, family (Cruciferae)
IV–VI
Herbage
Tea, salad
Oil of mustard glycoside, bitter principles
For "blood purification"
Large quantities may irritate the stomach and kidneys.

14
Tuberous corydalis, or **hollow root** (*Corydalis cava* L.)
Poppy family (Papaveraceae)
III–V
Palsy, trembling, excitement

15
Woodland strawberry, or **common strawberry** (*Fragaria vesca* L.)
Rose family (Rosaceae)
Leaves, roots, ripe fruit
Tannins, essential oils, vitamin C
(F) Leaves and roots for gastric and intestinal disorders, fruit for improving the function of the biliary and hepatic systems
Possible allergic reactions

16
Fig buttercup, pilewort, or **lesser celandine** (*Ranunculus ficaria* L.)
Buttercup, or crowfoot, family (Ranunculaceae)
III–V
Fresh herbage for spring salads
Protoanemonin, anemonin, saponins, vitamin C
Excessive amounts lead to irritation of the stomach, intestines, or kidneys.

13 Cuckoo flower, lady's smock, apple pie

15 Woodland strawberry, common strawberry

14 Tuberous corydalis, hollow root

16 Fig buttercup, pilewort, lesser celandine

*G*ermander speedwell, wild germander, or bird's-eye (*Veronica chamaedrys*), is popularly known as **speedwell**, because the blue flowers fall from the plant shortly after they are picked. It is a member of the genus *Veronica,* in which only two stamens project above the corolla. This figwort was dedicated to Saint Veronica. In medieval lyrics, the flower was sung about as "gamandré," the beloved harbinger of springtime. In folk medicine, the "European tea" made from this plant was recommended for bronchitis, asthma, rheumatic pains, and gout, but has since proven to be unjustified.

Because the lovely, featherlike leaves of the **dewcup,** or **lady's mantle** (*Alchemilla vulgaris,* aggregate species), are frequently used to decorate the head of gothic Madonnas, they are often referred to as "Virgin Mary's cloak." This member of the rose family, with its greenish-yellow, inconspicuous flowers, is also known as "dew weed" and "dew cloak," as dewdrops can be found in the leaf axils on humid summer days. These drops are actually excess water that is exuded by the plant itself. The early alchemists hoped to change base metals into gold with the aid of this "water from heaven," which accounts for the genus name *alchemilla*. Folk medicine recommended the use of the dewcup for female complaints. Today, however, because of its high concentration of tannins, the only recognized indications are "nonspecific" diarrhea and gastrointestinal disorders.

During the springtime, the tender umbels of **wild chervil, cow parsley,** or **cow weed** (*Anthriscus sylvestris*), blanket the region in and around Bad Wörishofen. This plant has an angular stem and glistening, green leaves with two or three very fine leaflets. The herbage smells unpleasant and tastes somewhat bitter. The ingestion of this plant may result in mild visual disturbances and blurred vision similar to that caused by alcoholic intoxication, hence its epithet "crazy chervil." In addition, greater sensitivity to sunlight may be experienced, possibly causing skin irritation.

The **common periwinkle,** or **running myrtle** (*Vinca minor*), is considered to be a garden refugee from old monastery gardens and as such carries with it traditional lore. Couples who eat leaves together from this messenger of spring supposedly become even more closely united. Wreaths of this plant set out before a window are said to protect against lightning. In 1961, the chemical formula of the plant's primary component, vincamine, was finally clarified. This substance, isolated in the form of a tablet, selectively induces the cerebral blood flow. However, it has been shown that there is a risk of adverse effects, making its administration unjustified.

17
Germander speedwell, wild germander, or **bird's-eye**
(*Veronica chamaedrys* L.)
Figwort, or snapdragon, family
(Scrophulariaceae)
V–VIII
Tannins, bitter principles, flavonoids
18
Dewcup, or **lady's mantle**
(*Alchemilla vulgaris* L.)
Rose family (Rosaceae)
V–IX
Herbage
Tea
Tannins, bitter principles, flavonoids, essential oils
(F) Spasmolytic, astringent, female disorders, gastrointestinal disorders, impurities of the skin
19
Wild chervil, cow parsley, or **cow weed** (*Anthriscus sylvestris* L.)
Parsley, or carrot, family
(Umbelliferae)
IV–VIII
Furocoumarin
Sensitivity to light (photosensitization), possibly causing skin irritation
20
Common periwinkle, or **running myrtle** (*Vinca minor* L.)
Dogbane, or periwinkle, family
(Apocynaceae)
III–IV
Herbage
Vincamine
There is a risk of adverse effects!

17 Germander speedwell, wild germander, bird's-eye
19 Wild chervil, cow parsley, cow weed

18 Dewcup, lady's mantle
20 Common periwinkle, running myrtle

The **lawn daisy,** or **marguerite** (*Bellis perennis*), grows wild in meadows, fields, and lawns, and is also cultivated. Its Latin name comes from *bellus,* which means "beautiful" or "lovely," and *perennis,* which means "enduring," indicating that this tidbit for geese is a flowering, perennial plant. The lawn daisy has finely haired basal leaves in a rosette arrangement near the ground. From these leaves arise crinose (hairy) stalks topped by a singular flower with a yellow disk and white or rose-colored rays. In folk medicine, the lawn daisy was used to "purify the blood" and to bring down inflammations, and it also played a role in "spring cures." However, today its primary use is as a gentle laxative, although it has also proven to be beneficial for colds, coughs, and stomach problems, as well as external injuries.

A creeping perennial plant, the **mountain wood sorrel** (*Oxalis acetosella*) favors cool, shady forests. Because it is often seen in beechwood forests, it is also known as "beech sorrel." Its genus name has to do with its high concentration of oxalic acid. The mountain wood sorrel has well-developed trefoil leaves that fold up in the evening and during rain showers. Not all of the flowers open, and the seeds are disseminated quite a distance from the fruit capsules. As part of a "spring cure," the leaves are added to soups and salads to invigorate the organism, stimulate the appetite, and aid digestion. But only small quantities of these leaves should be eaten, as the potassium oxalate found in them in high concentrations is poisonous.

The lovely **true forget-me-not,** or **water forget-me-not** (*Myosotis scorpioides*), already begins blossoming during May in damp environments. This plant grows to a height of ½ meter (about 1 ½ feet) and has a pleasant scent. Because of their blue color, the flowers are a symbol for faithfulness and love.

The tender flowers of the **blackthorn,** or **sloe** (*Prunus spinosa*), which appear before the leaves develop, adorn the area around Bad Wörishofen as early as March. A member of the rose family, the blackthorn bush has thorns on its branches. Like the whitethorn, it can live as long as 600 years, so it was once assumed to be a useful agent against magic and illness. The blackthorn can be traced back to the Stone Age, when its fruit was used as a nutrient by lake dwellers. Today, the fruit is employed as a component of jam, stewed fruit, wine, and liquor. Its extremely hard wood is appreciated by carpenters and wood turners. Sebastian Kneipp recognized the flowers of this plant as being a "faultless laxative," and they are still recommended as a mild laxative, especially for children. In addition, blackthorn is known to be beneficial for stomach and bladder disorders and skin problems.

21
Lawn daisy, or **marguerite** (*Bellis perennis* L.)
Composite, or daisy, family (Compositae)
III–XI
Flowers and leaves
Tea, tincture
Saponins, bitter principles, anthroxanthin
Laxative, treatment for colds, coughs, stomach problems, external injuries
(F) "Blood purifying," appetite-stimulating, anti-inflammatory

22
Mountain wood sorrel (*Oxalis acetosella* L.)
Wood-sorrel family (Oxalidaceae)
IV–V
Oxalic acid and its salts
Eaten as a vegetable, as well as in salads and soups
Digestive problems, heartburn, lack of appetite
Large concentrations may be harmful!

23
True forget-me-not, or **water forget-me-not** (*Myosotis scorpioides* L.)
Borage, or forget-me-not, family (Boraginaceae)
V–VII

24
Blackthorn, or **sloe** (*Prunus spinosa* L.)
Rose family (Rosaceae)
III–IV
Flowers, fruit, leaves
Tea, jam, stewed fruit, plant juices
Amygdalin, coumarin, tannins, bitter principles, vitamin C
(F) Tea as a mild laxative, a mild diuretic

21 Lawn daisy, marguerite

22 Mountain wood sorrel

23 True forget-me-not, water forget-me-not

24 Blackthorn, sloe

The bright-blue flowers of the **common grape hyacinth** (*Muscari botryoides*) are among the first indicators of spring. This member of the lily family is native to the eastern Mediterranean area. As a result of overfertilization of meadowlands, the wild population of this species has become endangered and is thus protected.

Members of the mint, or dead-nettle, family, the **henbit dead-nettle** (*Lamium amplexicaule*) and the **spotted henbit** (*Lamium maculatum*) flourish even in barren habitats and can reach a height of up to a meter (about 3 feet). The nettle-like leaves, however, do not sting, as they are "dead." Because their flowers are widespread from May to August, these are excellent honey plants and are known in some places as "suck of a bee." The spotted henbit is thought to have a calming effect on female disorders, and it is also used to calm the respiratory tract. But its primary use is as a component of tea, rounding off the aroma.

The **common bugle,** or **creeping bugle** (*Ajuga reptans*), also belongs to the mint, or dead-nettle, family. This plant is a close relative of the well-known rosemary, which is originally from the Mediterranean region. Its name is derived from its creeping offshoots. With its whorls of dark-blue blossoms, the common bugle lends a wonderful accent to spring meadows.

25
Common grape hyacinth
(*Muscari botryoides* L.)
Lily family (Liliaceae)
IV–V
Wild populations are endangered and thus protected.
26
Henbit dead-nettle (*Lamium amplexicaule* L.)
Mint, or dead-nettle, family (Labiatae)
III–V
27
Common bugle, or **creeping bugle** (*Ajuga reptans* L.)
Mint, or dead-nettle, family (Labiatae)
V–VIII
28
Spotted henbit (*Lamium maculatum* L.)
Mint, or dead-nettle, family (Labiatae)
IV–IX
Flowers of the white dead-nettle (*Lamium album*)
Tea
Saponins, mucilage, tannins, flavonoids
(M) Catarrh of the upper respiratory tract, gastric and intestinal disorders
(F) Female disorders

25 Common grape hyacinth

27 Common bugle, creeping bugle

26 Henbit dead-nettle

28 Spotted henbit

In the springtime, **elephant ears,** or **pig squeak** (*Bergenia crassifolia*), blooms a brilliant red. Native to Asia, it is a member of the saxifrage family. When its leaves wither, they turn black as if they had been burned. This discoloration is due to the oxidation of arbutin, a substance found in high concentrations in this plant (as well as in the bearberry). Arbutin acts as an antibacterial agent against infections of the urinary tract. But unfortunately elephant ears is not effective as a cure for inflammations of the bladder or the kidneys. The plant also has a great deal of tannin, which is not tolerated well by the gastrointestinal tract.

Of the anemones, the most common is the white wood anemone. But the mildly poisonous **yellow woodland anemone,** or **yellow wind-flower** (*Anemone ranunculoides*), is also frequently encountered. Sometimes called "wind-flower," this plant has delicate leaves that sway in the wind and demonstrate a distinct day–night rhythm. Because of its several stamens and their overproduction of pollen, the yellow woodland anemone attracts more than its share of insects. Its small fruit is distributed by ants, which hold this delicacy in high esteem.

A member of the poppy family, the poisonous **greater celandine, garden celandine,** or **swallowwort** (*Chelidonium majus*), grows along the roadside and on fences and hedges. Its fruit is podlike and has a white, fleshy appendage, and its stem is hairy. The yellow flowers begin blooming in April. When the flowers are picked, a sticky, yellowish sap flows from the broken part of the stems. This sap contains sugar and attracts ants. In his *Doctrine of Signatures,* Paracelsus made the point that the external form of a plant can be a clue to its possible effects, so it was claimed that this bilelike sap is effective against disorders of the liver and biliary system. And in fact extracts from the plant's roots, which are especially rich in active components, are used as ingredients of spasmolytic cholagogues (agents that stimulate the bile flow). The sap has also shown to be effective in treating warts; it is dabbed externally on the warts three or four times a day. Yet this plant can be highly poisonous, especially for children, and should be used only after consulting a physician.

Garlic mustard (*Alliaria officinalis*), also known as **Jack-in-the-bush,** is very common to the forests around Bad Wörishofen. The leaves are similar to those of the nettles, the stem is four-sided, and the inconspicuous cruciform flowers stand in a corymbose formation. If you rub the plant between your fingers, you'll release a strong aroma similar to that of garlic. Therefore, it is very good for seasoning soups and salads.

29
Elephant ears, or **pig squeak**
(*Bergenia crassifolia*)
Saxifrage family (Saxifragaceae)
IV–V
Arbutin, tannins
Gastrointestinal intolerance
30
Yellow woodland anemone, or **yellow wind-flower** (*Anemone ranunculoides* L.)
Buttercup, or crowfoot, family (Ranunculaceae)
III–V
31
Greater celandine, garden celandine, or **swallowwort** (*Chelidonium majus* L.)
Poppy family (Papaveraceae)
V–IX
Herbage, root
Tea, tincture, external application of the yellow, milky latex
Alkaloids (chelidonium, sanguinarine), saponins
(M) Mildly spasmolytic in the upper gastrointestinal tract, functional disturbances in the biliary tract
(F) Disorders of the liver and biliary system, cramping
Yellowish, milky plant latex for treating warts
To be used only after consulting a physician
32
Garlic mustard, or **Jack-in-the-bush** (*Alliaria officinalis*)
Mustard, or cabbage, family (Cruciferae)
IV–VI
Leaves as a seasoning agent

29 Elephant ears, pig squeak

31 Greater celandine, garden celandine, swallowwort

30 Yellow woodland anemone, yellow wind-flower

32 Garlic mustard, Jack-in-the-bush

A member of the geranium, or cranesbill, family, the **long-stalk cranesbill,** or **pigeon's foot** (*Geranium columbinum*), has rose-colored flowers that grow in pairs. Its fruit is stretched out long like a crane's bill and covered with glandular hairs. When ripe, the bearded fruit bends over with the humidity of the air, flinging its seeds a great distance for dissemination.

The many remedies attributed to **narrow-leaf plantain, ribgrass, ribwort plantain,** or **lance-leaf plantain** (*Plantago lanceolata*), may compensate for its lack of beauty. Alexander the Great used it for headaches. Dioscorides and Galen recommended it for healing wounds. Sebastian Kneipp even praised the sap from this plant for its wound-healing properties, saying it "closes a gaping, lacerated wound as with a golden thread." Its genus name comes from the Latin *planta,* meaning "sole of the foot." Narrow-leaf plantain grows everywhere and was called "footprints of the white man" by Native Americans, as it was seen to spring up in the tracks of the white settlers. Plantain tea and juice from the plant have contrastimulatory, expectorant, and astringent effects. Its crushed leaves pressed onto an insect sting relieve the pain and inhibit the swelling. This plant is also employed for catarrhs of the upper respiratory tract as well as for inflammations of the skin and the mucous membranes.

Black medick (*Medicago lupulina*), also known as **millet** and **yellow clover,** has been cultivated in England since the seventeenth century. It is generally seen along paths and in meadows, and is fond of soil with a high nutrient level. Black medick varies quite extensively depending on its location, fertilization, the cultivated crop, and the degree of grazing. Although it is very rich in nutrients as a feed, it is cultivated only in areas where crimson clover and alfalfa grow poorly, for it has a low-yield productivity.

The **dwarf milkwort** (*Polygala amarum*) can be spotted in swampy meadows during May and June. The bitter taste associated with all parts of this plant has to do with its concentration of bitters. Bitters are characterized by a bitter principle that acts on the mucous membranes of the mouth and stomach, increasing appetite and promoting digestion. Dwarf milkwort is therefore recommended for strengthening the gastrointestinal tract. Over the course of many centuries, various species of *polygala* have been used to relieve nervous eye complaints and to heal snakebites. The genus name *polygala* means "much milk" in Latin and indicates the stimulating effect of this plant on the milk secretion of nursing mothers.

33
Long-stalk cranesbill, or **pigeon's foot** (*Geranium columbinum* L.)
Geranium, or cranesbill, family (Geraniaceae)
V–VII
34
Narrow-leaf plantain, ribgrass, ribwort plantain, or **lance-leaf plantain** (*Plantago lanceolata* L.)
Plantain family (Plantaginaceae)
V–X
Leaves, herbage
Tea, juice from the plant
Glycosides (aucibin), mucilage, bitters
(M) Catarrh of the upper respiratory tract
(F) Application of the leaf against insect bites and stings
35
Black medick, millet, or **yellow clover** (*Medicago lupulina* L.)
Pea family (Papilionaceae)
V–VII
36
Dwarf milkwort (*Polygala amara* L.)
Milkwort family (Polygalaceae)
V–X
Bitter principles

33 Long-stalk cranesbill, pigeon's foot
35 Black medick, millet, yellow clover

34 Narrow-leaf plantain, ribgrass, ribwort plantain, lance-leaf plantain
36 Dwarf milkwort

An evergreen dwarf shrub in the heath family, the **bearberry** (*Arctostaphylos uva-ursi*) thrives in dry or sandy soil. Its coriaceous (leathery) leaves are similar to those of the cowberry. Due to the leaves' high concentration of tannin, they are used for tanning fine morocco (saffian) leather and as a black coloring agent. The flowers are pink or white and grow in widely dispersed terminal clusters. The bearberry is one of the true medicinal plants of the north. In Iceland, bearberry was applied to the skin to ward off evil spirits. The important curative effects of the plant's leaves against kidney and bladder complaints were recognized by physicians long ago. Its active ingredients (arbutin and methylarbutin) are first broken down in the urine, where antibacterial and disinfectant compounds are formed that are active in the urinary tract. However, in order for them to be effective, the urine must be alkalized, so bearberry should always be taken with bicarbonate of soda. But you need to use caution, as excessive use of bearberry can upset the stomach and prolonged use can cause chronic poisoning.

During the spring, on a mountain slope near Bad Wörishofen, it's possible to spot the **pasque flower,** or **windflower** (*Anemone vernalis*), laden with blossoms. Another name for this poisonous plant, "kitchen bell," comes from its bell-shaped flowers. In the Tyrol (an alpine region in western Austria and northern Italy), it is also known as the "hairy little man" because of its "fur." This plant is endangered and therefore protected.

The **common plantain, greater plantain,** or **waybread** (*Plantago major*), is often caught sight of growing in fields as well as along the roadside. It has broad, rounded leaves traversed by seven "nerves," which is why it was once called "nerve weed." The spike of this plant is a long "rat tail" with greenish-white flowers. Hikers place the leaves of this plant in their shoes to refresh and invigorate their feet. As a wild vegetable, the leaves can be used for soups and salads. Medicinally, common plantain has been employed for coughs, hoarseness, and stomach, bladder, and respiratory problems, as well as for external wounds and insect bites.

Cultivated for their use as a spice, **caraway** (*Carum carvi*) plants also grow wild along the roadside and in sparse pastures, where grazing animals often search them out. Unlike other plants bearing umbels such as chervil, hogweed, and cow parsnip, caraway has accessory leaves close to the ground. The small flowers can be white or yellow and appear in a compound umbel with rays of differing lengths. The two-seeded fruit typically has white stripes and is suitable for making liqueurs and spirits. As with many other spices, caraway is known to have strengthening effects on digestion. It is also used in the form of a tea, tablets, or drops, to stimulate the gastric juices and the appetite, relieve spasms or convulsions, reduce a feeling of fullness, and counteract flatulence. In addition, knowledgeable cooks use it as an ingredient in meals that can cause gas, as when preparing cabbage, sauerkraut, or beans.

37
Bearberry (*Arctostaphylos uva-ursi* L.)
Heath family (Ericaceae)
III–IX
Leaves
Tea (cold extract)
Arbutin, methylarbutin, hydroquinone
(M) Inflammatory illnesses of the efferent urinary passages
Avoid long-term therapy!

38
Pasque flower, or **windflower** (*Anemone vernalis* L.)
Buttercup, or crowfoot, family (Ranunculaceae)
IV–VI
Sharp substances and related glucosides (protoanemonin, anemonin)
Contact may result in skin blisters.

39
Common plantain, greater plantain, or **waybread** (*Plantago major* L.)
Plantain family (Plantaginaceae)
VI–X
Fresh leaves as a wild vegetable
Leaves as a refreshing insole in shoes
Stomach, bladder, and respiratory problems, coughs, hoarseness, external wounds and insect bites

40
Caraway (*Carum carvi* L.)
Parsley, or carrot, family (Umbelliferae)
V–VIII
Fruit, essential oil
Tea, herb, drops, tablets
Essential oils (carvone, dihydrocarvone, carveol)
A feeling of fullness, flatulence cramplike disorders of the gastrointestinal tract

37 Bearberry
39 Common plantain, greater plantain, waybread
38 Pasque flower, windflower
40 Caraway

A deciduous tree, the **sycamore maple** (*Acer pseudo-platanus*) can reach as high as 30 meters (100 feet). Its leaves are similar to those of the plane trees, earning it the name *pseudo-platanus.* Its flowers grow in hanging racemes, ultimately bearing the winged fruit. Wood from this tree is suitable as a veneer, and in the past was even used for making wooden tableware and string instruments. The bark has mildly astringent properties, and it has been used as a wash for skin problems and as an eyewash for tired, sore eyes. The inner bark, with its sap, has been employed externally to dress wounds.

The **red chestnut** (*Castania rubra*) is a type of horse chestnut. The **horse chestnut** (*Aesculus hippocastanum*) is a magnificent tree that can grow to a height of 25 meters (more than 75 feet) and live as long as 200 years. It derives its name from the stipules of the fallen leaves, as they are shaped not unlike a horse's hoof. This tree offers something special three times a year: In the spring it displays its silver-haired, hand-shaped leaves; later it blooms with red, yellow, or white candlelike flowers; and in the late summer it presents its prickly, green fruit. Especially in Bavaria, chestnut trees can be seen decorating many beer gardens, where they are also a wonderful source of shade. Medicinally, the seeds, leaves, and bark of the horse chestnut are used in ointments, drops, and tablets to treat a number of ailments, from varicose veins, hemorrhoids, and sunburn to diarrhea, bronchitis, and respiratory problems.

The **European black currant** (*Ribes nigrum*) is cultivated and also grows wild in moist soil and shallow marshes. This bush is valued for its sour berry, which is high in vitamin C and often made into juices and jams. Medicinally, the berries and their juice are used to treat kidney disorders and colic. The dried berries, in the form of a gargle, can reduce inflammations in the mouth and throat, and, as a mouthwash, can be used for bleeding gums. A tea made with the leaves stimulates the kidneys and is also beneficial for rheumatic disorders as well as arteriosclerosis. Drinking the tea cold is helpful for hoarseness and a sore throat.

Rosemary (*Rosmarinus officinalis*) is native to Mediterranean countries and can reach a height of up to 2 meters (more than 6 feet). However, special skills and a bright habitat protected from frost are necessary to get this shrub through the winter. The fine, needlelike leaves are highly valued as a seasoning and are often used to flavor lamb, chicken, and pork. In earlier times, wreaths for winners were braided out of rosemary, laurel, and myrtle. Today, in some places, wedding guests are still decorated with sprigs of rosemary as a symbol of eternal life. Rosemary is a plant with a range of medicinal uses. During the Middle Ages, it was an important part of the herb gardens of the Benedictine order. This member of the mint, or dead-nettle, family was one of Sebastian Kneipp's favorite plants. He especially recommended rosemary wine for "heart shortcomings" and for strengthening weak and elderly patients. The tart essential oil of rosemary, with its "rosemary camphor" that activates the circulation, is used today in stimulating and reviving bath products and in aromatic soaps and perfumes. As an aromatherapy oil, it is a tonic for the nerves and the heart as well as for circulation and digestion. The refreshing aroma is also used to combat tiredness, increase concentration, and clear the mind. When applied externally, rosemary is used to treat rheumatic disorders, eczema, bruises, and wounds. Taken internally, it improves digestion and circulation. However, when rosemary is used in large quantities internally, there is a danger of poisoning, and it should definitely not be taken internally by pregnant women.

41
Sycamore maple (*Acer pseudo-platanus* L.)
Maple family (Aceraceae)
IV–V
Astringent, dressing for wounds, the treatment of diarrhea, bronchitis, respiratory problems
42
horse chestnut (*Aesculus hippocastanum* L.)
horse chestnut family (Hippocastanaceae)
IV–V
Seeds, leaves, bark
Ointment, drops, tablets
Triterpene saponins (escin), flavonoids, coumarin
Chronic venous complaints, mobilization of fluids, anti-inflammatory
43
European black currant (*Ribes nigrum* L.)
Saxifrage family (Saxifragaceae)
IV–V
Leaves, berries
Tea, plant juice, fresh fruit, lozenges, gargle
Vitamin C, flavonoids, procyanidines, potassium salts
Kidney ailments, rheumatic disorders, arteriosclerosis, colic, mouth and throat inflammations, bleeding gums, hoarseness, sore throat
44
Rosemary (*Rosmarinus officinalis* L.)
Mint, or dead-nettle, family (Labiatae)
III–V
Leaves, essential oil
Tea, plant juice, wine, aromatic oil, heart ointments, bath products, herb
Essential oil ("rosemary camphor"), resin, triterpenic acids
For indigestion, as a circulatory tonic

41 Sycamore maple

43 European black currant

42 horse chestnut

44 Rosemary

The root of the **horseradish** (*Armoracia rusticana*) causes even the strongest among us to cry. Nevertheless, horseradish remains a popular herb and nutrient plant. It grows wild and is also cultivated. Some caterpillars protect themselves from being eaten by birds by ingesting horseradish leaves, thereby acquiring an acrid flavor. The roots are harvested between September and February. In order to be kept fresh, they are buried in sand in cool cellars. In the past, poultices with this herb that irritated the skin were applied to the neck and painful joints. The sharp taste of horseradish is due to the mustard oils, which are ascribed as having an antibacterial effect. Similar to antibiotics, horseradish is also used to treat infections. In addition, it stimulates the digestive juices and the flow of bile. Nevertheless, doses that are too high can result in stomach or skin irritation.

As early as December, the **stinking hellabore** (*Hellaborus foetidus*), which should not be confused with the white hellabore, waits for spring under the snow and ice. For this reason, it is also known as the "snow rose" and "Christmas rose." This member of the buttercup, or crowfoot, family, with its pale, bell-shaped flowers and hand-shaped, basal leaves, is quite conspicuous against the brown forest floor of deciduous leaves. In ancient times, the effects of the stinking hellabore on the heart were already recognized, although some cases of poisoning were also reported. The rootstock, which has since been found to be poisonous, was previously used to make sneezing powder and snuff.

Like the common bugle, or bugle weed, the related **blue bugle** (*Ajuga genevensis*) is a member of the Labiate family. The German name Günsel is derived from the Latin *consolido,* meaning "to make firm" or "to heal."

The **red lampflower, campion,** or **catchfly** (*Melandrium rubrum*), with its bright-purple flowers, can be spotted along the banks of brooks and in damp, deciduous forests. It can reach a height of up to 1 meter (more than 3 feet) and, with its five cleft petals and swollen calyxes, is easily recognized as a member of the pink, or campion, family. As a dioecious plant (in which the male flowers are on one plant and the female flowers on another), the female calyxes are somewhat more glomerate than the male calyxes. The flowers are open during the daytime, because, in contrast to white lampflowers, they are visited by day-flying butterflies. Hungry bumblebees bite through the calyx from the outside without bringing about any pollination, as the length of their proboscis is too short to reach the bottom of the long flowers.

45
Horseradish (*Armoracia rusticana* L.)
Mustard, or cabbage, family (Cruciferae)
V–VII
Root
Herb, trituration (finely ground) with sugar, poultice with paste
Mustard oils, vitamin C, potassium salts
Antibacterial, antibiotic
Infections of the urinary tract, bronchitis
Doses that are too high may cause skin or stomach irritation.
46
Stinking hellabore (*Hellaborus foetidus* L.)
Buttercup, or crowfoot, family (Ranunculaceae)
III–IV
Cardioactive glycosides
Poisonous rootstock!
47
Blue bugle (*Ajuga genevensis* L.)
Mint, or dead-nettle, family (Labiatae)
V–IX
48
Red lampflower, campion, or **catchfly** (*Melandrium rubrum* L.)
Pink, or campion, family (Caryophyllaceae)
V–IX

45 Horseradish
47 Blue bugle

46 Stinking hellabore
48 Red lampflower, campion, catchfly

The bright-yellow, gullet-shaped, labiate flowers of the **yellow archangel** (*Lamium luteum*) are frequently glimpsed in damp, green forests and meadows. Usually there are six blossoms in the leaf axis, which take on the form of false whorls. The sharp tip of the lower lip of the flowers has brown stripes. This plant propagates by means of stolonization (offshoots).

One day, I was surprised to happen upon the flower of a **yellow marsh-marigold, bog arum,** or **water dragon** (*Calla palustris*), in the pond of an herb garden. This plant, which can be poisonous, is also known as a "snake plant" and is a member of the arum, or campion, family. The flower's inflorescence reminds one of an ear, and it is surrounded by a decorative spathe (bract whorl), making it a popular flower for bouquets. Today, as a result of the drainage of swampland and the filling in of boggy shorelines, the yellow marsh-marigold is an endangered plant.

The **large bitter cress** (*Cardamine amara*), with its small, paniculate clusters of flowers, is frequently observed on the banks of brooks and in oak forests. Because it is often confused with watercress, a plant favored more as an ingredient in salads, it is also known as "false watercress." However, its young leaves and the tips of its shoots are also used in salads as well as in soups, adding a pleasant, slightly bitter flavor.

The slender, red panicles of the **red-vein dock, common sorrel,** or **wood sorrel** (*Rumex sanguineus*), are seen from May to June. Regardless of how benevolently we regard this plant, with its persistence and toughness it must still be classified as a weed. The pointed, light-green leaves develop slightly rust-colored edges and contain a lot of fluid. The small, green, sexually separated flowers are inconspicuous and appear twice a year, in the spring and during midsummer. Although farmers are not fond of seeing red-vein dock in their pastures, it is valued as an herb for soups because of its sour taste and vitamin C con-

tent. Yet the plant also contains a great deal of oxalic acid, and was previously employed as an initial substance in the production of potassium oxalate, used in dyeing and bleaching. For this reason, fresh common sorrel should not be used in salads.

49
Yellow archangel (*Lamium luteum*)
Mint, or dead-nettle, family (Labiatae)
IV–VII
50
Yellow marsh-marigold, dog arum, or **water dragon** (*Calla palustris* L.)
Arum, or calla, family (Araceae)
V–VII
May be poisonous, cyanogen!
Sharp substances
51
Large bitter cress (*Cardamine amara* L.)
Mustard, or cabbage, family (Cruciferae)
IV–VII
52
Red-vein dock, common sorrel, or **wood sorrel** (*Rumex sanguineus* L.)
Milkwort family (Polygonaceae)
V–VIII
Herbage
Fresh herbage, tea
Potassium oxalate, oxalic acid, flavone gylcosides, vitamin C
The tea and wine are no longer used.
Vomiting, diarrhea, disturbances while urinating

34

49 Yellow archangel
51 Large bitter cress

50 Yellow marsh-marigold, dog arum, water dragon
52 Red-vein dock, common sorrel, wood sorrel

*I*t's not uncommon to see meadows splashed with the flowers of the **ox-eye daisy** (*Chrysanthemum leucanthemum*), also known as the **golden daisy, white daisy,** and **herb Margaret.** The flowers have a yellow disk and white rays, and they are popular in wildflower bouquets. This plant also goes by the name of "profiteering flower," which describes the rapid manner in which its flowers flourish. Who is not familiar with the famous oracle described by Goethe in the garden scene of *Faust,* "she loves me . . . she loves me not . . ."? According to legend, many of these flowers are thrown into the air at the same time in order to seek information about the future. The number of flowers that a person could catch on the back of the hand, for instance, would signify the number of children he or she would have. Although the ox-eye daisy is not used much as a medicinal plant anymore, in the past it was employed to promote sweating and to treat urinary disorders and pulmonary diseases.

The **bistort,** or **snakeweed** (*Polygonum bistort*), tends to grow in moist meadows and gets its name from its snakelike stalks and offshoots. At one time, snakeweed was used as an agent against snakebite, unfortunately without any positive effects. Because of its cylindrical, reddish heads, the plant is known as "bottle brush" in some places. As a member of the buckwheat family, it has a knotted stem with only a few leaves. This plant contains a high concentration of tannins, especially in the rootstock. It is therefore used to treat diarrhea and gastrointestinal disorders. However, it is not recommended if you have a sensitive stomach. As a mouthwash, bistort can be used as a remedy for gum problems and inflammations of the mouth. Externally, it can be applied to wounds to stop the bleeding.

During May in Bad Wörishofen and its surroundings, there is a symphony in yellow where the meadows are blanketed with the yellow, pinnatisect flowers of blooming **dandelion** (*Taraxacum officialis*). Worldwide, there are about 500 different species of this perennial plant, which is known to have a white latex in all parts, but especially in its hollow stem. The dandelion demonstrates a distinct day–night rhythm. The head of the flower opens in the morning and closes in the evening or during damp weather. Playing children as well as the wind distribute the parachutelike seeds. Valued as good grazing fodder, dandelion is also known in some places as "milk flower." Sebastian Kneipp recommended dandelion soup and dandelion dumplings. He also felt that it was unfortunate that this lovely flower, because it grows everywhere, is not regarded highly enough, as "it is very beneficial for health." The roots and the foliage contain bitter principles and mineral salts, which function choleretically (stimulate bile flow) and diuretically as well as increase the appetite. A "spring cure" in the form of plant juices, teas, and herbal lozenges has been known to relieve the effects of rheumatic disorders. The delicate leaves, shaped like a crosscut saw, when harvested by the end of May, are a good, healthful addition to salads. The flowers are used for herbal liqueurs, and the roasted taproot is suitable as a substitute for coffee.

53
Ox-eye daisy, golden daisy, white daisy, or **herb Margaret**
(*Chrysanthemum leucanthemum* L.)
Composite, or daisy, family (Compositae)
V–X
54
Bistort, or **snakeweed**
(*Polygonum bistort* L.)
Milkwort family (Polygonaceae)
V–VII
Tea, poultices, partial baths
Tannins
Treatment for diarrhea, gastrointestinal disorders, gargle for inflammations of the mouth and throat, external application for wounds
Not suitable for individuals with a sensitive stomach
55/56
Dandelion (*Taraxacum officinalis* L.)
Composite, or daisy, family (Compositae)
IV–V
Roots and herbage
Tea, plant juices, plant lozenges, tincture, salad
Bitter principles, triterpenes, sterols, flavonoids, minerals inducing the excretion of bile and urine, indigestion, appetite-stimulating
Do not use in the event of an inflammation or an obstruction of the biliary ducts or the intestines.

53 Ox-eye daisy, golden daisy, white daisy, herb Margaret
55 Dandelion (blossoming)

54 Bistort, snakeweed
56 Dandelion (familiar puffballs that succeed the flowers)

$\mathcal{L}$eopard's bane (*Doronicum grandiflorum*), with its bright-yellow composite flowers, is found growing wild, especially on dry, rocky mountain slopes. It is also cultivated as an ornamental plant.

Likewise, **wild chive, garlic chive,** or **leek** (*Allium schoenoprasum*), is both cultivated and wild. Leek is a mild-tasting relative of the onion. We seldom get the chance to view the wonderful flower of this plant, as its freshly cut, long stems are used as an herb. The glomerate flower develops during the second year of life, if the plant is not harvested during the first year. Should the stem of the flower be cut off while it is sprouting, the plant will attempt to multiply vegetatively by producing small offshoot bulbs. These "false cocktail onions" are edible. Chives are known to stimulate the appetite and promote digestion. They also contain iron and arsenic (in small quantities), so they may be helpful if you are anemic.

In a part of a forest that is rich in herbs and protected from inclement weather, I encountered a blossoming **European columbine, common columbine,** or **columbine herb** (*Aquilegia vulgaris*). This slightly poisonous *aquilegia* species, which bears dark-blue and brownish blossoms, has become very rare and is therefore under wildlife protection. Medicinally, the plant's root can be used to curb diarrhea, and its flowers, taken with wine, are known to promote perspiration. European columbine has a stalk with three to ten long-stemmed, nodding flowers. The fruit is husked. The paired, three-pieced leaves, with their notched pinnatifid ends, show that the European columbine, like the **European globeflower** (*Trollius europeus*), is a member of the buttercup, or crowfoot, family.

The globeflower, with its glomerate, yellow blossoms, grows sociably in moist meadows and is characteristic of alpine regions. The botanical name *Trollius* comes from the Old French *truiller* ("to enchant"), and in fact the golden flowers are a joy to many hikers. Like most of the members of the buttercup, or crowfoot, family, this plant is slightly poisonous and not permitted to be collected.

57
Leopard's bane (*Doronicum grandiflorum* L.)
Composite, or daisy, family
(Compositae)
VII–VIII

58
Wild chive, garlic chive, or **leek**
(*Allium schoenoprasum* L.)
Lily family (Liliaceae)
VI–VII
Stimulates the appetite, promotes digestion

59
European columbine, common columbine, or **columbine herb**
(*Aquilegia vulgaris* L.)
Buttercup, or crowfoot, family
(Ranunculaceae)
VI–VII
Endangered and therefore protected!
Slightly poisonous (magnoflorine), skin irritations!

60
European globeflower (*Trollius europeus* L.)
Buttercup, or crowfoot, family
(Ranunculaceae)
V–VI
Endangered and therefore protected!
Slightly poisonous (magnoflorine), skin irritations!

57 Leopard's bane
59 European columbine, common columbine, columbine herb

58 Wild chive, garlic chive, leek
60 European globeflower

*E*urasian Solomon's seal (*Polygonatum multiflorum*) blossoms in dry forests during May and June, at the same time as the lily of the valley. The Latin name of this plant from the lily family, *Polygonatum,* comes from *poly,* for "many," and *gony,* for "knee," as the root has many joints on its knotted extensions. The leaves, which are similar to those of the lily of the valley, hang from the arched stalk, and the white flowers dangle from the leaf axes like little bells. The berries, which are first red and then turn very dark blue, are poisonous. However, when employed externally, Eurasian Solomon's seal is safe and can be used to treat inflammations, bruises, wounds, and skin problems.

The **spring meadow pea, or everlasting pea** (*Lathyrus vernus*), with its initially reddish-violet, then blue, and finally greenish papilionaceous (butterfly-shaped) flowers, is found blooming during spring in the damper parts of forests. It has no tendrils but only a small leaf apex. As a member of the pea family, this plant naturally has legumes, or pods.

The light-pink, somewhat fragrant flowers of the **dog rose, or brier rose** (*Rosa canina*), can be spotted growing in fields and along fences and roadsides during the spring. Rose hips are the fruit of the dog rose and are rich in vitamin C. The fruit, either with or without the seeds, is used to prepare mildly purgative juices and a somewhat sour-tasting tea, to which hibiscus flowers are frequently added. Sebastian Kneipp recommended dog rose tea in cases of renal or urinary disorders because of its mild diuretic properties. The fruit is also used in the preparation of vitamin-rich marmalades, sauces, and soups, as well as an excellent wine, because of its pectin, sugar, and fruit-acid contents. The vitamin C in the fruit is especially good for strengthening the defense mechanisms and fighting colds. In the past, the shrub's hard wood was used to make knife handles.

Another member of the rose family, the **queen of the meadow, or meadowsweet** (*Filipendula ulmaria*), is commonly encountered in damp meadows and on the banks of brooks. The umbels of this plant, which bears a resemblance to cotton candy, are quite extraordinary, and for this reason it has also been called "queen of the valley." The name meadowsweet is derived either from its sweet fragrance or its earlier use as an aromatic agent in the production of mead, wine, and beer. In addition to the essential oil vanillin, the herbage contains tannins, mucilage, and especially salicylic compounds. These pharmacological agents are used for their antirheumatic and pain-relieving effects in the form of diaphoretic teas and as ingredients in ointments.

61
European Solomon's seal
(*Polygonatum multiflorum* L.)
Lily family (Liliaceae)
V–VI
External applications
Berries are poisonous!

62
Spring meadow pea, or everlasting pea (*Lathyrus vernus*)
Pea family (Papilionaceae)
V–VII

63
Dog rose, or brier rose (*Rosa canina* L.)
Rose family (Rosaceae)
VI
Fruit (rose hips)
Tea, marmalade
Vitamin C, minerals, fruit acids, sugar
To strengthen the defense mechanisms, for colds, mild purgative, mild diuretic

64
Queen of the meadow, or meadowsweet (*Filipendula ulmaria* L.)
Rose family (Rosaceae)
VI–VIII
Herbage
Tea, ointment
Salicylic compounds, mucilage, essential oils
Anti-inflammatory, diaphoretic (sweat-inducing), and diuretic

61 European Solomon's seal
63 Dog rose, brier rose

62 Spring meadow pea, everlasting pea
64 Queen of the meadow, meadowsweet

As May comes to a close, the **bluebell,** or **spring squill** (*Scilla anemone*), with its light-blue flower stalk, can be seen blooming in many herb gardens. This member of the lily family traveled to Central Europe as an ornamental plant from Constantinople around the end of the sixteenth century. The genus includes about a hundred different species, the most common of which is the red squill, or sea onion. This plant is found along the coasts of the Mediterranean in two different forms: The red sea onion can grow as large as a pumpkin, whereas the white sea onion is only about the size of a household onion. The cardioactive effects of the bluebell were already known about during the eighteenth century. But this plant can be poisonous and can irritate the skin.

On warm evenings in deciduous forests and parks, the strong smell of garlic and onions reveals the habitat where **ramsons** (*Allium ursinum*) can be found. This aroma has also given the plant the names "bear's garlic," "hog's garlic," and "gypsy onion" in some places. The strong scent is actually quite out of place considering the dainty, white umbels of this lily, which frequently carpets the forest floor like a layer of snow. The overpowering scent comes from the sulfur-containing alliaceous oils (garlic oils). Not only do wild animals appreciate this plant, but it has also proven to be a good herb. The medicinal effects on cardiovascular and intestinal disorders are similar to those known for garlic.

A member of the parsley, or carrot, family, **fennel** (*Foeniculum vulgare*) is both cultivated and found growing wild. The plant has a long, carrot-shaped root, finely grooved stems, and yellow flowers that appear in large, compound umbels. The medicinal uses of fennel date back to ancient times. The use of the fruit was even reported in the medical papyri of Egypt. In the Middle Ages, Hildegard von Bingen and Albertus Magnus recommended fennel for red spots on the face, coughs, eye ailments, flatulence, and digestive complaints, as well as to stimulate milk secretion in nursing mothers. Sebastian Kneipp also referred to its comforting effects, saying, "Fennel is effective against cramping and strengthens the stomach." Parents appreciate the wondrous spasmolytic effects of fennel tea when given to crying babies in their milk bottles. Especially today, when eating unusual whole-grain foods is not uncommon, the mixture of fennel with anise and caraway as a tea or in tablet form can work wonders for that "bloated" feeling. Fennel can also be used to season foods that tend to cause flatulence (cabbage, whole-grain bread, and fatty sauces, for example). In addition, the root can be used as a vegetable and an ingredient in salads.

The **common comfrey, comfrey root, boneset,** or **healing herb** (*Symphytum officinale*), is a perennial plant that thrives in moist meadows. Its blossoms of various colors are pollinated primarily by bumblebees. The main component of this plant is allantoin, a substance that has demonstrated a regenerative effect on the tissues. Common comfrey is also known as "bruisewort" in some places, indicating its application in earlier times. It was believed that a paste made from the roots and applied as a poultice would stimulate callus formation. The Latin name *Symphytum*, from *sympho,* meaning "to grow together," represents this action. The anti-inflammatory and soothing effects of the chopped root (wallwort) is often made use of in healing ointments and pastes for poultices. However, comfrey should not be used internally or on open wounds, nor should it be used by pregnant women.

65
Bluebell, or **spring squill** (*Scilla anemone* L.)
Lily family (Liliaceae)
III–V (cultivated)
Poisonous, cardioactive glycosides
May result in skin irritations.
66
Ramsons (*Allium ursinum* L.)
Lily family (Liliaceae)
V–VI
Fresh herbage (spring), bulbs (fall)
Herb, drops, granular powder
Flavonoids, sulfur-containing compounds, vitamin C
As a preventive agent against arteriosclerosis, against elevated blood lipid values, antibacterial, for gastrointestinal disorders
Sharpness hinders overdose.
67
Fennel (*Foeniculum vulgare*)
Parsley, or carrot, family (Umbelliferae)
VII–X
Fruit
Tea, herb, cough syrup
Essential oils (anethole, fenchone), fixed oil, protein, sugar
(M) Against bloating and cramping in the gastrointestinal region, mucolytic during coughing, antiseptic
68
Common comfrey, comfrey root, boneset, or **healing herb** (*Symphytum officinale* L.)
Borage, or forget-me-not, family (Boraginaceae)
V–VII
Root
Ointments, poultices, tinctures
Allantoin, rosemary acid, tannins, mucilage
Externally for intact bone fractures, strains, sprains

65 Bluebell, spring squill
67 Fennel

66 Ramsons
68 Common comfrey, comfrey root, boneset, healing herb

Sweet-scented bedstraw, sweet woodruff, or master of the wood (*Asperula odorata*), is found in shady deciduous forests and easily recognized because of its characteristic whorl of leaves. The inconspicuous little flowers, which appear in May, stand long-stalked in small, white umbels. Especially after drying, the plant develops an intensive fragrance similar to the smell of hay. It is therefore frequently used as a substitute for lavender and placed in laundry. The source of the fragrance is coumarin, a substance that also provides the aroma in Maibowle ("May wine"). This much-appreciated white-wine punch was previously attributed as having cardiotonic and liver-strengthening effects. We still don't know whether the headaches that sometimes develop after drinking this wine come from the coumarin content or from the alcohol. In an altered form, coumarin is used to reduce blood coagulation, and thus the danger of thrombosis, and is applied medicinally following myocardial infarctions.

The **herb Paris,** or **one berry** (*Paris quadrifolia*), with its four-leafed whorl, is sometimes glimpsed under moist bushes. The plant is also known in some places as "wolf's berry," and it may have previously been used to poison predatory animals. The Latin *Paris* comes from *parparis*, meaning "all equal," and pertains to the plant's four leaves, four sepals, four petals, four stamens, and four stigmas. In spite of its flower structure and its rosulate leaves, this plant is a member of the lily family. Blue–black huckleberries develop from its singular, greenish spring flowers. These mildly poisonous berries can cause attacks of agitation, earning the plant the names "angry nightshade" and "crazy weed" during the Middle Ages. Herb Paris is believed to symbolize the selection made by Paris in Greek mythology. The four leaves represent the three goddesses Juno, Minerva, and Venus, as well as the Trojan prince Paris (the most beautiful leaf, standing in the middle).

Blossoming from May to October, the **white dead-nettle** (*Lamium album*) is thus an important source of honey. Children also like to pull the sweet nectar from the plant's corolla tube (perianth). Five to eight false whorls are present in the leaf axes and have a helmetlike upper lip that is occasionally pink on the outside. As a member of the Labiate family, the plant has a four-sided stem and decussate (crosswise or opposite), typically heart-shaped nettle leaves. Like the spotted henbit, also in the Labiate family, the white dead-nettle is used to calm the respiratory tract and thought to have a calming effect on female disorders. Its flowers, also like those of the spotted henbit, are used to round off the aroma of tea.

The **shepherd's purse, rattle pouches,** or **St. James' weed** (*Capsella bursa-pastoris*), is a ubiquitous, undemanding, and inconspicuous plant that commonly grows in fields and along the roadside. Like the white dead-nettle, this weed has followed humans wherever they have gone. Its name has to do with the similarity of its seed pods to the leather pouches previously carried by shepherds. A sign of coming starvation, when shepherd's purse is found in abundance in the spring farmers have been known to predict a poor year for grain. Back in the Middle Ages, the herbage from this member of the mustard, or cabbage, family was used as the only known agent to still bleeding. Today, shepherd's purse is employed as a supportive agent for nosebleeds and severe menstrual bleeding. As birds are very fond of the taste of the seeds, they are frequently mixed in birdfeed.

69
Sweet-scented bedstraw, sweet woodruff, or **master of the wood** (*Asperula odorata* L.)
Bedstraw, or madder, family (Rubiaceae)
V
Blossoming herbage
Tea, "May wine"
Coumarin glycosides, asperuloside, bitter principles
(F) For liver and gastrointestinal disorders, disturbed sleep
Overdose leads to headaches.
70
Herb Paris, or **one berry** (*Paris quadrifolia* L.)
Lily family (Liliaceae)
V
Saponins, organic acids
All parts (but especially the berries) are mildly poisonous.
71
White dead-nettle (*Lamium album* L.)
Mint, or dead-nettle, family (Labiatae)
IV–VIII
Flowers
Tea, irrigations
Saponins, mucilage, tannins, essential oils
(M) Catarrhs of the upper respiratory tract, gastrointestinal disorders
(F) Female disorders
72
Shepherd's purse, rattle pouches, or **St. James' weed** (*Capsella bursa-pastoris* L.)
Mustard, or cabbage, family (Cruciferae)
II–XI
Herbage
Flavonoids, potassium salts, peptides
(F) Against bleeding and for "blood purification"

69 Sweet-scented bedstraw, sweet woodruff, master of the wood
71 White dead-nettle

70 Herb Paris, one berry
72 Shepherd's purse, rattle pouches, St. James' weed

oltsfoot (*Tussilago farfara*) is an easily satisfied, tough perennial plant that tends to grow in wet areas. The fleshy scapes (leafless flower stalks), with their brownish scales, develop in February before the leaves unfold. Later in the year, the weed's somewhat hoof-shaped leaves appear, earning it the name coltsfoot. The flowers are reminiscent of an old straw hat. The Latin name *Tussilago* means "I repel coughs" and is an indication of the plant's esteemed medicinal effects. Sebastian Kneipp valued coltsfoot as a "true whiskbroom for the thorax." The soothing effects of the mucins in the leaves are an ideal complement to their expectorant actions. Thus, coltsfood is beneficial for hoarseness, coughs, colds, and bronchitis. After drying, the leaves can also be smoked in the form of "asthma cigarettes." In addition, the leaves can be applied externally for comforting relief in the case of insect bites, inflammations, and burns. However, a tea made from this plant should not be taken for longer than four weeks because of the presence of specific alkaloids, and during pregnancy and nursing it should be avoided altogether. Amateur herbalists frequently confuse the leaves of the coltsfoot with those of the butter bur, so only products that have been investigated and guaranteed should be used for infusions (brewed teas).

The tubular, bright-red, quadripartite flowers of the **paradise plant, daphne,** or **mezereon** (*Daphne mezereum*), are seen in forest clearings on the Moosberg (a mountain near Bad Wörishofen) and in front yards as early as March. All parts of this protected plant are extremely poisonous, the ripe red berries in late summer being a dangerous temptation especially for children. The leaves that unfold after the fragrant flowers bloom are similar in form to those of the laurel, hence the botanical name *Daphne*, which means "laurel" in Greek. The plant's tough bark was previously used in producing string.

A dwarf shrub with yellow blossoms, the **German broom** (*Genista germanica*) is fre-

quently found in oak forests. The leaves are somewhat thorny and, like the stems, are slightly crinose (hairy). The papilionaceous flowers have bristlelike bracts that are longer than the stem of the flower. Because of their content of cardioactive glycosides, the broom species are poisonous!

The **common buckbean, bogbean,** or **marsh trefoil** (*Menyanthes trifoliata*), has only the tripartite leaves (*trifolii*) in common with other clover, or trefoil, species. This protected swamp plant is a member of the gentian family. Like the yellow gentian, it too contains a large amount of bitter principles and is therefore also known as "bitter swamp-clover" in some places. Because of its dainty, succulent, crinose, five-folded flowers, it appears somewhat exotic. Sebastian Kneipp recommended the bogbean for a weak stomach, flatulence, and liver disturbances. In folk medicine, the leaves are used in tea to lower a fever. As a substitute for hops, the leaves are sometimes added to beer.

73
Coltsfoot (*Tussilago farfara* L.)
Composite, or daisy, family (Compositae)
III–IV
Leaves, flowers
Tea
Mucilage, tannins, bitter principles, flavonoids
Against hacking coughs and mucous congestion, bronchitis
Carcinogenic effects or liver damage may possibly occur following constant use; not to be used by pregnant women!
74
Paradise plant, daphne, or **mezereon** (*Daphne mezereum* L.)
Mezereon, or spurge-laurel, family (Thymelaeaceae)
II–IV (endangered and therefore protected!)
Daphnane derivatives (glycoside), sharp substances, sitosterols
Because it's extremely poisonous, this plant should not be used!
75
German broom (*Genista germanica* L.)
Pea family (Papilionaceae)
V–VI
Poisonous!
76
Common buckbean, bogbean, or **marsh trefoil** (*Menyanthes trifoliata*)
Gentian family (Gentianaceae)
V–VI (Endangered and therefore protected!)
Leaves
Tea
Bitter principles, tannins, flavonoids
Gastrointestinal disorders, fermentative dyspepsia

73 Coltsfoot
75 German broom

74 Paradise plant, daphne, mezereon
76 Common buckbean, bogbean, marsh trefoil

The buttercup, or crowfoot, family includes more than 400 different species, the best-known of which is the **crowfoot buttercup,** or **bachelor's button** (*Ranunculus acris*), with its yellow blossoms. The members of this family are fond of moist environments, growing where the frogs live (*ranunculus* is Latin for "little frog"). The name crowfoot buttercup has to do with the form of the leaf, as it resembles the shape of a crow's foot. Along with the dandelion, this plant is largely responsible for the yellow color of fields. The crowfoot buttercup contains a sharp, vesicant substance that is quite poisonous and can irritate the skin and mucous membranes. Yet the effects of this poison are absent after drying, so the presence of buttercups in feed is not harmful to livestock.

The whorl of the leaves of the **false baby's breath,** or **hedge bedstraw** (*Galium mullago*), is similar to that of sweet woodruff, showing clearly that the two plants are related. Like rennin in the stomach of cattle, the herbage of this plant also causes milk to curdle. The high, soft panicles are topped with tiny, white flowers. The undersides of the leaves are covered with light hair. Both grazing animals and bees are fond of false baby's breath because of its pleasant aroma.

Whereas the **mountain lungwort** (*Pulmonaria montana*) has red flowers, the common lungwort (*Pulmonaria officinalis*) is also known in some places as "unlike sisters," because it has first red and then violet-blue blossoms. Previously, the common lungwort, which contains mucolytic substances, salicylic acid, and tannins, was used as a tea against respiratory disturbances, but today it no longer has much medicinal significance.

The **pestilence wort,** or **butter bur** (*Petasites hybrides*), is common to loamy brook banks and sides of woods. It has a scaly stalk, where the flowers appear before the leaves. With a diameter of more than 30 centimeters (about 1 foot), the leaves are some of the largest observed in local flora. In fact, in the past they were even used to pack butter. At one time, the leaves were employed as an antitussive (cough remedy) and to relieve nervous stomach complaints, but they have been found to contain dangerous alkaloids.

77
Crowfoot buttercup, or **bachelor's button** (*Ranunculus acris* L.)
Buttercup, or crowfoot, family (Ranunculaceae)
V–X
Protoanemonin, saponins, tannins
Fresh herbage is poisonous and can irritate the skin and mucous membranes.

78
False baby's breath, or **hedge bedstraw** (*Galium mullago* L.)
Bedstraw, or madder, family (Rubiaceae)
VI–X
Salicylic acid, tannins, organic acids
Yellow spring bedstraw, lady's bedstraw, curdwort, or yellow bedstraw (*Galium verum*), has a diuretic effect.

79
Mountain lungwort (*Pulmonaria montana* L.)
Borage, or forget-me-not, family (Boraginaceae)
III–V
Mucilage, flavonoids, allantoin
Common lungwort (*Pulmonaria officinalis*) as a tea
Sore throat, cough, mucous congestion

80
Pestilence wort, or **butter bur** (*Petasites hybrides* L.)
Composite, or daisy, family (Compositae)
III–V
Not to be used because of pyrrolizidine alkaloids!

77 Crowfoot buttercup, bachelor's button
79 Mountain lungwort

78 False baby's breath, hedge bedstraw
80 Pestilence wort, butter bur

The **European false hellebore,** or **American white hellebore** (*Veratrum album*), is generally found in alpine pastures like the moist meadows of the Zillertal (a valley in the Austrian Alps). A highly poisonous plant, it reaches a height of 1½ meters (almost 5 feet) and is also known as "sneeze root" in some places. Many consider this member of the lily family to be a detested, space-consuming weed. Its inflorescence is occasionally confused with that of the yellow gentian. Yet its leaves, in contrast to those of the yellow gentian, are alternate and have a downy back. The large, yellowish-green flowers are partially hermaphroditic (both male and female) and appear in a clustered panicle. Cattle avoid this plant, as it causes vomiting and colic. As far back as the Middle Ages, European false hellebore was known to be a very harsh medicine. In Elizabethan England, the powdered root was mixed in snuff. The hammer-shaped rootstocks contain highly active alkaloids, so they should be applied only under the supervision of a physician or in very diluted homeopathic agents, for the treatment of nerve pains, cramps, a weak heart, or gastrointestinal disorders.

Because of its reflective, white-mottled leaves, the **milk thistle,** or **lady's-thistle** (*Silybum marianum*), is frequently used as an ornamental plant. A lovely example of it can be observed growing in the monastery garden here. As with many herbs of the Mediterranean region, the milk thistle has medicinal effects that have been known about since antiquity. In the Middle Ages, it was considered to be a miraculous plant. It can be seen in pictures of the Virgin Mary—for instance, in the famous painting from the fifteenth century entitled *Garden of Paradise,* hanging in the Frankfurt Städel Museum. The seeds are used medicinally together with the husk, for the effective agents are found directly under the husk. Because the effective complex, the silymarin, is not very water soluble, extracts in the form of tablets and drops are used primarily instead of a tea. Silymarin detoxifies the liver and is especially helpful as supportive therapy for severe hepatic disturbances following hepatitis, as well as for alcohol and drug abuse. Even the fatal consequences of consuming certain mushrooms that result in liver destruction can be halted through the administration of high concentrations of silymarin.

The inconspicuous **common self-heal,** or **heal-all** (*Prunella vulgaris*), brings forth its reddish-violet blossoms in woods and fields from May to October almost without being noticed. It is a member of the Labiate family, whose stamens resemble a halberd. Because of this plant's toughness and immunity to the weather, it is distributed throughout the world. As its name implies, heal-all has a host of medicinal uses. It can be employed as a tea for internal healing, as a wash for external wounds, as a gargle for throat irritations, and as an astringent for hemorrhage and diarrhea. This plant has also been known to help stop fits and convulsions.

The **high mallow, common mallow,** or **blue mallow** (*Malva sylvestris*), is cultivated and can also be spotted growing wild in fields and along fences and roadsides. Typical of the plant are its light-purple flowers with darker stripes. The leaves of this plant, also known as the "cheese-flower," contain as much as 8 percent mucilage. In pectoral teas, mucilage has an anti-inflammatory effect on the upper respiratory tract and helps to dilute thick secretions that can then be expectorated. The teas are thus good for coughs, hoarseness, bronchitis, laryngitis, and emphysema. The red–violet flowers of the mallow also add a pleasing visual component to the teas.

81
European false hellebore, or
American white hellebore
(*Veratrum album* L.)
Lily family (Liliaceae)
VI–VIII
Alkaloid
This plant is highly poisonous!

82
Milk thistle, or **lady's-thistle**
(*Silybum marianum* L.)
Composite, or daisy, family
(Compositae)
VI–IX (cultivated)
Fruit without the crinose crown
Tea, tablets, drops
Silymarin, tannins, essential oil
Liver protection, liver regeneration,
indigestion

83
Common self-heal, or **heal-all**
(*Prunella vulgaris* L.)
Mint, or dead-nettle, family (Labiatae)
V–X
Internal healing, treating external
wounds, relieving throat irritations,
controlling hemorrhage and diarrhea,
terminating convulsions

84
High mallow, common mallow,
or **blue mallow** (*Malva sylvestris*)
Mallow family (Malvaceae)
V–IX
Flowers, herbage, leaves
Tea
Mucilage, essential oil, tannins
Relief in cases of coughing, hoarseness, sore throat, bronchitis

81 European false hellebore, American white hellebore
83 Common self-heal, heal-all

82 Milk thistle, lady's-thistle
84 High mallow, common mallow, blue mallow

*M*eadowsweet (*Spiraea* aggregate species) shrubs, including the whitethorn, the blackthorn or sloe, and the strawberries, are members of the rose family. These plants, which are native to southeastern Europe, decorate the slopes and roadsides around the Waldsee (a nearby lake) with their multitude of small, fragrant, white blossoms. Because of their clustered, or panicled, inflorescence, some of the thirty types of plants in this genus are cultivated as hardy, ornamental shrubs and are found in many parks and gardens.

The **false horsetail, bottle brush, Dutch rush,** or **scouring rush** (*Equisetum arvense*), is among the thirty-two different species of the horsetail family that still exist today. These rush-like, flowerless plants, found all over the world, go back many million years before the evolution of blossoming plants. They are "living fossils," originating from the Carboniferous period (300 million years B.C.). Horsetails belong to the classification of ferns and mosses, and are therefore flowerless, multiplying by way of spores. Two types of stems are produced. In the spring, one type appears, bearing on top a brown, spindle-shaped spike containing spores. It soon dies, and in the summer is replaced by the sterile, green, jointed stem, with its whorls of delicate branches. It is this type that is used medicinally and likened in form to a horsetail. When collecting this plant, swampy sites should be avoided, as the poisonous marsh horsetail is found there. Because of their high concentration of crystalline salicylic acid, horsetails are a suitable ingredient in polish for silverware. Their high concentration of salicylic acid also makes them appropriate for bath products, as it helps to strengthen the connective tissues. Sebastian Kneipp noted that, when taken internally and used in abdominal vapor baths, horsetail has "versatile and excellent effects." In the form of teas, the field horsetails have proven to be a mild diuretic agent for washing out the urinary tract and for the elimination of renal gravel.

The juice from the horsetail is said to strengthen the lungs and promote blood coagulation. Used externally as a wash, horsetail is good for wounds, sores, and skin problems. As a mouthwash, it brings down mouth and gum inflammations.

The **field chickweed, mouse ear,** or **starry grasswort** (*Cerastium arvense*), is a plant that is noticed frequently along the paths around Bad Wörishofen. The nonblossoming stems form a thick lawn, whereas the stems with flowers stand upright. A member of the pink, or campion, family, the plant is crinose (hairy) all over. Capsules extend from the flower calyx like arched horns.

A member of the rose family, the **common blackberry, bramble,** or **dewberry** (*Rubus fruchticosus*), grows in the forests around Bad Wörishofen. In contrast to those of the raspberry, the leaves of the blackberry are darker and more crinose, all originating from a single site. The tips of the lower sprouts take root, making the typical "blackberry arch." According to legend, if we crawl under one of these arches the thorns will protect us from any trouble. Because of their high concentration of tannins, the leaves of the common blackberry are effective as a mild agent against diarrhea. When fermented, the leaves become darker and more aromatic, making them a good substitute for black tea. In this form, the leaves are also used to alter the taste of many household teas. The juice from this plant has been shown to reduce hoarseness.

85
Meadowsweet (*Spiraea* aggregate species)
Rose family (Rosaceae)
V–VII
86
Field horsetail, bottle brush, Dutch rush, or **scouring rush**
(*Equisetum arvense* L.)
Horsetail family
(Equisetaceae)
III–IV
Herbage
Tea, plant juice, bath extract
(M) Catarrhs of the kidneys and efferent urinary tract
(F) Cough, bronchial complaints, rheumatic disorders, promotes blood coagulation and "blood purification" Externally, for strengthening the connective tissues, healing wounds, lessening mouth and gum inflammations
87
Field chickweed, mouse ear, or **starry grasswort** (*Cerastium arvense* L.)
Pink, or campion, family
(Caryophyllaceae)
VI–IX
88
Common blackberry, bramble, or **dewberry** (*Rubus fruchticosus*)
Rose family (Rosaceae)
VI–IX
Leaves, berries
Tea, plant juice
(M) Mild cases of diarrhea, household tea, juice for hoarseness

85 Meadowsweet
87 Field chickweed, mouse ear, starry grasswort
86 Field horsetail, bottle brush, Dutch rush, scouring rush
88 Common blackberry, bramble, dewberry

*G*arden valerian, common valerian, or **allheal** (*Valeriana officinalis*), bushes reach a height of up to 2 meters (more than 6 feet) and can be seen growing along the damp, shady banks of brooks in the Zillertal (a valley in the Austrian Alps). This plant spends the winter as a cylindrical rootstock, and the underground runners are important for its propagation. The umbelliferous panicles at the ends of the stems consist of countless white or pink, funnel-shaped, fragrant, small blossoms. Fertilization occurs primarily by way of flies. The plant's name in German, *Baldrian,* can be traced to the Germanic god of light, Baldur. The Latin name probably comes from *valeo,* meaning "I feel well," and is an indication of the medicinal effects attributed to the root. Common valerian is both soothing and sleep-inducing. It is also effective for nervous cardiac complaints and digestive disorders, as well as phobias over examinations and other types of stress. Sebastian Kneipp said that "its use as a soporific [sleeping drug] is highly valued." Because the harvesting of the rootstock leads to the loss of the plant, it is cultivated primarily. The typical fragrance exudes from the roots after they are dried. The essential oils have a balancing effect on humans, whereas the intense odor makes cats "high." Because of its strong odor, valerian has frequently been used for magic tricks. A plant often linked with superstition, valerian was believed to protect people from plagues, evil spirits, and the devil. Farmers believed that, when added to the drinking water of livestock, together with wild marjoram and dill, valerian protected animals from witches.

The **purple avens, drooping avens,** or **nodding avens** (*Geum rivale*), with its drooping flowers, is also found in moist habitats. As a member of the rose family, it has five round sepals and pinnatifid leaves. After the purplish flowers blossom, the long-stalked collective fruit appears with a hook at the end, extending outward like a pig's tail. The rootstock, when taken with milk and sugar, can be used for diarrhea, digestive problems, and a lack of appetite. The whole plant can be used for an infusion (brewed tea) to clear up congestion and combat nausea. However, consuming too much can cause disagreeable side effects.

The classical feed clover, **red clover** (*Trifolium pratense*) is found all over meadows. The spherical little flower of this member of the pea family has an aroma much like that of honey. The plant is also known as "sugar bread" in some places, as children like to suck out the sweet "honey." Bees are unable to reach the nectar of this clover due to their short proboscises, so it must be pollinated by bumblebees with longer proboscises. Not only has the cloverleaf been used as a symbol for luck, given as a love charm, and employed as protection against witches, but it has also been used in artistic forms—take, for example, the cloverleaf tracery in Gothic churches, the "club" in playing cards, and its use as a symbol for the trinity in Irish coats of arms. Although red clover is important mainly as a feed plant, it is also a popular plant in folk medicine with many usages, including reducing inflammation.

Into June, the **pale-yellow iris, water flag**, or **yellow flag** (*Iris pseudacorus*), blossoms in the moist biotope of the herb garden. This protected, slightly poisonous plant grows to a height of up to 1 meter (about 3 feet). The orris root, good for treating water retention, coughs, a sore throat, and colic, and used to scent toothpaste, comes from the rootstock of another species, the Florentine iris, which has an aroma like that of violets.

89
Garden valerian, common valerian, or **allheal** (*Valeriana officinalis* L.)
Valerian family (Valerianaceae)
V–IX
Root
Tea, tincture, plant juice, tablets, bath oils
Essential oils
(M) Soothing, sleep-inducing, for nervousness, nervous complaints of the gastrointestinal system

90
Purple avens, drooping avens, or **nodding avens** (*Geum rivale* L.)
Rose family (Rosaceae)
IV–V
For diarrhea and digestive problems, to stimulate the appetite, to clear up congestion, to counteract nausea
Consuming too much can cause unpleasant side effects!

91
Red clover (*Trifolium pratense*)
Pea family (Papilionaceae)
V–IX
Flowers
Tannins (glycosides, isoflavones)
(F) Inflammation of the mucous membranes

92
Pale-yellow iris, water flag, or **yellow flag** (*Iris pseudacorus* L.)
Iris family (Iridaceae)
VI–VI (endangered and therefore protected!)
Bitter principles
The yellow-blossomed wild plant is slightly poisonous!

89 Garden valerian, common valerian, allheal
91 Red clover

90 Purple avens, drooping avens, nodding avens
92 Pale-yellow iris, water flag, yellow flag

From the end of April to the beginning of June, the fields around Bad Wörishofen are blanketed in yellow from **cultivated rape, colza,** or **cole** (*Brassica napus*). As with all members of the Cruciferae family, the petals and sepals are four-fold and crossed, or opposite. After blossoming, the flower develops into a long, narrow pod with glomerate seeds only a few millimeters in diameter (up to about 1/8 inch). These seeds are about 25 percent protein, 20 percent carbohydrate, and as much as 50 percent fat in the form of rapeseed oil. Through cultivation, attempts are presently being made to increase the concentration of the plant's essential, unsaturated fatty acids. Mixed with poppyseed and linseed oil, rapeseed oil is used as a salad oil and in the production of margarine. Technically, rapeseed oil is employed as a lubricating and leather oil.

The **codlins and cream, hairy willow herb, great willow herb,** or **apple pie** (*Epilobium hirsutum*), from the evening-primrose, or willow-herb, family, is recognizable because of its glandular, hairy stamens. As with the dandelion, the propagation of the different species of willow herb is carried out by the wind, making them a much-feared weed in many gardens. A plant with small blossoms, hairy willow herb is applied in folk medicine for the treatment of benign complaints of the prostate.

Buckthorn, blackthorn, or **alder blackthorn** (*Rhamnus frangula*), bushes are frequently found in damp parts of oak forests and in the surrounding areas. Reaching a height of up to 3 meters (about 10 feet), this member of the buckthorn family is easily identified through the light, axillary, corklike tufts on its grayish-brown bark. In the springtime, this bark peels off the branches. The berries, which are unpalatable for humans, are consumed by thrushes without any ill effects. Buckthorn is also known as "powder wood" or "shooting wood" in some places, as the wood was previously charred in charcoal kilns to make black

gunpowder. Before the discovery of aniline dyes, the bark and berries were used to produce yellow, green, and blue coloring agents, depending on their particular stage of ripening. The anthracene glycoside of the buckthorn's well-seasoned bark has proven to be effective as a mild laxative. The bark is aged for at least a year before it is used, as beforehand it not only smells rotten but also causes stomachaches when administered. However, as a laxative, it is not suited to long-term use, and should not be used at all during pregnancy or in cases of intestinal obstruction.

When hiking around Bad Wörishofen, it's not unusual to encounter the **common nipplewort** (*Lapsana communis*) along the edges of paths. The hairless stalk has many branches, and all of the sepals of the calyx are shaped like a tongue. This plant is considered the "vegetable for the poor man." After they triumphed over Pompeii, Caesar's troops joked in a satirical verse that their reward was having to nourish themselves from the *Lapsana*.

93
Cultivated rape, colza, or **cole** (*Brassica napus* L.)
Mustard, or cabbage, family (Cruciferae)
VI–IX

94
Codlins and cream, hairy willow herb, great willow herb, or **apple pie** (*Epilobium hirsutum*)
Evening-primrose, or willow-herb, family (Onograceae)
VII–VIII
Herbage
Beta-sitosterol, flavonoids
Tea
(F) Relief from benign complaints of the prostate

95
Buckthorn, blackthorn, or **alder blackthorn** (*Rhamnus frangula* L.)
Buckthorn family (Rhamnaceae)
V–VI
Bark, seasoned for one year
Tea, coated tablets
Anthracene glycosides (glucofrangulin, frangulin)
Mild, stool-softening laxative, not suitable for long-term use, not to be used by pregnant women or in cases of intestinal obstruction

96
Common nipplewort (*Lapsana communis* L.)
Nipplewort family (Liguliflorae)
VII–IX

93 Cultivated rape, colza, cole
95 Buckthorn, blackthorn, alder blackthorn

94 Codlins and cream, hairy willow herb, great willow
herb, apple pie
96 Common nipplewort

The large, compound flowers of the **eltrot, masterwort,** or **hogweed** (*Heracleum sphondylium*), dominate the fields of the Bavarian Algau region into the summer. Its botanical name is derived from the Greek hero Heracles (also known as Hercules). The umbels are usually populated by flies, beetles, and butterflies. The large, pinnatisect leaves have petioled sheaths at their base. This plant has an unpleasant odor and is fed to livestock only while the feed is still young. In Russia, the shoots are eaten like asparagus. In Poland, a strong beer is brewed from the seeds. Yet masterwort has been known to increase sensitivity to sunlight and thus to irritate the skin.

The inconspicuous and less common **northern bedstraw,** or **cheese rennet** (*Galium boreale*), tends to grow in sparsely wooded habitats. There are 300 different species of this genus, of which a hundred are native to Europe. The northern bedstraw's stalk is erect, usually has offshoots, and is covered with horizontal hairs. The leaves have four verticils and a lanceolate (or thorny) tip. Three veins traverse the leaves along the longitudinal axis without presenting a clear vein network. The small white or yellow flowers secrete honey that is released at easily accessible sites, so insects with a short proboscis can benefit from it too; in addition, flies and beetles can distribute the pollen with their legs. Another species, the yellow spring bedstraw, lady's bedstraw, curdwort, or yellow bedstraw (*Galium verum*), has a mild diuretic effect and is also used for healing wounds.

The **horsebean,** or **broad bean** (*Vicia faba*), which is cultivated in the fields of the Moosberg (a mountain near Bad Wörishofen), is an erect plant that reaches a height of up to 1 meter (about 3 feet). Its bluish-gray color lends the fields an unusual appearance. The papilionaceous flower has a black spot on the standard, and the vexillum has reddish veins. This bean, which is also known as "pig bean" in some places, serves primarily as a feed for livestock.

From May to June, the **meadow foxtail** (*Alopecurus pratensis*) is a common sight in the meadows of the Zillertal (a valley in the Austrian Alps). As a perennial top grass, it is very hardy. The heads of this high-quality grass, which look like pink pipe cleaners, can grow to a thickness of up to 1 centimeter (almost ½ inch). The shape of the head has led to the plant's also being called "donkey's tail," "dog's tail," "rat's tail," and "fox's brush" in some places. The meadow foxtail is an ingredient of the "hay pack" in a Kneipp thermotherapy.

97
Eltrot, masterwort, or hogweed
(*Heracleum sphondylium* L.)
Parsley, or carrot, family
(Umbelliferae)
V–X
Photosensitization, causing skin irritation

98
Northern bedstraw, or cheese rennet (*Galium boreale* L.)
Bedstraw, or madder, family
(Rubiaceae)
VI–VIII
Salicylic acid, tannins, flavonoids
Galium verum species is mildly diuretic and also used for healing wounds.

99
Horsebean, or broad bean (*Vicia faba* L.)
Pea family (Papilionaceae)
V–VII
Protein, amino acids, minerals
Livestock feed

100
Meadow foxtail (*Alopecurus pratensis* L.)
Grass family (Gramineae)
V–VII
Used in the "hay pack" of a Kneipp thermotherapy

97 Eltrot, masterwort, hogweed
99 Horsebean, broad bean

98 Northern bedstraw, cheese rennet
100 Meadow foxtail

Often associated with magic power and poison, the **deadly nightshade,** or **belladonna** (*Atropa belladonna*), is a glandular, crinose (hairy) bush encountered in pastures and mountain forests. According to popular lore, the devil himself makes use of this plant, so it has also been called "devil's cherries," "devil's herb," "naughty man's cherries," and "Satan's apple" in some places. The "black mandragora" of the ancients was probably our belladonna. The genus name *Atropa* is derived from Atropos, one of the three Fates among the Greeks and Romans; it was she who deprived individuals of life by cutting the mortal thread. Atropine, a substance that paralyzes the muscles that contract the pupils, can be attained from the plant's leaves and roots. Ophthalmologists make use of this dilatory effect on the pupils by using drops with this agent to examine the retina. During the Renaissance, women put drops with belladonna extracts into their eyes to acquire large, alluring eyes, thus becoming a "lovely woman" (*bella donna*). But, as a result, they saw their sweethearts through blurred vision. Today, in the hands of physicians, in a minute, precise concentration, atropine plays an important role as a strong spasmolytic agent. However, belladonna is an extremely poisonous plant and is not suitable for self-medication. Three to four of the shiny, black berries are enough to constitute a deadly dose for humans. These berries are recognizable through their five-fold calyx in the form of a saucer. Birds, on the other hand, can eat the berries without experiencing any ill effects, thereby propagating these bushes throughout fields and forests.

The **dove pincushions,** or **small scabious** (*Scabiose columbaria*), with its blue-violet flowers, is very common to the drier meadows around Bad Wörishofen. Its genus name is derived from scabies, because the plant was previously and erroneously used to treat this contagious illness. It has also been known as "thunder flower," as some superstitious people thought this member of the teasel, or scabious, family offered protection from thunderstorms.

The **brown knapweed** (*Centaurea jacea*), which grows to a height of 1 meter (about 3 feet), is similar in appearance to a red-violet cornflower. In some places, it is called "tufted flower," from the white tufts observed in its early stages of blossoming. As a hardy plant, it is also known as "iron herbage." The thick heads of the flowers have led some to call it "fat head" and "trouser button." The mythical centaur Chiron, famed for his knowledge of medicine and the arts, allegedly recognized the healing properties of this plant, providing the basis for the genus name *Centaurea*. In the Middle Ages, brown knapweed was believed to have a therapeutic effect on bone fractures, injuries, cholera, and inflammations of the urinary tract. These effects, however, could not be verified.

In the fresh, flowing waters around Bad Wörishofen, it's not unusual to see the bright **watercress,** or **tall nasturtium** (*Nasturtium officinale*), with its small, yellowish-white flowers. In France, the plant is known as "bard's herb," as it is said to cause a husky voice to attain a radiant tone. As with mustard and horseradish leaves, the pungent, aromatic leaves of the watercress plant contain a saccharate compound of the mustard oils, bitter principles, and vitamins A, C, and D. Watercress is therefore a very popular ingredient in soups, salads, and sauces. Because of its high concentration of iodine, it is considered by some to be a good prophylactic agent against goiters. Its digestive effects were praised by Sebastian Kneipp, who said, "The fresh-pressed juice is not only blood-purifying but also strengthens the stomach." Watercress is also known to have diuretic and expectorant effects. Nevertheless, excessive or prolonged use is not recommended, and may be especially harmful for pregnant women.

101
Deadly nightshade, or **belladonna** (*Atropa belladonna* L.)
Tomato, or nightshade, family (Solanaceae)
VI–VIII
Standardized contents from the leaves, herbage, root
Deadly poisonous plant, not suitable for self-treatment
Atropine, hyocyamine, scopalamine, as well as alkaloids
Useful in the hands of physicians as a finished spasmolytic preparation and for ophthalmology

102
Dove pincushions, or **small scabious** (*Scabiose columbaria* L.)
Teasel, or scabious, family (Dipsacaceae)
VII–IX

103
Brown knapweed (*Centaurea jacea* L.)
Composite, or daisy, family (Compositae)
VI–X

104
Watercress, or **tall nasturtium** (*Nasturtium officinale*)
Mustard, or cabbage, family (Cruciferae)
V–VIII
Herbage
Salad, plant juice
Mustard oil glycoside, potassium, iron, vitamins
Mild diuretic, "blood purification," disturbances of the liver and biliary systems
Excessive or prolonged use can irritate the stomach, and can be especially harmful for pregnant women.

101 Deadly nightshade, belladonna
103 Brown knapweed

102 Dove pincushions, small scabious
104 Watercress, tall nasturtium

A highly valued medicinal plant, the **German chamomile, wild chamomile,** or **chamomile** (*Matricaria chamomilla*), is cultivated and also seen growing wild in fields and along the roadside. Chamomile tea is the epitome of medicinal teas and is used for a range of problems, from nervous conditions and insomnia to rheumatic disorders and rashes. This plant has a hollow stem, from which arises the solitary, terminal flower, consisting of a yellow disk with white rays. The genus name *Matricaria* is derived from the Latin *mater,* for "mother," and alludes to the previous use of this plant for women during childbirth. In certain places, it is still also known as "mother's herbage." The chamomile plant is considered to be holy by some and has been associated with the Germanic sun god Baldur. Its effective components—bisabolol, chamazulene, and water-soluble flavones, in an essential oil—have been researched thoroughly and are responsible for the high esteem attributed to this plant. These components supplement one another with their spasmolytic, anti-inflammatory, wound-healing, antibacterial, and carminative (against flatulence) effects. When used internally, chamomile can benefit gastrointestinal disorders. Externally, it can be used to treat inflammations of the skin and mucous membranes and poorly healing wounds; it is also an ingredient in cosmetic preparations. The inhalation of chamomile can relieve inflammations and irritations of the respiratory tract. Sebastian Kneipp made use of chamomile primarily as a bath additive and for poultices.

Creeping thyme, mother-of-thyme, or **wild thyme** (*Thymus serpyllium*), is cultivated widely for its use as a spice. With its little, reddish-purple flowers that are whorled in clusters, this small shrub is also spotted growing wild in dry meadows and on the sides of cliffs. Although thyme has a broad range of culinary applications, it is most commonly used as a seasoning for pizza, pasta, and roasts. Medicinally, the herb is often used in bath additives for relief of rheumatic disorders, bruises, and sprains, and as a filling for relaxing herbal pillows (in some places, it is also known as "Maria's bed straw"). Because of their antiseptic effect, the essential oils from this plant are employed as an ingredient in gargles and bronchial teas, and are applied externally on wounds. When administered internally, thyme can be used to treat a number of conditions, including gastrointestinal disorders and diarrhea. However, excessive internal use should be avoided, as it can lead to poisoning.

English lavender (*Lavandula officinalis*) comes from the warmer countries in the Mediterranean region. In France, especially around Grasse, it is cultivated in fields for its aromatic flowers. The harvest of this important basic material for the perfume and cosmetic industries is celebrated there annually. This small shrub is also appreciated in gardens because of its lovely flowers and pleasant aroma. The plant has purple, tubular flowers arranged along its gray–green stem at various stages. The five flowers blossom consecutively from the lower level upward. Lavender has sedative, spasmolytic, carminative, choleretic, and antiseptic effects. According to Sebastian Kneipp, lavender oil should be a part of all home medicine cabinets. Lavender is a perfect plant for aromatherapy and, when used in this way, is said to balance the emotions, lift the spirits, and restore strength and vitality. Also, as an environmentally friendly, fragrant insecticide for use against moths, a lavender sack is an effective device for linen cupboards.

The **creeping buttercup** (*Ranunculus repens*) is commonly found along the edges of waterways and paths. This member of the buttercup, or crowfoot, family has individual, 50-centimeter (about 1½ foot) long, hairy stems with creeping offshoots and golden-yellow flowers.

105
German chamomile, wild chamomile, or **chamomile** (*Matricaria chamomilla* L.)
Composite, or daisy, family (Compositae)
V–IX
Flowers, oil
Tea, extract, ointment, oil, bath additive, inhalant
Essential oil (chamazulene, bisabolol), coumarin
Gastrointestinal disorders, inflammations of the skin and mucous membranes, illnesses of the respiratory tract, wound healing, anti-inflammatory, spasmolytic, carminative

106
Creeping thyme, mother-of-thyme, or **wild thyme** (*Thymus serpyllium*)
Mint, or dead-nettle, family (Labiatae)
IV–IX
Herbage, oil, cough syrup, inhalant, bath additive, herb
Essential oil (thymol, carvacrol), flavonoids
Spasmolytic, disinfectant, coughs and bronchitis, catarrhs, gastrointestinal disorders

107
English lavender (*Lavandula officinalis* L.)
Mint, or dead-nettle, family (Labiatae)
IV–IX
Tea, bath additive, aromatherapy
Essential oil, coumarin, tannins, flavonoids
Sedative, spasmolytic, carminative, choleretic, and antiseptic effects

108
Creeping buttercup (*Ranunculus repens*)
Buttercup, or crowfoot, family (Ranunculaceae)
V–VIII

105 German chamomile, wild chamomile, chamomile
107 English lavender

106 Creeping thyme, mother-of-thyme, wild thyme
108 Creeping buttercup

The **hawthorn,** or **whitethorn,** species *Crataegus oxyacantha, Crataegus laevigata,* and *Crataegus monogyna* are not only important sources of drugs but also give us a great deal of pleasure because of their luxuriant inflorescence. The flowers, however, are more pleasant to the eye than to the nose because of their intensive odor. Growing as either a shrub or a tree, the hawthorn can reach a height of 10 meters (more than 30 feet), and is seen along the edges of forests and paths around Bad Wörishofen. Carpenters and wood turners are fond of the wood from the hawthorn because of its hardness and ruggedness. Hawthorn was first used as a medicinal herb during the nineteenth century. Its leaves, blossoms, and fresh, red berries are all employed therapeutically. As a tea or in the form of tablets and drops, hawthorn extracts are used to normalize blood pressure by regulating the heart. Moreover, pharmacological investigations have shown that hawthorn, as a "friend of the heart," is an ideal agent for treating a reduced functional capacity of the heart (a geriatric heart), a sensation of constriction in the region of the heart, and mild forms of cardiac irregularity.

The **common Saint-John's-wort, rose of Sharon,** or **Klamath weed** (*Hypericum perforatum*), blooms a brilliant yellow and can be found growing in the dry soil along the edges of woods and paths. Common Saint-John's-wort has strong leaves that appear to be perforated, also earning it the name "hard spotted hay" in certain places. Much lore has centered around this plant as an effective agent against demons and lightning. But it also has a long history as a medicinal plant with varied uses. Paracelsus considered an extract made from the fresh flowers, in a sunflower or olive oil base, to be an unparalleled agent for healing wounds. Sebastian Kneipp praised common Saint-John's-wort as a "marvelous balm against swelling, lumbago, and luxations due to gout." Its soothing effects on the psyche were first revealed during the nineteenth century. Because of its mood-elevating and antidepres-

sive agent, hypericin, preparations administered internally are used primarily to strengthen the nervous system. However, hypericin can increase sensitivity to the sun, heightening the risk of sunburn. When Saint-John's-wort is taken in the form of teas, plant juices, drops, or tablets, it is therefore important to avoid direct sunlight as much as possible.

The **common barberry, European barberry, holly-leafed barberry,** or **sowberry** (*Berberis vulgaris*), is a deciduous shrub that is fond of warm, dry forests. Botanically interesting, the stamens of this plant, which are sensitive to tactile stimulation, move rapidly up the pistil after being touched. The yellowish wood is extremely hard. The leaves serve as a secondary host for the dangerous black rust that sometimes afflicts grains. Its red, cylindrical berries have a sour taste. Aside from the alkaloid berberine, which is mildly but not dangerously poisonous, the berries contain fruit acids and are thus used in marmalades and juices. Medicinally, barberry is employed for various liver ailments, as a laxative, and to lower blood pressure and a fever.

A tree with bushy clusters of yellow flowers, the **small-leafed lime, little-leaf linden,** or **common linden** (*Tilia cordata*), exudes a captivating fragrance, especially at night. The leaves are smaller than those of the broad-leafed lime, large-leafed lime, or big-leafed linden (also known in some places as "summer linden"), which has an even stronger aroma. Linden trees can reach an age of up to 1,000 years. A particularly impressive example is one in Schöneschach from the year 1648. Linden trees are revered and sung about in various cultures. Many place names also make use of the lindens. The soft wood is used for carving and is fondly known as "holy wood." The carefully dried flowers, collected shortly after blossoming, are used medicinally as a sweat-inducing tea in cases of feverish colds.

109
Hawthorn, or **whitethorn**
(*Crataegus oxyacantha* L.,
Crataegus laevigata L., and
Crataegus monogyna L.)
Rose family (Rosaceae)
V–VI
Flowers, leaves, fruit
Tea, plant juices, coated tablets, drops
Proanthocyanidin, flavone gylcosides
(rutin, hyperoside, vitexin, etc.)
(M) Reduced physical powers, heart problems

110
Common Saint-John's-wort, rose of Sharon, or **Klamath weed** (*Hypericum perforatum* L.)
Saint-John's-wort family (Guttiferae)
VI–VIII
Blossoms, oil, tincture
Flavonoids (hypericin, hyperoside, rutin, etc.), essential oil
(M) Restlessness, sleep disturbances, depression, digestive disorders, skin care
Causes sensitivity to light

111
Common barberry, European barberry, holly-leafed barberry, sowberry (*Berberis vulgaris* L.)
Barberry family (Berberidaceae)
V–VI
Mildly poisonous alkaloid (berberine)
Ripe fruit is not dangerous.
For liver ailments, as a laxative, to lower blood pressure

112
Small-leafed lime, little-leafed linden, or **common linden** (*Tilia cordata* L.)
Linden, or lime, family (Tiliaciae)
VI–VII
Inflorescence, wood coal
Tea, inhalant, bath oil
Flavonoids (rutin, quercitrin)
(M) Diaphoretic (sweat-inducing) in the event of feverish colds

109 Hawthorn, whitethorn
111 Common barberry, European barberry, holly-leafed barberry

110 Common Saint-John's-wort, rose of Sharon, Klamath weed
112 Small-leafed lime, little-leafed linden, common linden

Hikers frequently encounter the **sweetbrier** (*Rosa villosa,* subspecies *pomifera*) when walking near Kirchdorf. This short shrub has a layer of soft hair and is closely related to the dog rose. The round false fruit is about 1 to 2 centimeters (about ½ to 1 inch) in diameter and differs in appearance from that of the dog rose.

The **columbine meadow rue** (*Thalictrum aquilegifolium*) is found in moist habitats of the Zillertal (a valley in the Austrian Alps). It is quite noticeable in forests because of its delicate, light-violet flowers that grow in a cyme (a single terminal blossom). The narrower leaves are frequently covered with a bluish frost. The columbine meadow rue belongs to the buttercup, or crowfoot, family, which is made up of about eighty-five different species. This species bears a pollinic flower and is propagated by means of insects. Its trigonal fruit is winged.

Unlike the aromatic, angular Solomon's seal, the rarer **pink Solomon's seal** (*Polygonatum verticillatum*) grows in the shady forests of the Moosberg (a mountain near Bad Wörishofen). The names of the different types of Solomon's seal are based on the characteristic appearance of their snakelike rhizomes. As a member of the lily family, pink Solomon's seal is closely related to the lily of the valley. Its stalk is rather erect with numerous broad leaves, the last of which appears in a terminal position. The berries are considered poisonous. Various superstitions have given rise to a number of other names for this plant, including "bewitched weed," which is a reference to the "bewitched" cows that were consequently unable to give milk.

The **bog blueberry, bog bilberry,** or **wortleberry** (*Vaccinium uliginosum*), is also known locally as "moss berry" and "swamp blueberry." This member of the heath family grows in moist areas of the Moosberg. Its drooping, light-pink, jug-shaped blossoms appear in multiples at the end of the stem. Its leaves are convolved to a certain extent and bluish-green in color. This plant loses its leaves during the winter. The dark-blue berries are whitish inside and can be eaten. Although the bog blueberry is called "intoxicating berry" in some places, the berries have no intoxicating effects, but may cause headaches and vomiting when large quantities are eaten.

113
Sweetbrier (*Rosa villosa,* subspecies *pomifera*)
Rose family (Rosaceae)
VI–VII
Fruit is not used medicinally.

114
Columbine meadow rue (*Thalictrum aquilegifolium* L.)
Buttercup, or crowfoot, family (Ranunculaceae)
V–VII

115
Pink Solomon's seal (*Polygonatum verticillatum*)
Lily family (Liliaceae)
V–VI
Berries may be poisonous.

116
Bog blueberry, bog bilberry, or **wortleberry** (*Vaccinium uliginosum* L.)
Heath family (Ericaceae)
V–VI
Fruit, leaves
Arbutin, acids, minerals, tannins
The effects claimed are controversial—it may even be mildly poisonous.

113 Sweetbrier
115 Pink Solomon's seal

114 Columbine meadow rue
116 Bog blueberry, bog bilberry, wortleberry

The **corn poppy,** or **corn rose** (*Papaver rhoeas*), can be spotted growing on rocky cliffs and in fields and meadows. This plant's lovely, crimson-red flowers are often the radiant, central point of the symbolic wreath bound after harvesting and of bouquets of meadow flowers, although they soon lose their petals. The flowers grow singularly at the end of a hairy stalk. Even through many insects are known to be blind to the red color, and the flower of the corn poppy doesn't smell, they are able to find this blossom by means of its ultraviolet light that is visible only to insects' eyes. In certain places, the corn poppy is also known as the "rattling rose," as the seeds rattle in the ripe poppy capsules. Through a ring of holes in the upper margin, these seeds are flung from the capsule into the wind. All parts of this plant have a white, somewhat poisonous, milky latex. The genus name *Papaver* comes from the Celtic word *papa,* meaning "mash," and in fact the pressed juice from the corn poppy was previously mashed into food for babies because of its calming effect. The Egyptians and the Romans used the aromatic corn poppy seeds for baking and as a seasoning. However, the poppy seeds that we use today in baking are obtained from the opium poppy.

Although **kitchen sage,** or **garden sage** (*Salvia officinalis*), grows wild, it is mainly cultivated for its use as a spice. However, sage not only adds flavor to soups, sauces, poultry, and meats, but is also a medicinal herb with a long history and many applications. Its essential oil has destructive and inhibitory effects on bacteria, fungi, and viruses, and is thus employed in gargles and mouthwash. Sage is also used in gargles to reduce inflammations of the mouth, throat, and gums. Because of its bitter principle and tannin content, sage taken internally is effective against gastrointestinal disorders, intestinal catarrhs, and flatulence. In addition, sage teas have been known to combat increased perspiration, especially night sweats. In the past, it was even recommended that sage be rubbed on the teeth so that they would remain strong and clean. Sebastian Kneipp recommended sage for every garden. This shrublike plant has stems covered in fine hair, opposing, oblong-shaped leaves, and purple, blue, or white two-lipped flowers that grow in whorls forming terminal racemes.

Like the **common velvet-grass,** or **Yorkshire-fog** (*Holcus lanatus*), the **stinging nettle, common nettle,** or **greater nettle** (*Urtica dioica*), is a widespread weed that is difficult to eliminate. This plant is dioecious (has male flowers on one plant and female flowers on another). The male inflorescence stands upright, whereas the female cluster hangs and forms more side shoots. Young nettle plants can be eaten in salads and as a vegetable. However, old plants must be cooked thoroughly to be safe, as ingesting uncooked, old plants can lead to poisoning. Nettle ichor is suitable as both a fertilizer and a pesticide for the garden. As an additive to chickenfeed, nettle gives egg yolks a nice yellow color. Its genus name *Urtica* comes from the Latin word *urere,* "to burn," and in fact the bristly hairs of this plant do hurt when touched, so be careful when handling it. The stinging nettle has a long tradition as a medicinal plant. Roman physicians recommended whipping the body with nettles in order to stimulate blood flow. Sebastian Kneipp was aware that a canvaslike material was made of the nettle, but he also praised its "invaluable healing powers." These effects are frequently made use of today in the form of nettle lotions for the scalp, which stimulate the flow of blood, and diuretic teas and extracts from the nettle root, which have a soothing effect on benign prostate problems. However, nettle should not be used in cases of venous stasis or edema resulting from reduced cardiac or renal function.

117
Corn poppy, or **corn rose**
(*Papaver rhoeas* L.)
Poppy family (Papaveraceae)
V–VII
Flowers
Alkaloid (rhoeadine), coloring agent, organic acids, saponins as auxiliary agents in teas, but may be poisonous and are no longer used
118
Kitchen sage, or **garden sage**
(*Salvia officinalis* L.)
Mint, or dead-nettle, family (Labiatae)
VI–VII
Leaves, essential oil
Tea, tincture, tablets, spice
Essential oil (thujone, cineole, camphor), tannins, flavonoids
(M) Inflammations of the mouth, throat, and gums
Emphractic (reduces sweating), gastrointestinal disorders
119
Common velvet-grass, or
Yorkshire-fog (*Holcus lanatus* L.)
Grass family (Gramineae)
VI–VIII
120
Stinging nettle, common nettle,
or **greater nettle** (*Urtica dioica* L.)
Nettle family (Urticaceae)
VI–X
Herbage, roots, fruit (seeds)
Tea, tonic, plant juices, coated plant tablets, scalp lotions
Sterols, phenylpropane, lignans, flavonoids, amino acids
(M) Diuretic, problems in urination, benign prostatic enlargement, rheumatism, gout, disturbances of the biliary system; stimulates the flow of blood when applied externally

117 Corn poppy, corn rose

118 Kitchen sage, garden sage

119 Common velvet-grass, Yorkshire-fog

120 Stinging nettle, common nettle, greater nettle

*O*f this beloved plant has not yet been picked by hikers, the graceful **European lily of the valley** (*Convallaria majalis*) can be found in small clusters in the sparsely wooded forests around Bad Wörishofen. Along with the violet and the forget-me-not, the lily of the valley has some of the most appealing flowers, which grow in dainty, white, bell-shaped florets and exude a captivating aroma. The Latin name of the genus, *Convallaria,* means "valley lily"; the species name *majalis* is derived from the goddess of the earth and of May, Maya, and is an indication of the month in which it blossoms. The lily of the valley is a self-pollinating plant. The pea-sized, scarlet-red berries, which are less poisonous than the rest of the plant, develop in late summer. The lily of the valley is similar to the foxglove with regard to its beauty and toxicity. But whereas that plant dies after blossoming, the lily of the valley, with its rootstock, is a perennial. The lily of the valley contains cardioactive glycosides, which can be administered by physicians for the treatment of acute cardiac insufficiency. The plant also can be used as a diuretic and a laxative. However, because its contents are poisonous, it is not suited for self-medication.

The **German iris** (*Iris germanica*), with its violet blossoms, and the **Florentine iris** (*Iris florentina*), with its blue-veined, yellow-fringed white flowers, are seen in many gardens. The rootstock of the latter species, known as the orris root, is a good diuretic and helps to sooth the pain of teething infants. This species grows wild in the Mediterranean region as well as in Mexico, and its commercial production is based in Florence, Italy. A powder made from the orris root is frequently used in the perfume and cosmetic industries.

A plant with a sweet and pungent aroma, **sweet basil,** or **common basil** (*Ocimum basilicum*), grows wild and is also cultivated as a spice. From its bushy stems arise often purplish leaves and two-lipped flowers in the form of racemes. Its species name, *basilicum,* comes from the Latin *basilisca* or the Greek *basilikon,* both meaning "royal," and indicates the esteem attributed to this seasoning plant since antiquity. Sweet basil is an annual plant that demands fertile soil and a sunny location. If these demands are fulfilled, it rewards us with an herb with an incomparable aroma that is also kind to the stomach. When used in the form of an aromatherapy oil, sweet basil helps to soothe and strengthen the nerves, clear and activate the mind, and lift the spirits.

The **yellow rattle** (*Alectorolophus glaber*) is a partially parasitic plant found growing in meadows. The flowers have plain, yellow throats and conspicuous, inflated calyxes. The unusual shape of the flowers is reflected in the plant's genus name: In Latin, *alector* means "rooster" and *lophus* "comb." The erect upper lip has violet teeth. When you walk through meadows, it is sometimes possible to detect the clattering of the seeds in their compressed pods. As a semiparasitic plant, the yellow rattle turns black when it dries.

121
European lily of the valley
(*Convallaria majalis* L.)
Lily family (Liliaceae)
V–VI
Endangered and therefore protected!
Leaves
Standardized tablets or drops prescribed by a physician
Cardioactive glycosides (convallatoxin, convallatoxol)
Chronic cardiac injuries, cardiac insufficiency, diuretic, laxative
Contents are poisonous, not suitable for self-medication!

122
German iris (*Iris germanica* L.) and **Florentine iris** (*Iris florentina* L.)
Iris family (Iridaceae)
V–VI
The orris root is used medicinally and in perfumes and cosmetics.

123
Sweet basil, or **common basil** (*Ocimum basilicum* L.)
Mint, or dead-nettle, family (Labiatae)
V–VII (cultivated)
Herbage without the roots, leaves
Herb, tea
Essential oil, tannins, flavonoids
(M) Flatulence, gastric disorders, lack of appetite, restlessness

124
Yellow rattle (*Alectorolophus glaber*)
Figwort, or snapdragon, family (Scrophulariaceae)
V–VIII

121 European lily of the valley

122 German iris

123 Sweet basil, common basil

124 Yellow rattle

Growing in meadows and pastures, the **meadow salsify, yellow goat's-beard,** or **goat's-beard** (*Tragopogon pratensis*), has yellow blossoms similar in form to those of the dandelion. Demonstrating an unusual daily rhythm, the solitary flowers open between nine and ten in the morning, turn with the sun, and already close again around noon. The long, narrow leaves envelop the flower stalk. When the sepals of the ligulate flowers are dry, they hang down and turn away from the head of the flower receptacle, resembling a billy goat's beard. Like the dandelion, this plant also has a white, milky latex and a taproot with a pleasant taste when young. Medicinally, this root is used for its diuretic effect.

The **lingonberry, cranberry,** or **red bilberry** (*Vaccinium vitis-idaea*), is a dwarf shrub that is encountered very rarely in our forests. Its brown leaves are more leatherlike than those of the blueberry, and they are convoluted backward and do not drop off in the winter. Its nodding, reddish flowers are grouped in small clusters. The tart berries (cranberries) carry the dried calyx as a "crown." In addition to malic and citric acids, vitamins A and C are regarded as active components. In the form of a preserve, cranberry sauce is a popular side dish, especially with turkey. Like the leaves of the bearberry, cranberry leaves contain arbutin, a urinary antiseptic, so they have been used in the form of a tea for bladder problems. A tea made with these leaves has also been used as a diuretic and to curb diarrhea. However, excessive usage can cause nausea and vomiting.

The inconspicuous **small cow-wheat** (*Melampyrum sylvaticum*) is a semiparasitic plant with yellowish-brown tubular florets. The genus name *Melampyrum* comes from the Latin *melas* ("black") and *pyros* ("wheat"), as the seeds are colored black and look like wheat. Because of their nectarlike sap, the seeds are frequently collected by ants. Quails are allegedly fond of them as well.

The **meadow hawksbeard** (*Crepis biennis*) has blossoms and leaves similar to those of the dandelion and a milky sap found in all parts. Its stalk, however, is not hollow. This tall, unpretentious, branched plant grows on rocky cliffs and walls as well as along paths. The seeds serve as canary feed, so in some places it is also known as "bird thistle."

125
Meadow salsify, yellow goat's-beard, or **goat's-beard**
(*Tragopogon pratensis* L.)
Composite, or daisy, family (Compositae)
V–VI
Diuretic

126
Lingonberry, cranberry, or **red bilberry** (*Vaccinium vitis-idaea* L.)
Heath family (Ericaceae)
V–VII
Leaves, berries
Tea, fruit, juice, sauce
Organic acids, arbutin, vitamins, minerals
(F) Tea against diarrhea, water retention, bladder problems
High doses, no longer administered, can lead to nausea and vomiting.

127
Small cow-wheat (*Melampyrum sylvaticum* L.)
Figwort, or snapdragon, family (Scrophulariaceae)
VI–X

128
Meadow hawksbeard (*Crepis biennis* L.)
Composite, or daisy, family (Compositae)
V–IX

125 Meadow salsify, yellow goat's-beard, goat's-beard
127 Small cow-wheat

126 Lingonberry, cranberry, red bilberry
128 Meadow hawksbeard

The **great globe-thistle** (*Echinops sphaerocephalus*) grows wild in groups or individually in meadows, vineyards, and quarries, as well as along rocky slopes and railway embankments. This valuable honey plant is also found in many gardens as an ornamental plant. The globe-thistles are tall, perennial plants with alternating pinnatisect leaves. The habitat of the seventy or so species is centered in the Mediterranean region. The genus name is derived from the Greek *echinos* ("hedgehog") and *ops* ("appearance"), as the heads of the flowers can be thought to resemble rolled-up hedgehogs.

The **field bindweed** (*Convolvulus arvensis*), with its large, white, funnel-shaped corolla, is scattered over meadows and fields and often seen climbing fences. The leaves stand alternately along the stem. Bearing five red stripes, the white, funnel-shaped corollas are positioned in the leaf axils. The pleasantly fragrant blossoms close in the evening and when it rains. A member of the morning-glory family, this plant is feared as a weed in grain fields, as it weighs down the stalks and is difficult to wipe out because of its deep rootstock. It is therefore also known in some places as "devil's twine" or "devil's bowels."

The common, delicate **silverweed cinquefoil,** or **wild agrimony** (*Potentilla anserina*), has golden-yellow, five-petaled blossoms and is in the rose family. The flowers are pinnatisect and have a white, hairy back. The name of the species, *anserina,* comes from the Latin word *anser,* meaning "goose," as geese consider this small, creeping plant to be a delicacy. Silverweed cinquefoil is also called "cramp weed" in some places, and in fact Sebastian Kneipp praised the leaves as being effective against stomach and abdominal cramps. Because of the leaves' high concentration of tannins, a tea brewed from them is used to curb diarrhea. Applied externally, the tea can be employed as an astringent for skin problems and inflammations in the mouth. In folk medicine, silverweed cinquefoil is known to be helpful in treating women's complaints.

An ornamental plant, the **European white water lily,** or **white water lily** (*Nymphaea alba*), thrives in the moist biotope of the herb garden. The genus name *Nymphaea* comes from *nymphe,* the Greek water nymph who supposedly swung on the leaf in the moonlight. The nymph myth also connects evil water spirits with this water lily. The plant grows wild in swampy, shallow rivers and lakes throughout Europe. As a result of their hollow, air-filled cavities, the leaves float on the water's surface. This plant's deep roots are like ropes, and the stems can be as thick as an arm. Because of their four canoe-shaped sepals, the aromatic blossoms, which open in the morning and close in the evening, are also able to float.

129
Great globe-thistle (*Echinops sphaerocephalus* L.)
Composite, or daisy, family (Compositae)
VII–VIII
130
Field bindweed (*Convolvulus arvensis* L.)
Morning-glory family (Convolvulaceae)
V–X
131
Silverweed cinquefoil, or **wild agrimony** (*Potentilla anserina* L.)
Rose family (Rosaceae)
V–VIII
Herbage without roots
Tea, tincture, irrigations, as a gargle
Tannins, bitter principles, flavonoids
(M) Inflammations of the mouth and the throat
(F) For women's diseases
Mild diarrhea, weak spasmolytic
132
European white water lily, or **white water lily** (*Nymphaea alba* L.)
Water-lily family (Nymphaeaceae)
VI–IX

129 Great globe-thistle
131 Silverweed cinquefoil, wild agrimony

130 Field bindweed
132 European white water lily, white water lily

$\mathcal{I}$nnumerable grasses, sedges, and rushes grow in the fields and along the paths around Bad Wörishofen. They are monocotyledonous plants and can be differentiated as false grasses, sedges, meadow grasses, reeds, and rushes. Alone, the reed genus includes more than 500 species, which are difficult for even experienced botanists to tell apart based on their stalk or leaf formation or their specific type of spike.

The light-brown spikes of the **reed canary-grass** (*Phalaris arundinacea*) blossom decoratively in moist habitats. They are often seen near climbing plants along the banks of brooks and streams.

Chee reed-grass (*Calamagrostis epigeios*), also known as **wood small-reed**, is feared by farmers as a useless and annoying offshoot grass. The panicle is coiled, and the spikes are short-stemmed. Because of its creeping rootstock that forms a compact entanglement of runners, this grass is especially suitable for holding back sand and inclines.

With a panicle full of button-sized spikes, the **cock's foot, or orchard grass** (*Dactylis glomerata*), blossoms in June on the Moosberg (a mountain near Bad Wörishofen). Its Latin name comes from *dactylis* ("fingerlike") and *glomerare* ("convolute") and has to do with the form of the flower. As a productive, high-quality meadow grass favored by grazing animals, cock's foot is valued highly in agriculture. Nevertheless, it must be harvested early enough so that it doesn't silicify too extensively.

The **common velvet-grass, or Yorkshire-fog** (*Holcus lanatus*), begins to blossom about the same time as cock's foot. This troublesome weed gets its name from the wool-like hair covering the leaves. Because of this hair, it is avoided by grazing animals and thus eaten only at times when no other feed grasses are available.

Whereas the meadow grasses like forest millet grass, forest hair-grass, and wood club-rush grow commonly in forests, the grasses described above, along with brome-grass, smooth-stalked meadow-grass, rye grass, crested dog's tail, meadow fescue, and meadow Timothy grass, are frequently found in fields. These grasses are the most common components of "hay flowers," which, when carefully harvested, dried, and cut, serve as fillers for Kneipp "hay sacks." The pleasant, typical fragrance of hay comes primarily from the aromatic sweet vernal-grass (*Anthoxanthum odoratum*). Because of its high concentration of coumarin, this plant has the distinct odor of sweet woodruff, especially after being dried. In the past, mainly the seeds that fell through the gaps in the threshing floor were used to fill these Kneipp sacks, but today studies have shown that finely cut hay is just as effective.

133
Reed canary-grass (*Phalaris arundinaceae* L.)
Grass family (Gramineae)
VI–VIII

134
Chee reed-grass (*Calamagrostis epigeios*)
Grass family (Gramineae)
V–VIII

135
Cock's foot, or **orchard grass** (*Dactylis glomerata* L.)
Grass family (Gramineae)
V–VI

136
Common velvet-grass, or **Yorkshire-fog** (*Holcus lanatus* L.)
Grass family (Gramineae)
VI–VIII

133 Reed canary-grass
135 Cock's foot, orchard grass

134 Chee reed-grass
136 Common velvet-grass, Yorkshire-fog

*C*hicory, blue dandelion, blueweed, coffeeweed, or succory (*Cichorium intybus*), plants are fond of heavy, loamy soil and are commonly found along the edges of paths. This plant is an unusual combination of dainty, sky-blue blossoms on robust, roughly haired, ramified stalks. The leaves have a jagged edge. The thin, spindle-shaped taproot can be roasted and ground to be used as a substitute for coffee. This Cichorium coffee was frequently drunk during periods of war. Chicory is also cultivated from the wild chicory and used to flavor coffee. Because of their mildly bitter taste, the leaves from this edible plant are valued highly as salad greens. Medicinally, the bitter agents of the chicory are effective against stomach complaints and a lack of appetite. Chicory has a long tradition as a medicinal plant. The Greek physician Galen recognized it as being "a friend of the liver," and it has been used in folk medicine as a skin remedy.

Spearmint, garden mint, or **spire mint** (*Mentha spicata*), is considered important especially because a mixture of this plant with the water mint results in a sort of hybrid, the peppermint (*Mentha piperita*), which is medicinally quite highly regarded. Spearmint prefers moist meadows, the banks of streams, and the edges of trenches. From the glabrous, square stems arise oblong, unevenly serrate leaves and spikes of purple flowers. Spearmint is probably the species of mint first employed medicinally. Like peppermint leaves, spearmint leaves are used in a tea for a number of ailments, from indigestion and heartburn to nervousness and insomnia.

A particularly nice specimen of the **European sage** (*Salvia sclarea*) is cultivated in the garden of the Dominican monastery at Bad Wörishofen. Due to its essential oils, the head of the flower offers essences for the perfume and cosmetic industries. Similar to the uses of common sage (*Salvia officinalis*), the leaves of this plant are employed as an herb that stimulates digestion, as a tea for reducing perspiration, and as a disinfectant gargle.

Because of its blue blossoms, the **bluebell, bellflower,** or **harebell** (*Campanula rotundifolia*), is easily recognized as a field and roadside flower. Its genus name *Campanula* is derived from the Latin word *campanula,* meaning "little bell." The stalk thus represents the campanile, or bell tower. The various species are differentiated mainly through the form of their leaves. Children sometimes turn the flowers over on their hand to break them with a bang. The superstition that the flowers attract thunderstorms gave rise to the alternative name "thunder flower."

137
Chicory, blue dandelion, blueweed, coffeeweed, or **succory** (*Cichorium intybus* L.)
Composite, or daisy, family (Compositae)
VII–IX
Herbage, roots
Tea
Bitter principles, tannins
(M) Tonic, amarus bitter in cases of lacking appetite, disturbances of the liver and biliary systems
(F) Skin impurities

138
Spearmint, garden mint, or **spire mint** (*Mentha spicata* L.)
Mint, or dead-nettle, family (Labiatae)
VII–IX
Herbage
Tea
Essential oil (without menthol, with carvone, etc.)
(F) Flatulence
Indigestion, heartburn, nausea, abdominal pains, nervousness, insomnia

139
European sage (*Salvia sclarea* L.)
Mint, or dead-nettle, family (Labiatae)
VI–VII (cultivated)
Leaves, herbage
Essential oil
(F) Stimulates digestion, emphractic (reduces the action of the sweat glands)

140
Bluebell, bellflower, or **harebell** (*Campanula rotundifolia* L.)
Bluebell, or bellflower, family (Campanulaceae)
VI–IX

137 Chicory, blue dandelion, blueweed, coffeeweed, succory
138 Spearmint, garden mint, spire mint
139 European sage
140 Bluebell, bellflower, harebell

The inconspicuous **field sow-thistle** (*Sonchus arvensis*), with its golden-yellow blossoms, can be found growing sociably along the edges of meadows on the Moosberg (a mountain near Bad Wörishofen). The plant gets its name from its common occurrence and its use as a sown pig feed, and is also known in some places as "pig cabbage." A perennial plant, field sow-thistle has a milky sap, and a paste can be made from the young leaves. The stalk, which reaches a height of up to 150 centimeters (almost 5 feet), extends from cylindrical, creeping offshoots. The hollow, broad leaves are lanceolate, sinuate, and pinnatisect with a coarse-thistled denticulation. As a weed in grain fields, it stretches above the upper level of the grain, whereas the corn poppy and the corn-flower remain below this level.

The **western touch-me-not, touch-me-not balsam,** or **jewelweed** (*Impatiens noli-tangere*), is often encountered in the damp forests around Bad Wörishofen. The lemon-yellow flowers that hang from the stems are similar in form to a cornucopia. The flower's inner surface bears red spots, and the tip has a spur bent backward. The Latin name of the species means "do not touch me" and is an indication of the unusual action of the plant's ripe, three-fold fruit capsules. The slightest contact causes these capsules to spring open and fling their seeds far away. According to superstition, the plant is startled.

In contrast to the flower of the true chamomile, the **disc mayweed,** or **pineapple-weed** (*Matricaria matricarioides*), flower doesn't have the white rays surrounding the yellow glomerate head. As with the chamomile, this flower is recognized along the edges of pastures and on the roadside through the typical chamomile fragrance. The disc mayweed, unlike the chamomile, is not used medicinally.

As with other types of dock, or sorrel, the **broad dock, broad-leafed dock,** or **bitter dock** (*Rumex obtusifolius*), is often discovered growing on rocky slopes and in ditches. One of the large-leafed types of sorrel, it has thus also been known as "ox's tongue," "sow's tongue," and "wild tobacco." The inflorescence of this species of sorrel has also caused it to be called "foxtail." The epithets "half a nag," "half a horse," "wild horse," and "half a cow" refer to the unkempt appearance of the plant when it bears fruit. In folk medicine, the large leaves are laid on swollen, inflamed parts of the body and on wounds, and the fruit is cooked together with pig fat to be used as an agent against dysentery.

141
Field sow-thistle (*Sonchus arvensis* L.)
Composite, or daisy, family (Compositae)
VII–X
142
Western touch-me-not, touch-me-not balsam, or **jewelweed** (*Impatiens noli-tangere* L.)
Borage, or forget-me-not, family (Boraginaceae)
VI–X
Salicylic acid, tannins, organic acids
143
Disc mayweed, or **pineapple-weed** (*Matricaria matricarioides* L.)
Composite, or daisy, family (Compositae)
VI–VIII
144
Broad dock, broad-leafed dock, or **bitter dock** (*Rumex obtusifolius* L.)
Milkwort family (Polygonaceae)
VI–VIII
(F) Externally used to treat inflammations and wounds, internally used for dysentery

141 Field sow-thistle

142 Western touch-me-not, touch-me-not balsam, jewelweed

143 Disc mayweed, pineapple-weed

144 Broad dock, broad-leafed dock, bitter dock

*L*ike most of the species of knotweed, or knotgrass, the **tasteless water-pepper** (*Polygonum mite*) is fond of damp, rocky sites on the Moosberg (a mountain near Bad Wörishofen). This annual plant has an erect stalk, but it doesn't taste as sharp as that of other knotweed species, although, as with the others, it contains calcium oxalate. The different species of knotweed, which vary a great deal in appearance, frequently have extensive rhizomes and bisexual blossoms that are combined in false clusters.

The **lamb succory** (*Arnoseris minima*) tends to like sandy soils and is also found in pine forests. Although they can handle dry periods very well, these plants (especially the older ones) are quite sensitive to frost. The small flower heads have twenty to twenty-five umbels forming a disk, and they are fondly visited by flies. A one-year-old plant has a spindle-shaped, whitish-yellow root. The base of the stalk is covered in red, and the upper part is thickened like a club and hollow, especially when the plant blossoms.

The **common plantain, greater plantain,** or **waybread** (*Plantago major*), can be differentiated from the narrow-leafed lance-leaf plantain, or ribgrass, mainly because of the form of its leaves. Broad and rounded, common plantain leaves are covered with veins, which can be pulled out when the leaves are torn. In a game used to foretell how long someone will live, each of these veins stands for ten years. The common plantain was brought to North America by the early pioneers, so the indigenous people called it "white man's foot." In the past, the plant was known as "nerve weed" and erroneously claimed to have a nerve-strengthening effect. As with lance-leaf plantain, or ribgrass, this species, however, does have a number of medicinal effects. It can be used to treat coughs, hoarseness, respiratory problems, and gastrointestinal ailments, as well as external wounds. Common plantain is also used as a vegetable in soups and salads. In addition, hikers have been known to lay the broad leaves in their shoes to refresh and invigorate their feet. A related species, fleaseed, or flea wort (*Plantago psyllium*), provides us with fine, flealike seeds. When mixed in water, these seeds swell a great deal, forming a pulpy mass. This swelling property makes them useful as a mild, harmless laxative.

The **white clover** (*Trifolium repens*) is found creeping in fields and along the roadside. Its name is derived from its light-pink, oval flowers that smell like honey. When near the ground, the stem takes root, and the flower head once again becomes erect after the offshoots have continued on. The leaf is the national symbol for Ireland. According to legend, Saint Patrick used the three-fold leaf in his sermons to explain the Trinity. The cloverleaf is also frequently encountered in Gothic buildings as an ornament in the stone.

145
Tasteless water-pepper
(*Polygonum mite*)
Milkwort family (Polygonaceae)
VII–X
Calcium oxalate

146
Lamb succory (*Arnoseris minima* L.)
Composite, or daisy, family (Compositae)
VI–IX

147
Common plantain, greater plantain, or **waybread** (*Plantago major* L.)
Plantain family (Plantaginaceae)
VI–X
Herbage
Tea, juice, soups, salads, leaves (externally)
Mucilage, bitter principles, salicylic acid, aucubin
(F) Antitussive, mild antibiotic effect
Treatment of coughs, hoarseness, respiratory problems, gastrointestinal ailments, external wounds, insect bites

148
White clover (*Trifolium repens* L.)
Pea family (Papilionaceae)
V–IX
Tannins, glycosides

145 Tasteless water-pepper
147 Common plantain, greater plantain, waybread

146 Lamb succory
148 White clover

*Y*ellow willow herb, yellow loosestrife, or **common loosestrife** (*Lysmachia vulgaris*), with its golden-yellow blossoms, brings a radiant spot of color to many herb gardens. Thriving in moist areas, the plant gets its name yellow willow herb from the similarity of its leaves to those of the willow. Nevertheless, it is a member of the primrose family. Its racemes are situated in the leaf axes, with a whisklike arrangement of the leaves. The five tips of the flower cup have a red margin, and the petals are deeply grooved. The corolla tube, which is typical of the primrose family, is evident for only a short time and is therefore noticed rarely.

Fond of moist, shady places, the **curly plumeless thistle,** or **welted thistle** (*Carduus crispus*), is often found in meadows alongside rivers in high mountain habitats, especially around alder and poplar trees. Here in Wörishofen, this biennial weed can be seen along the shores of the Wertach. This plant can reach a height of 2 meters (more than 6 feet) and has a spindle-shaped taproot. The fragile, branched upper stalks are hairy and have thorns, and give rise to purple, three- to five-fold blossoms. The flower of this plant is the heraldic flower of Scotland. According to the premise of Paracelsus in his *Doctrine of Signatures,* the curly plumeless thistle is effective against sharp, internal pains because of its thorny exterior.

With its impressive violet flowers, the **introduced sage,** or **meadow clary** (*Salvia pratensis*), is very conspicuous along the paths around Bad Wörishofen. The stalk of this plant is four-sided, hairy, and sticky. If a bumblebee lands on the typically lipped flower, the hidden stamens are pressed out through a specific linkage that results in the pollination of the back of the bee. Lore concerning the meadow clary goes back to ancient times. In the Middle Ages, it was believed that this plant would thrive when the man of the household was doing well and that its drying out or dying was a sign of unfavorable times. The pleasant-smelling flower is considered to have effects similar to those of the common, or garden, sage flower. The essential oil, in a gargle, has a disinfectant effect and, used internally, provides relief from gastrointestinal disorders as well as night sweats.

False baby's breath, or **hedge bedstraw** (*Galium mollugo*), is very widespread. A member of the madder family, it has full, soft panicles covered with small, white flowers. Its eight-leafed whorls are reminiscent of the leaves of the sweet woodruff. The plant's pleasant fragrance makes it a favorite of bees and grazing animals. Its genus name *Galium* comes from the Latin word *gala,* meaning "milk," as the plant, like the rennet of a cow's stomach, causes milk to curdle.

149
Yellow willow-herb, yellow loosestrife, or common loosestrife (*Lysmachia vulgaris* L.)
Primrose family (Primulaceae)
VI–VIII
150
Curly plumeless thistle, or **welted thistle** (*Carduus crispus* L.)
Composite, or daisy, family (Compositae)
VII–IX
151
Introduced sage, or **meadow clary** (*Salvia pratensis* L.)
Mint, or dead-nettle, family (Labiatae)
V–VIII
For mouth inflammations, gastrointestinal disorders, night sweats
152
False baby's breath, or **hedge bedstraw** (*Galium mollugo* L.)
Bedstraw, or madder, family (Rubiaceae)
VI–X

149 Yellow willow-herb, yellow loosestrife, common loosestrife
151 Introduced sage, meadow clary

150 Curly plumeless thistle, welted thistle
152 False baby's breath, hedge bedstraw

Reversed clover (*Trifolium resupinatum*) can be spotted growing on the Moosberg (a mountain near Bad Wörishofen) and is an annual plant. Initially, it grows close to the ground and then becomes more erect. The little leaves are oval. The species name comes from the Latin *resupinare,* meaning "turned back upon itself," as the corona of the flower is structured in such a way that the standard is turned outward and the carina faces inward. One plant has as many as fifty-seven axillary inflorescences. Around noon, the plant, which otherwise has no odor, exudes a strong honey fragrance. This type of clover is fond of saline soil and grows in pastures and fields, as well as barren land. In Persia, it has been cultivated for a long time as a rich, good fodder. However, reversed clover's cultivation north of the Alps is not especially lucrative because of its demand for warmer temperatures.

A low, perennial plant, the **silverweed cinquefoil,** or **wild agrimony** (*Potentilla anserina*), not surprisingly, has leaves that are generally five-fold. The flowers are bright yellow and grow at the top of long peduncles. This member of the rose family is found primarily in moist habitats, as in the lower mountain areas of the Palatinate (in southwest Germany). It is also called "goose-finger weed" in some places, an indication of how much geese like it. Silverweed cinquefoil has been used medicinally to curb diarrhea, relieve cramps, bring down inflammations in the mouth and throat, and treat skin problems.

Scarlet elderberry (*Sambucus racemosa*) grows wild here and is also cultivated. Because of its clusters of small, scarlet-red berries, which contain a high concentration of vitamin C, it is also known in some places as "red elder" or "grape elder." The blossoms of the oval panicles are yellowish-green, and the leaves are pinnate with about five leaflets. The plant grows up to 4 meters (more than 12 feet) and has a light-brown pith. Animals avoid it, as scarlet elderberry contains a glycoside from which small concentrations of hydrocyanic acid are derived. However, the berries are used to make a tasty, nutritious jam, and the root is employed medicinally as a purgative and a diuretic. The bark is also used medicinally, as it contains bast, tannins, and bitter principles, as well as a laxative resin.

153/156
Scarlet elderberry (*Sambucus racemosa* L.)
Honeysuckle family (Caprifoliaceae)
VI–VIII
Berries, bark, root
Vitamin C (berries), tannins, bitter principles, resin (bark)
Purgative, diuretic (root)
154
Reversed clover (*Trifolium resupinatum* L.)
Pea family (Papilionaceae)
IV–VI
155
Silverweed cinquefoil, or **wild agrimony** (*Potentilla anserina*)
Rose family (Rosaceae)
V–VIII
Herbage without roots
Tea
Tannins, bitter principles, flavonoids
(M) Inflammations of the mucous membranes in the mouth and throat (rinsing), diarrhea, cramplike complaints of the gastrointestinal tract

153 Scarlet elderberry
155 Silverweed cinquefoil, wild agrimony

154 Reversed clover
156 Scarlet elderberry

*I*n Bad Wörishofen, the **European black elder,** or **European elder** (*Sambucus nigra*), is frequently found in gardens and leaning against sheds in fields. When it blossoms, the June breezes are filled with its enchanting fragrance. In the form of a bush or a small tree, the European black elder bears yellowish-white blossoms that develop into berries. The Teutons believed that Freya, the goddess of love, beauty, and fecundity, and the protector of house and home, lived in an elderberry bush. Therefore, it was a common practice to plant elder bushes near houses. Sebastian Kneipp said, "There should be no house without the elderberry as a fellow lodger." The blossoms, which contain glycosides, essential oil, fruit acids, and vitamin C, are harvested in the summer. After being washed, the blossoms can be covered in a pancake batter and then deep-fried, to make a treat eaten with powdered sugar. Tea from elderberry blossoms serves as a diaphoretic (sweat-inducing) drug in the event of feverish colds and helps to stimulate bronchial secretion. The berries are used in tasty, nutritious jams and sauces. However, use caution when collecting the berries yourself, as the unripe berries are slightly poisonous. The young elderberry twigs, with their soft, white pith, are used by children to make pea-shooters.

The blue blossoms of the perennial **spreading bellflower** (*Campanula patula*) are well known and frequently collected for use in meadow-flower bouquets. According to superstition, as with many of the "thunder flowers," picking them leads to rain showers or thunderstorms. This species has a violet-blue corolla that is funnel-shaped and separated at the midpoint into five long, ovular lobes. The lowest leaves are elliptical, the leaves that follow are ligulate, and the uppermost ones are lanceolate.

The **Norwegian angelica, angel's wort, angelica,** or **archangel** (*Angelica archangelica*), is cultivated and also grows wild in moist habitats. The stems are branched near the top and produce greenish-white blossoms in large, compound umbels. The root has a spicy, pleasing aroma when fresh, and contains essential oil, bitter principles, tannins, sugar, starch, and resins. During the plagues of the fourteenth century, through which 30 million people died in Europe alone, the Archangel Raphael supposedly pointed out the curative powers of this plant, and it was thus named in his honor. The pleasant, spicy essential oil is a component of several liqueurs and adds a refinement to many dishes. The Dutch artist Hieronymus Bosch said, "Angel's wort stimulates the desire to eat and the digestion, and is especially good for the heart." In fact, it has been found to stimulate the production of gastric juices and to alleviate flatulence, a feeling of fullness, and complaints of the gastrointestinal tract. Nevertheless, excessive consumption can have harmful side effects.

Chinese rhubarb (*Rheum officinalis*) is one of the oldest-known medicinal plants. It comes from Tibet, and the Chinese already knew about it during the third century B.C. In contrast to the related garden rhubarb, whose mildly stimulating effects on digestion are brought about by the fruit acids and plant fibers in the stalk, the Chinese rhubarb root contains laxative glycosides that also serve as a gastric stimulant for promoting the appetite. At higher dosages, the peeled root has proven to be a highly effective laxative through its stimulation of the large intestine. Because of the increased flow of blood in the pelvic area during its use, however, it is not recommended for pregnant or nursing women or for individuals suffering from hemorrhoids or intestinal obstruction.

157
European black elder, or
European elder (*Sambucus nigra* L.)
Honeysuckle family (Caprifoliaceae)
VI–VII
Blossoms, fruit
Tea, cooked juice, sauces, jams
Glycosides, essential oil
(M) Diaphoretic (sweat-inducing) for treating feverish colds, influenza
Unripe berries are slightly poisonous!

158
Spreading bellflower
(*Campanula patula* L.)
Bluebell, or bellflower, family
(Campanulaceae)
V–VIII

159
Norwegian angelica, angel's wort, angelica, or **archangel**
(*Angelica archangelica* L.)
Parsley, or carrot, family
(Umbelliferae)
VII–VIII
Root
Tea, wine
Essential oil, bitter principles, tannins, furanocoumarins, resins
Appetite-stimulating, digestant, carminative (against flatulence)
Overdosage leads to paralysis of the central nervous system, development of photosensitization with possible skin irritation

160
Chinese rhubarb (*Rheum officinalis*)
Milkwort family (Polygonaceae)
V–VII (cultivated)
Root
Tea, coated tablets, powder
Anthracine derivatives, tannins
(M) Laxative
Not recommended in cases of intestinal obstruction, hemorrhoids, during pregnancy or nursing

157 European black elder, European elder
159 Norwegian angelica, angel's wort, angelica, archangel

158 Spreading bellflower
160 Chinese rhubarb

Summer

*W*hitespot, or **hedge woundwort** (*Stachys sylvatica*), is frequently observed in damp deciduous forests and oak groves. It is also known in some places as "forest nettle," as its lipped flowers are similar in appearance to those of the dead-nettle. The flowers, which reach a height of up to 120 centimeters (almost 4 feet), appear at the heads of spikes. The use of this plant as a diaphoretic (sweat-inducing) agent cannot be verified. Betony (*Stachys officinalis*), a related species, is used in folk medicine because of its tannin and bitter principle contents.

In June, the white-blossoming **mountain clover** (*Trifolium montanum*) is often seen on the Moosberg (a mountain near Bad Wörishofen). The hairy stalk gives rise to long, sharply serrated leaves with no petiole. The flowers have a pleasant fragrance.

The reddish-violet blossoms of the **brown knapweed** (*Centaurea jacea*) generally stand individually in a glomerate involucre at the end of a high stalk and are similar in appearance to the blossoms of the cornflower (also known as the bachelor's-button, bluebonnet, bluebottle, or blue centaury). The involucre is made up of five-lobed, tubular florets that carry their nectar internally. Depending on the moisture of their habitat, these plants demonstrate varying forms of leaves. Because of its flower's wide, glomerate head, brown knapweed is also known in some places as "fat head" or "trouser button." As with the milfoil, or yarrow, the genus name *Centaurea* refers to the legend of the mythical centaur, Chiron, famed for his knowledge of medicine and the arts, who allegedly discovered the healing properties of these plants for the treatment of fractures and internal injuries.

The **Bird's-foot deervetch,** or **bird's-foot trefoil** (*Lotus corniculatus*), is found throughout the summer as a yellow spot of color in many meadows and pastures. The individual papilionaceous (butterfly-shaped) flowers stand five-fold in a long-stemmed umbel. The two-paired, pinnate leaves are not typical for a type of clover and take a nocturnal position during the night. Bees and bumblebees make use of a "plunging" pollinating mechanism when they visit these honey-producing plants. As they alight on the flower, the carina of the flower is pressed down; the filaments of the stamens then press the sticky pollen out from the tip of the carina onto the abdomens of the nectar-sucking insects. "Horn clover" is another name for this popular, leguminous feed plant and is based on its hornlike curvature.

161
Whitespot, or **hedge woundwort** (*Stachys sylvatica* L.)
Mint, or dead-nettle, family (Labiatae)
VI–VIII
(F) Betony (*Stachys officinalis*) is used medicinally due to its tannin and bitter principle contents.

162
Mountain clover (*Trifolium montanum* L.)
Pea family (Papilionaceae)
V–VIII

163
Brown knapweed (*Centaurea jacea* L.)
Composite, or daisy, family (Compositae)
VI–X

164
Bird's-foot deervetch, or **bird's-foot trefoil** (*Lotus corniculatus* L.)
Pea family (Papilionaceae)
V–IX

161 Whitespot, hedge woundwort
163 Brown knapweed

162 Mountain clover
164 Bird's-foot deervetch, bird's-foot trefoil

The Latin name *Myosotis* is used to classify the forget-me-not species of the borage family and means "mouse ear." These species are known for their blue flowers, which have been a symbol for faithfulness since ancient times. The **field forget-me-not** (*Myosotis arvensis*) species is shown here.

The **European Venus' looking glass** (*Legousia speculum-veneris*) is a very rare plant that can now be found on the Moosberg (a mountain near Bad Wörishofen). It had been missing from our flora for a long time. This annual, gnarled weed, with its dark-violet blossoms, was rediscovered as a nature trail for studying grains was set out on the Moosberg and the biotope was finally corrected. The European Venus' looking glass is fond of clayey fields and is a member of the bluebell, or bellflower, family.

Creeping Jenny, creeping Charlie, or **moneywort** (*Lysimachia nummularia*), is often seen in ditches and creeping along the banks of rivers and streams, as its name implies. This member of the primrose family is relatively common. It can be recognized through its individual, lemon-yellow flowers, whose inner surface has red spots, and its round, opposite leaves that are frequently undulated. The species name *nummularia* comes from the Latin *nummula,* which means "little coin." In folk medicine, it is used for coughs and colds, rheumatic disorders, gout, and diarrhea.

The members of the spurge, or wolf's milk, family get their family name as a result of the poisonous, white "milk" that exudes from their stems when they are broken off. The **cypress spurge** (*Euphoribia cyparissias*) species is a bushlike perennial plant. The species name *cyparissias* indicates its cypresslike leaves. This 30-centimeter (nearly 1 foot) plant is striking in that is has a multiradiate umbel in which the blossoms are situated. Each ray holds two flowerlets. The cuplike, greenish-yellow perianth has a pistil and a number of male flowers, as well as yellow, crescent-shaped glands. The small leaves are similar in form to pine needles. Because of its poisonous "milk," this plant is not recommended for either internal or external use.

165
Field forget-me-not (*Myosotis arvensis* L.)
Borage, or forget-me-not, family (Boraginaceae)
V–VII
166
European Venus' looking glass (*Legousia speculum-veneris* L.)
Bluebell, or bellflower, family (Campanulaceae)
VI–VIII
167
Creeping Jenny, creeping Charlie, or **moneywort** (*Lysimachia nummularia* L.)
Primrose family (Primulaceae)
V–VII
Herbage
Tea
Tannins, saponins, salicylic acid, enzymes (primverase)
(F) For coughs, colds, rheumatism, gout, diarrhea
168
Cypress spurge (*Euphoribia cyparissias* L.)
Spurge, or wolf's milk, family (Euphoribiaceae)
IV–VII
Milky sap contains poisonous, sharp substances (euphorban)!
Used externally, it may lead to skin blistering; used internally, vomiting, stomach pains, and diarrhea can result!

165 Field forget-me-not
167 Creeping Jenny, creeping Charlie, moneywort

166 European Venus' looking glass
168 Cypress spurge

The rootstock of the **erect cinquefoil, tormentil,** or **bloodroot** (*Potentilla erecta*), is used medicinally. After being cut, this root immediately turns blood-red in color, hence the name bloodroot. The rootstock is dug up between March and May or in the late fall and contains 15 to 20 percent catechin tannin, which gradually turns red during storage. Tea made from tormentil should be boiled for at least 10 minutes. This strongly astringent extraction is used internally against complaints of the gastrointestinal tract and diarrhea. However, caution is advised when it is taken internally, as excessive amounts can cause stomach problems and nausea. Externally, it is used as a gargle against inflammations of the gingiva and mucous membranes, and as a wash for poorly healing wounds. The plant's medicinal applications can be traced back as far as the fourth century. In herb books dating from the sixteenth century, tormentil, also known as "devil's bite," was attributed as having an effect against "Black Death," or the plague. Sebastian Kneipp praised the plant, insisting, "Tormentil . . . is very good. I have already prepared tormentil powder and achieved remarkable successes with it." In contrast to other members of the rose family, like the closely related cinquefoil, or wild agrimony, tormentil has yellow blossoms with only four petals. The more frequent three-fold and five-fold basal leaves wither before the plant blooms. The Latin word *tormentum,* from which tormentil is derived, means "torment" or "torture." Panel paintings from the Middle Ages therefore made use of this plant as a symbol for the toils of Jesus.

The **two-leafed false Solomon's seal** (*Maianthemum bifolium*) can be seen blanketing the shady floor of oak groves. Beneath the inconspicuous raceme are two layers, each with two pointed, heart-shaped leaves. Only a single leaf sprouts from the plant before blossoming. The berries, which are initially white and later turn red, are poisonous.

The many species of **hawkweed** (*Hieracium* aggregate species) are frequently mistaken for the dandelion because of their similar blossoms. The name is supposedly derived from the fact that the plant is frequently found in places where hawks nest. In contrast to the dandelion, the stalk is not hollow and the plant blossoms from May to October, frequently in forests and stony sites. The leaves are situated as a rosette at the base of the stalk.

The **St. Bernard's lily** (*Anthericum liliago*) is considered to be one of the remnants of the warm period before the last Ice Age. Its inflorescence is an unbranched, terminal cluster of middle-sized, stalked, white flowers. The genus includes about fifty different species that are primarily common to Africa. This plant is fond of rocky slopes, sandy pastures, and dry forests. The suffix "ago" in the species name indicates its similarity to the lily.

169
Erect cinquefoil, tormentil, or
bloodroot (*Potentilla erecta* L.)
Rose family (Rosaceae)
V–VIII
Rootstock
Tea, gargle, bath additive, tincture
Catechin tannin, phlobatannin derivative (phlobaphene)
Mouth and throat infections, complaints of the gastrointestinal tract, diarrhea; stomach problems and vomiting in the event of overdose
170
Two-leafed false Solomon's seal
(*Maianthemum bifolium* L.)
Lily family (Liliaceae)
IV–VI
171
Hawkweed (*Hieracium* aggregate subspecies)
Composite, or daisy, family (Compositae)
V–IX
172
St. Bernard's lily (*Anthericum liliago* L.)
Lily family (Liliaceae)
V–VII

169 Erect cinquefoil, tormentil, bloodroot
171 Hawkweed

170 Two-leafed false Solomon's seal
172 St. Bernard's lily

Along with the marsh marigold, cuckoo flower, red lampflower, and creeping bugle, the **ragged robin** (*Lychnis floscuculi*) is found here growing in meadows. From the Greek, *Lychnis* indicates the plant's luminous body and *flos* the flower. The blossoms are situated as cymes (single terminal flowers). Typical for this member of the pink, or campion, family are the petals with their four slits that can reach a height of up to half a meter (about 1½ feet). Because of its disorderedly appearing flower tips, this plant is also known in some places as "messy maid." Similar to the cuckoo flower, the ragged robin is a plant also frequently covered with "cuckoo's spit" from the larva of the spittle bug.

Another special member of the pink, or campion, family is the **maiden's tears** (*Silene inflata*), which received its species name as a result of the inflated flower cup beneath the white, star-shaped inflorescence. Although it is also known as the "catchfly," the ring of sticky sap around the stalk that is present to protect the red German catchfly from visits made by ants or beetles, for instance, is lacking here. The blossoms are occasionally dioecious (female flowers on one plant, male flowers on another). The calyx has twenty veins that are interconnected. Because this flower cup can be exploded with a bang, the plant is also known in some places as "bang weed," "bang-smack," and "gun buffer." Only moths, with their long proboscis, are able to suck the nectar from the base of the blossom and are consequently also able to pollinate the flower. For this reason, the blossoms generally open during the evening.

An annual weed, the **brittlestem hemp nettle** (*Galeopsis tetrahit*) is very common on the Moosberg (a mountain near Bad Wörishofen). The genus name *Galeopsis* has to do with the similarity of the blossom to the head of a polecat, as, in Latin, *gale* means "weasel" and *opsis* "appearance." The relationship of this member of the labiate family to the nettle is recognized through its nettlelike leaves, and in some places is it also known as "common nettle." The stalk, which is often very strong, usually has numerous articulations with bristles pointing backward. The abundant false whorls are often nearly glomerate and have bracts that are thorned. In folk medicine, herbage of a related species, *Galeopsis segetum,* is used to treat coughs and skin problems.

The **peachleaf bellflower** (*Campanula persicifolia*) is found growing wild in dry forests and along forest paths and is also cultivated in gardens. Its long, finely serrated leaves are reminiscent of peach leaves, and its broad, bluish-violet, bell-shaped flowers stand in racemes with only a few blossoms. The fruit capsule in its upright position looks like a top that has burst open in the middle.

173
Ragged robin (*Lychnis floscuculi* L.)
Pink, or campion, family (Caryophyllaceae)
V–IX

174
Maiden's tears (*Silene inflata*)
Pink, or campion, family (Caryophyllaceae)
V–IX

175
Brittlestem hemp nettle (*Galeopsis tetrahit* L.)
Labiate family (Labiatae)
VII–X
Salicylic acid, tannins, saponins
(F) Herbage of the hemp nettle (*Galeopsis segetum*) against coughs (internally) and skin impurities (externally)

176
Peachleaf bellflower (*Campanula persicifolia* L.)
Bluebell, or bellflower, family (Campanulaceae)
VI–VIII

173 Ragged robin
175 Brittlestem hemp nettle

174 Maiden's tears
176 Peachleaf bellflower

With its violet racemes, the **cow vetch,** or **tufted vetch** (*Vicia cracca*), creates a radiant carpet of color on the Moosberg (a mountain near Bad Wörishofen). The genus name *Vicia* comes from *vincere,* Latin for "shoots," which are one of the plant's more pronounced characteristics. This plant is found here along the nature trail for studying grains, where its wrapping tendrils, seen at the end of the pinnate leaves, wind around the stalks of grain. The individual papilionaceous flowers can reach a length of up to 1 centimeter (almost ½ inch). The Roman naturalist Pliny considered the cow, or tufted, vetch to be a degenerated type of legume, and it was claimed that pigeons would no longer leave their lofts after eating these plants.

The **flat peavine** (*Lathyrus sylvestris*) is a wildflower that can also be found on the Moosberg. The ends of the leaves have no wrapping tendrils. The papilionaceous flowers demonstrate an astonishing change in color from pale pink to crimson red to blue.

Broadleaf enchanter's nightshade (*Circaea lutetiana*) is named after the city of Paris, which was known as Lutetia in Latin. This perennial weed reaches a height of up to 60 centimeters (almost 2 feet) and appears in groups. Here, it is found in the moist, shady forests of the Hartenthal (a valley in this region). The plant has a woody, long-limbed rootstock with horizontal, quill-like runners that are thicker at the terminal ends. The lower third of the stalk is round and smooth, whereas the upper parts are angular and brittle with fluffy hairs. Oval, heart-shaped leaves arise from a stem with furrows on the upper surface. The flower appears as a lengthened raceme with short, fluffy stalks. Broadleaf enchanter's nightshade is also known as "witches' weed" in some places; both names are probably derived from the genus name and its allusion to the sorceress Circe.

The **great burnet,** or **official burnet** (*Sanguisorba officinalis*), can be caught sight of in moist meadows and along the banks of brooks and streams around Schlingen (a town near Bad Wörishofen). The Latin name *Sanguisorba* is derived from *sanguis,* for "blood," and *sorbere,* "to resorb," as this weed has a hemostatic effect. Because of its dark-purple heads—with the male blossoms on top, the bisexual, or hermaphrodite, blossoms in the middle, and the female blossoms at the bottom—this member of the rose family is also known in some places as "little drops of blood." Petals are lacking, and the leaves are oddly pinnate. The hemostatic effect is based on the plant's high concentration of tannin. Therefore, great burnet is not only used to coagulate blood to stop hemorrhaging, but it is also effective in treating intestinal disorders and diarrhea. In folk medicine, it is employed externally for inflammations of the mouth, throat, and gums.

177
Cow vetch, or **tufted vetch** (*Vicia cracca* L.)
Pea family (Papilionaceae)
VI–VII

178
Flat peavine (*Lathyrus sylvestris* L.)
Pea family (Papilionaceae)
VII–VIII

179
Broadleaf enchanter's nightshade (*Circaea lutetiana* L.)
Evening primrose, or willow herb, family (Onograceae)
VI–VII

180
Great burnet, or **official burnet** (*Sanguisorba officinalis* L.)
Rose family (Rosaceae)
VI–IX
Herbage and root
Tea, irrigation
Saponins, bitter principles, flavones, vitamin C
(F) Inflammations of the mouth, throat, gums
Hemorrhaging, intestinal disorders, diarrhea

177 Cow vetch, tufted vetch
179 Broadleaf enchanter's nightshade

178 Flat peavine
180 Great burnet, official burnet

On a clearing in the woods on the Moosberg (a mountain near Bad Wörishofen) there are three magnificent species of foxglove growing in a very limited area: the purple foxglove, the straw foxglove, and the yellow foxglove. These biennial plants are fond of sandy soil that is lacking in calcium. In addition to growing wild, they are often planted in gardens as an ornamental flower. But it's always important to keep in mind, especially in the case of small children, that all parts of these plants are poisonous. In England, foxglove is therefore also known as "dead man's bell." Its genus name *Digitalis* comes from the Latin word *digitus,* for "finger," probably in reference to the characteristic solitary stalk.

In 1775, after obtaining information from an herb woman, the English physician William Withering was the first to describe the soothing effects on cardiac edema from a tea brewed with foxglove leaves. This was the start of "digitalis therapy." Once the extracts had become standardized, the healing dose had to be approached very carefully. The effective agents in foxglove are known as cardiac "glycosides," because they are bound to a sugar residue (glucose) in the plant. The manufacture of cardiac glycosides in a pure form took place for the first time in 1824. Today, every type of foxglove is known to contain the cardiac glycosides digoxin and digitoxin, although not all species are used medicinally. Physicians prescribe them in exact, low dosages in the form of standardized tablets for strengthening the cardiac muscle and reducing the heart rate.

The flowers of the **purple foxglove, digitalis, fairy glove,** or **fingerflower** (*Digitalis purpurea*), are generally rose-colored to purple on the outside and whitish with a red, spotty pattern on the inside. They hang on a hairy stalk that reaches a height of up to 1 meter (about 3 feet). The lower, oval, lancelet leaves are inconspicuous, as they lie flat against the ground in the form of a rosette. The plant blossoms during the second year and dies after the dispersal of its seeds. The terrible-tasting, notched leaves may lead to dizziness or vomiting and, at high doses, may even cause a fatal paralysis of the heart. Because of the narrow therapeutic range (the narrow margin between a healing dose and a dose with damaging side effects), any therapy with foxglove preparations must be supervised by a physician.

The **straw foxglove** (*Digitalis lutea*) is not observed very often, nor is it used medicinally. It has a smooth, erect stalk. The leaves, on the other hand, are covered with cilia (fine hair). The fruit capsule is situated in a small flower cup with a single-veined lobe.

The **yellow foxglove** (*Digitalis grandiflora*) is also known in some places as "forest bell" and "glove flower." Its strong stalk, which grows up to 1 meter (about 3 feet) in height, has blunt corners in the lower region. The light-green leaves are serrated and ciliated. The fruit capsule pappus is longer than the flower cup. This species is not used medicinally either.

The sight of these three splendid examples of the classical foxglove plant makes a hike worth taking through the forests of the Moosberg. But, remember, all three are considered endangered and are thus protected. And it must be emphasized again that foxglove is used in the production of intensive medical preparations and is not suitable as an herb for self-treatment in the sense that Sebastian Kneipp endorsed.

181/184
Purple foxglove, digitalis, fairy glove, or **fingerflower** (*Digitalis purpurea* L.)
Figwort, or snapdragon, family (Scrophulariaceae)
VI–VII (Endangered and therefore protected!)
Isolated substances from the leaves
Tablets
Glycosides (digitoxin, gitoxin), saponins, mucilage
Cardiac irregularities, weakening pump action of the heart muscle
Extremely poisonous—not suitable for self-treatment!

182
Straw foxglove (*Digitalis lutea* L.)
Figwort, or snapdragon, family (Scrophulariaceae)
VI–VIII (endangered and therefore protected!)
Not employed medicinally
Glycosides, saponins, mucilage
Extremely poisonous!

183
Yellow foxglove (*Digitalis grandiflora* L.)
Figwort, or snapdragon, family (Scrophulariaceae)
VI–IX (endangered and therefore protected!)
Not employed medicinally
Glycosides, saponins, mucilage
Extremely poisonous!

181 Purple foxglove, digitalis, fairy glove, fingerflower
183 Yellow foxglove

182 Straw foxglove
184 Purple foxglove, digitalis, fairy glove, fingerflower
(white-blossoming form)

The **creeping thistle,** or **Canada this-tle** (*Cirsium arvense*), usually blossoms from July to October on the clayey pastures and fallow land of the Palatinate's lower mountain regions. As a type of thistle, this plant has a glomerate head with numerous dioecious, violet, tubular florets that stand in loose clusters at the end of the stem. The lancelet leaves have a margin of fine thistles. The plant propagates by means of offshoots; therefore, it is a weed that is hard to kill and is feared by farmers. Goldfinches are often spotted hanging on to the composite flowers in order to peck out the seeds.

The plain and easily satisfied **gallant soldier,** or **galinsoga** (*Galinsoga parviflora*), is also known by a number of different names in Germany. Inasmuch as it is seen growing as a weed in rubble heaps, along the roadside, and even on walls, it is sometimes called "devil's weed" or "witches' weed." This plant has tiny, but still conspicuous, yellow heads surrounded by five white rays, so it is also known as "button weed" or "golden button." And its migration from Peru to Germany coincided with the invasion by France, earning it the name "French weed." The bushy plant is an annual and has a rounded, hexagonal stalk. The cymes (single terminal flowers) arise from the end of the stalk and from the leaf axes. The plant's rapid death as a result of the slightest frost is a further indication that it originated in South America.

An annoying perennial weed, **curly dock,** or **yellow dock** (*Rumex crispus*), is often found growing on the Moosberg (a mountain near Bad Wörishofen), as well as in farmlands and in rubble heaps. The genus of the docks, or sorrels, includes about 100 different species that tend to easily form new hybrids and can be difficult to differentiate. They are monogamist anemonophiles (wind-pollinated plants) with inconspicuous, pale-green blossoms, and are thus only rarely pollinated by insects. Because of their high concentration of oxalic acid and iron, various species are cultivated in gardens.

Livestock are very fond of some species when mixed with grass and clover. Curly dock reaches a height of up to 1 meter (about 3 feet) and has a carrotlike, almost woody rootstock. The flowers are androgynous or female. Curly dock has a long tradition as a medicinal plant, and it is still used as a laxative and a mild astringent tonic. It is also applied externally to treat inflammations, sores, and itching.

The **life root,** or **squaw weed** (*Senecio fuchsii*), is a member of a genus that includes about 1,300 different species. In the past, extracts from this plant, which is rather common here, were employed to stop bleeding (especially of the female organs) and to strengthen contractions of the uterus. But the use of this agent in self-treatment is urgently warned against today. The active ingredients in the composite flower are hepatotoxic as well as carcinogenic. The life root (*Fuchskreuzkraut* in German) was named here after Leonard Fuchs, who was born in Wemding, in Swabia, in 1501. He was a schoolteacher there initially and later became a professor of medicine in Tübingen. As a result of his renown as a physician and a botanist, he was raised to nobility by Emperor Charles V. A book Fuchs wrote forms the basis for popular phytotherapy. The fuchsia, which decorates many gardens, windows, and balconies, was also named after him.

185
Creeping thistle, or **Canada thistle** (*Cirsium arvense* L.)
Composite, or daisy, family (Compositae)
VII–IX

186
Gallant soldier, or **galinsoga** (*Galinsoga parviflora*)
Composite, or daisy, family (Compositae)
V–X

187
Curly dock, or **yellow dock** (*Rumex crispus* L.)
Borage, or forget-me-not, family (Boraginaceae)
III–V
Mucilage, flavonoids, allantoin
Laxative, mild astringent tonic, external applications

188
Life root, or **squaw weed** (*Senecio fuchsii*)
Composite, or daisy, family (Compositae)
VII–IX
Dangerous pyrrolizidine alkaloids
Not suitable for self-treatment!
Hepatotoxic, carcinogenic!

185 Creeping thistle, Canada thistle
187 Curly dock, yellow dock

186 Gallant soldier, galinsoga
188 Life root, squaw weed

The altitude and climate in the area around Bad Wörishofen make this region especially suited to growing grain. From the early part of the Middle Ages to the beginning of the twentieth century, the agricultural form of a three-field system was carried out in the Lower Algau. This system consisted of a cycle with a summer crop and a winter crop, followed by a period of fallow ground. As a result, field weeds like the corn cockle and the larkspur have since become extinct here. In the Algau of today, it is also rare to encounter corn poppies, cornflowers, field buttercups, and the common chamomile. However, the rediscovery of ecologically related weeds like the European Venus' looking glass, different species of the knotgrass family, and thistles and field rushes provide evidence of today's more natural method of cultivation. Of course, unlike the plant lovers and the botanists, many farmers in the area are not rejoicing in the change.

Common oats (*Avena sativa*) are the only type of grain in which the seeds are not found on a spikelet but hang on panicles. The production of grains, flakes, and groats requires the husking of the seeds in special mills. In addition to water, carbohydrates, minerals, and fiber, oats contain a relatively large concentration of proteins, together with eight essential amino acids, lecithin, and fat, consisting of 70 to 80 percent polyunsaturated fatty acids. Inasmuch as this fat is distributed in the starch cells of the nutrient tissues, rolled oats and oat bran are considered to be a highly nutritious food, especially recommended in cases of high cholesterol. In folk medicine, oats in various forms are used as a laxative, to lower cholesterol levels, and for treating nervous exhaustion, rheumatism, gout, and women's disorders.

Common barley (*Hordeum vulgare*), which is cultivated here in clayey soil, has either two-rowed or multi-rowed spikelets. Each joint of the spike has three grains with a long beard. The multi-rowed barley is generally cultivated as a winter crop. It serves as a fodder grain and is produced as pearl barley, groats, and malt coffee. On the other hand, the two-rowed barley, which is cultivated carefully as a summer crop, is used primarily as a brewing barley. Brewing barley has a high concentration of starch, whereas fodder barley has more protein. The cultivation of barley is even possible under the extreme conditions encountered in such places as Norway, Egypt, Australia, and Tibet. It can endure dry periods as well as frost and even high-saline soils. In worldwide production, it comes in fourth behind wheat, corn, and rice. When cooked, pearl barley is especially good for people with stomach and throat problems, as it soothes irritated tissue.

As the nearest relative of wheat, **common spelt**, or **German wheat** (*Triticum spelta*), was recommended by Sebastian Kneipp because of its high concentration of protein (vegetable gluten). The husking of this grain (its refinement) occurs in special mills. Typical spelt fields, with their ripe, horizontally aligned spikelets, can be seen in such places as southwestern Germany, Switzerland, and Belgium. Spelt is not a very demanding grain to grow when it comes to soil quality, weather conditions, soil cultivation, and insects and other pests. Spelt mash has been used as a filling morning meal for hundreds of years. Today, breads and pastas are baked using spelt. Unripe spelt has a high nutritive value, making it a healthful addition to soups, cakes, cookies, and dumplings.

Common wheat (*Triticum aestivum*) is considered to be a "naked cereal," for the grain already falls from its husk in the course of the threshing. This important type of grain is especially suitable for breads and other baked goods because of its high concentration of starch and gluten. In addition, wheat flour is used to make semolina for pasta. A top fermented beer of southern Germany is *Weizen* ("wheat beer"). Wheat bran, with its high concentration of aleurone protein, is an important source of dietary fiber.

189
Common oats (*Avena sativa* L.)
Grass family (Gramineae)
VI–VII
Fruit, herbage, green oats, oat straw
Amino acids, vitamins A, B, K, E, minerals, zinc, alkaloid (avenin)
Tea, rolled oats, oat bran, tincture, tablets, bath additives
(F) Laxative, cholesterol-reducing dietary fiber (bran), dietary agent (rolled oats), calmative, nervous exhaustion (tincture), rheumatism, gout (green oats), women's disorders (bath additive)
190
Common barley (*Hordeum vulgare* L.)
Grass family (Gramineae)
VI
Demulcent (soothes irritated tissue, especially mucous membranes)
191
Common spelt, or **German wheat** (*Triticum spelta* L.)
Grass family (Gramineae)
VI
Dietary fiber, carbohydrates, vitamins
192
Common wheat (*Triticum aestivum* L.)
Grass family (Gramineae)
VI–VII
Starches (85 percent), vitamin E
Flour, oil, capsules
Medicinal effects of wheat germ

189 Common oats
191 Common spelt, German wheat

190 Common barley
192 Common wheat

A member of the parsley family, the **giant hogweed** (*Heracleum mantegazzianum*) reaches a height of up to 3 meters (more than 9 feet) and is fond of moist habitats. Its white inflorescences are highly regarded as decorative components of flower arrangements and dried bouquets. However, this plant, with its unhindered proliferation, is now being combated because of the severe allergic skin reactions that develop following contact. The German name *Bärenklau* ("bear's claw") is derived from the form of the leaves. Its genus name, *Heracleum,* comes from the Greek hero Heracles (also known as Hercules).

Native to the Himalayas and eastern India, the **ornamental jewelweed,** or **Indian balsam** (*Impatiens glandulifera*), can now be found on the Moosberg (a mountain near Bad Wörishofen). This member of the balsam, or touch-me-not, family grows as high as 2 meters (more than 6 feet). Glands are located in the vicinity of the lower toothed region and along the knotty and jointed hollow stem. The cornucopialike, purplish-red flowers appear in clusters of two to fourteen blossoms and have a spur that bends backward. As with other touch-me-nots, this plant has a three-fold fruit capsule that, when ripe, flings its seeds far away upon the slightest contact.

The Latin name of the **crown vetch,** or **axseed,** (*Coronilla varia*) comes from *coronilla* ("little crown") and *varius* ("varied," pertaining to its colors). This plant has umbelliferous clusters of papilionaceous flowers, and can be seen blooming in the summer. The standard is pink, the wings are white, and the scutellum has a violet lip. The legume, or pod, has the form of a hatchet.

The **pot marigold, calendula,** or **common marigold** (*Calendula officinalis*), is an annual garden plant that blossoms throughout the summer. Another name for it, "ringlet flower," comes from the plant's knobby, rolled-up fruit that is shaped like a ring inside. In some places, the blossoms are known as "death flowers" because of their unpleasant odor of decay after having been picked. The ligulate crown of the composite flower is a radiant golden-yellow in color, and it has thus been used in makeup. When rain is threatening or with the early evening dampness, the blossoms close as an indicator of the weather. Sebastian Kneipp described this weather forecaster as follows: "The calendula is very clever. If it is still closed after seven in the morning, then it will certainly rain during the course of the day. If it opens between six and seven in the morning, however, it will definitely not rain." This plant has a range of medicinal uses. Father Kneipp said, "The calendula is the foremost agent for treating sores and ulcerations," and he praised the plant for its excellent anti-inflammatory, wound-healing, and skin-care effects. A tea made from calendula has diaphoretic (sweat-inducing) and spasmolytic results. When administered externally, an extract, brew, or tincture from this plant serves as a gargle for inflammations of the throat and for use as a poultice. In addition to essential oils, bitter principles, and glycosides, the blossoms contain carotinoids. For this reason, the plant was previously used to color butter, to embellish incense powders, and to replace the more expensive saffron.

193
Giant hogweed (*Heracleum mantegazzianum*)
Parsley, or carrot, family (Umbelliferae)
VI–VIII
Essential oil, furanocoumarins, bitter principles
Allergic skin irritation is common after contact.

194
Ornamental jewelweed, or **Indian balsam** (*Impatiens glandulifera*)
Balsam, or touch-me-not, family (Balsaminaceae)
VII–IX

195
Crown vetch, or **axseed** (*Coronilla varia* L.)
Pea family (Papilionaceae)
V–IX

196
Pot marigold, calendula, or **common marigold** (*Calendula officinalis* L.)
Composite, or daisy, family (Compositae)
VI–IX
Blossoms
Ointment, oil, tea (convalescent drug)
Essential oil, saponins, glycosides, carotinoids
(M) Externally for inflammations of the skin and mucous membranes, lacerations, contusions, burns; internally for its diaphoretic and spasmolytic effects

193 Giant hogweed
195 Crown vetch, axseed

194 Ornamental jewelweed, Indian balsam
196 Pot marigold, calendula, common marigold

The lemon-yellow flowers of the **common rockrose** (*Helianthemum nummularium*), which grows to a maximum height of 30 centimeters (about 1 foot), only open while the sun is shining and follow the sun with their leaf blades, as do sunflowers. *Helios* means "sun," and *anthros* "flower"; *nummularium* refers to the similarity of the flowers to coins. A low-lying shrub with a woody stalk, this plant is often seen along the edges of dry paths. When the flowers are touched, or when they are struck by sunlight, the numerous stamens lie flat against the petals, as with the mimosa.

A shrublike perennial plant, the **spiny restharrow,** or **thorny restharrow** (*Ononis spinosa*), does well in calcareous and poor soil, as found in the lower mountain areas of the Palatinate. Its rose-colored and white papilionaceous flowers can be seen blooming throughout the summer. Donkeys have been known to be fond of this plant, hence the genus name *Ononis,* Latin for "donkey's fodder." Its German name, *Hauhechel* ("hack hackle"), has to do with the fact that the plant's root, which extends nearly 60 centimeters (almost 2 feet) into the ground, must be "hacked" out of the earth. The second part of the German name, *Hechel,* meaning "cock's comb," as well as the plant's thorny fortification, indicate its similarity to the flax comb. Its thorns have also led to the name *Weiberkrieg* ("women's war") in Swabia. In terms of this plant's curative properties, the glycosides contained in the root have a diuretic effect and are effective agents for the prevention and washing out of renal gravel, without having a stimulating effect on the kidneys. However, the root should not be used in cases of edema resulting from cardiac or renal insufficiency. Externally, the root is employed to treat eczema and itching as well as other skin problems. In veterinary medicine, thorny restharrow is considered to be a good diuretic for horses that must be brought to urinate.

The **small cow-wheat** (*Melampyrum syl-vaticum*), a member of the figwort family, with plain, yellowish-brown, tubular florets, can be seen in the pine forests here. The genus name *Melampyrum,* from the Latin *melas,* for "black," and *pyros,* for "wheat," refers to the plant's seeds, which resemble dark grains of wheat. Because of their nectarlike sap, these seeds are frequently collected by ants. Quails also seem to be fond of them. Small cow-wheat is a semiparasitic plant, as its roots tap into those of neighboring plants.

The stringently protected **Martagon lily,** or **Turk's-cap lily** (*Lilium martagon*), is one of the more striking plants in the shady forests of the Moosberg (a mountain near Bad Wörishofen). A bulbous, perennial plant, it reaches a height of 30 to 100 centimeters (about a foot to more than 3 feet). The nodding flowers have curled-back petals and are situated in loose clusters of three to ten terminal blossoms. The erect, green stalk is speckled in red. The plant was previously also known in some places as "iron hyacinth" and "gold root," and its yellow bulb was considered by alchemists to have the power of changing metals to gold.

197
Common rockrose
(*Helianthemum nummularium* L.)
Rockrose family (Cistaceae)
V–IX
198
Spiny restharrow, or **thorny restharrow** (*Ononis spinosa* L.)
Pea family (Papilionaceae)
V–IX
Essential oil, flavonoids (ononins), triterpenes (onocerin), sterols
(M) To increase the amount of urine in the event of catarrhs of the renal pelvis or bladder, or urinary gravel, and to prevent the development of urinary calculi
Not to be used in cases of edema resulting from cardiac or renal insufficiency
Externally used for skin problems
199
Small cow-wheat (*Melampyrum sylvaticum* L.)
Figwort, or snapdragon, family (Scrophulariaceae)
VI–X
200
Martagon lily, or **Turk's-cap lily** (*Lilium martagon* L.)
Lily family (Liliaceae)
VII–VIII
Endangered and therefore protected!

197 Common rockrose
199 Small cow-wheat
198 Spiny restharrow, thorny restharrow
200 Martagon lily, Turk's-cap lily

The brilliant-yellow papilionaceous flowers of **dyer's greenweed, woadwaxen, dyer's broom, dyer's furze,** or **dyer's greenwood** (*Genista tinctoria*), can be spotted in woods, pastures, and meadows. The genus name *Genista* comes from the Celtic word *gen,* for "little shrub." This low-lying shrub has woody, slightly hairy, and branched stems. The herbage and blossoms contain bitter principles and exude an aroma similar to that of watercress. A very durable yellow dye is derived from the branches, leaves, and blossoms. Dyer's broom tea acts as a mild purgative and has been used for gravel and stones as well. Nevertheless, it should not be taken by people with high blood pressure, as it also raises it.

When the blossoms of the **prickly lettuce** (*Lactuca serriola*) are glimpsed from a distance on a sunny hill, they can barely be recognized as composite flowers. The Latin name *Lactuca* is derived from the word *lac,* meaning "milk," and indicates the plant's poisonous, milky sap. Pyramid-shaped panicles emanate from the plain, yellow, composite flower heads from June to October. The plant reaches a height of up to 1 meter (more than 3 feet). It is also known in some places as "compass lettuce," as, in dry, sunny sites, its leaves turn away from the sun and stand vertically in a north–south direction.

The **vervain mallow,** or **European mallow** (*Malva alcea*), is sometimes found scattered along the sides of paths on the Moosberg (a mountain near Bad Wörishofen). This perennial plant has an unbranched vine and a spindly root. The blossoms are pink to vibrant red and may have veins that are darker in color. Because of its mucilage, the vervain mallow is a good plant to use for poultices. In the Middle Ages, it was believed that this plant helped to protect people from accidents, and it was also carried as an amulet to strengthen the eyes.

The **Waldwitwenblume** (*Knautia silvatica*), as it is known in Germany, gets its genus name from the botanist Knaut, who died in Halle in 1716.

This plant is frequently encountered in moist habitats on the Moosberg during the summer. The flowers' violet heads can easily be confused with the blossoms of the small scabious (*Scabiose columbaria*), pictured on page 115. However, the leaves of this plant, which is also known as the "wood scabious" or "field scabious," are not parted or as notched.

201
Dyer's greenweed, woadwaxen, dyer's broom, dyer's furze, or **dyer's greenwood** (*Genista tinctoria* L.)
Pea family (Papilionaceae)
VI–VIII
Bitter principles
Mild purgative, also used for gravel and stones
To be avoided by those with high blood pressure

202
Prickly lettuce (*Lactuca serriola* L.)
Composite, or daisy, family (Compositae)
VII–IX

203
Vervain mallow, or **European mallow** (*Malva alcea* L.)
Mallow family (Malvaceae)
VI–IX
Mucilage, flavonoids, allantoin

204
Waldwitwenblume (*Knautia silvatica* L.)
Teasel, or scabious, family (Dipsacaceae)
VI–IX

201 Dyer's greenweed, woadwaxen, dyer's broom, dyer's furze, dyer's greenwood
203 Vervain mallow, European mallow

202 Prickly lettuce
204 Waldwitwenblume

A member of the teasel, or scabious, family, the **dove pincushions,** or **small scabious** (*Scabiose columbaria*), with its violet-blue flowers, is common to the fields around Bad Wörishofen. Typical of this plant is the five-lobed corolla, whereas the field scabious (shown on page 113) has a four-lobed corolla. As many as eighty individual petals are unified in one flower head. The leaves are parted and notched. As a "thunder flower," this plant supposedly offers protection from thunderstorms. The Latin name Scabiose is derived from *scabies* and indicates its use in folk medicine for treating skin problems.

Surprisingly, the **round-headed rampion** (*Phyteuma orbiculare*) is a member of the bluebell, or bellflower, family. Its glomerate, violet-blue flowers are often seen standing among the meadow grasses on the Moosberg (a mountain near Bad Wörishofen). The clawlike appearance of the flowers may explain the plant's German epithet *Teufel,* meaning "devil." The lengthy, arched, individual blossoms grow together at the tips.

Members of the cranesbill family can be distinguished through the typical form of their fruit, which stretch out in the shape of a crane or stork's bill, and their characteristically upright, glandular hairs. When the fruit is ripe, and as a result of the humidity in the air, the slender bristles bend, flinging their seeds outward. An especially lovely example from this family is the **meadow geranium,** or **meadow cranesbill** (*Geranium pratense*), with its large, violet-blue flowers, which we see on the sunny hills here during July. The Latin name *Geranium* comes from Greek *geranos,* meaning "crane," and indicates the typically bill-shaped fruit.

The **woolly burdock** (*Arctium tomentosum*), which grows in even the most desolate areas, is a member of the large, multiform family of composite flowers. The various species are generally not differentiated by the general public. They are biennial plants with many branches and have large, oval, deciduous leaves that are not typical of thistles. The woolly burdock is especially decorative when its thick, grayish-white, cobweblike heads stand out against its purplish-red blossoms. Water in which the root (especially from the great burdock) had been boiled was used as an agent for inducing hair growth. An extract from the root mixed with olive oil or almond oil ("burr-root oil") is still applied externally today to care for the scalp.

205
Dove pincushions, or **small scabious** (*Scabiose columbaria* L.)
Teasel, or scabious, family (Dipsacaceae)
VII–IX

206
Round-headed rampion (*Phyteuma orbiculare* L.)
Bluebell, or bellflower, family (Campanulaceae)
V–IX

207
Meadow geranium, or **meadow cranesbill** (*Geranium pratense* L.)
Geranium, or cranesbill, family (Geraniaceae)
VI–VIII

208
Woolly burdock (*Arctium tomentosum*)
Composite, or daisy, family (Compositae)
VII–IX

205 Dove pincushions, small scabious
207 Meadow geranium, meadow cranesbill

206 Round-headed rampion
208 Woolly burdock

The **Robert geranium, herb Robert, fox geranium,** or **red shanks** (*Geranium robertianum*), is an annual plant that tends to grow in rocky forests. Its species name *robertianum* is derived from the name Robert, or Rupprecht, the tutelary god of the house. This plant's long, stork's-bill-shaped fruit already extends from its mature flowers. It has soft, velvety leaves and a red, hairy stalk. In some places, it is also known as "stinking stork's-bill" because of its unpleasant odor. In the past, Robert geranium was used externally to stop bleeding, heal wounds, and treat painful joints and injuries. It's been said that the gladiators carried this small, pinkish-red herb with them. Today, the herb is used for gastritis, diarrhea, gout, and hemorrhages. However, as it contains tannins, excessive doses should be avoided.

Native to North America, **Canadian horseweed,** or **Canadian fleabane** (*Erigon canadensis*), grows here in the coarse, sandy soil in the lower mountain areas of the Palatinate. Together with the ragworts, it is one of the species that helps to protect young forest seedlings. Because of its many fruit, this plant can be quite a nuisance as a weed on cultivated land. It also has shown great resistance in the event of grass fires. Canadian horseweed has a bristly, hairy stem and numerous blossoms. As a member of the composite family, it is closely related to the asters (a stellate flower), although it has multiple rows of nearly filamentous, ligulate, green and white flowers. The genus name *Erigon* is derived from the Greek *eri* ("early") and *geron* ("aged"), as the plant can be seen to age early, with the white, hairlike crown of the fruit appearing shortly after blossoming. Because of its astringent and styptic (arresting bleeding) properties, it is helpful in cases of diarrhea, internal hemorrhage, and hemorrhoids.

Closely related to the potato, tomato, and eggplant, the **climbing nightshade, bittersweet, woody nightshade,** or **climbing bittersweet** (*Solanum dulcamara*), is a fairly common climbing perennial shrub that can be found in the Hartenthal (a valley in this region). The genus name *Solanum* is the Latin word for "consolation" or "appeasement," as pain-relieving and soporific effects were known for a number of species in the Solanaceae family (including, of course, belladonna). The blossoms of this plant can be differentiated from those of belladonna by their color (here, violet petals enclose the yellow stamen cone and have no yellow or green spots at their base). The ellipsoid, scarlet-red, hanging berries are often a temptation for children. Fortunately, they are only mildly poisonous. In the past, bittersweet was used as an agent against rheumatism and to sooth paralyzed limbs. In folk medicine, it has been employed to "purify the blood." The two- to three-year-old stalk has been prescribed for skin conditions arising during metabolic illnesses. Even though bittersweet is a relatively weak poison, it is not suitable for internal self-treatment.

The **purple loosestrife** (*Lythrum salicaria*), with its high purple spikes, blossoms splendidly in the moist fields and ditches near the Hartenthal beginning in July. The blossoms stand as false whorls and have two special characteristics: The pistils are found in three different lengths, and the longer filaments of the stamens develop green pollen whereas the shorter filaments develop yellow pollen. Insects eat this unripe yellow pollen and, at the same time, pick up the ripe green pollen in their covering "fur," which they then carry along on their further journeys. The plant was previously used to still bleeding because of its color (*lythron* is Latin for "blood"). It has also been used to treat diarrhea and gastroenteritis. *Salicaria* comes from *salix,* meaning "meadow," and is an indication that livestock are fond of the plant. Loosestrife blossoms were formerly a coveted source of dyes used in textiles.

209
Robert geranium, herb Robert, fox geranium, or **red shanks** (*Geranium robertianum* L.)
Geranium, or cranesbill, family (Geraniaceae)
V–X
Herbage, root
Tea, sap
Tannins, bitter principles, essential oil
(F) To stop bleeding, to lessen inflammations of the mouth and gingiva
To treat gastritis, diarrhea, gout, hemorrhages
Avoid overdose because of the tannins.

210
Canadian horseweed, or **Canadian fleabane** (*Erigon canadensis* L.) Composite, or daisy, family (Compositae)
VI–X
Tannins, essential oil
Tea
(F) Diarrhea, hemostyptic

211
Climbing nightshade, bittersweet, woody nightshade, or **climbing bittersweet** (*Solanum dulcamara* L.) Tomato, or nightshade, family (Solanaceae)
V–VIII
Stalk
Ointment
Bitter principles, steroid and triterpene saponins, solasonine
Antipruritic, antiallergenic, anti-inflammatory in cases of eczema and neurodermatitis
Berries are poisonous, especially when unripe!

212
Purple loosestrife (*Lythrum salicaria* L.)
Loosestrife family (Lythraceae)
VI–IX
Diarrhea, gastroenteritis

209 Herb Robert, fox geranium, red shanks
211 Climbing nightshade, bittersweet, woody nightshade, climbing bittersweet

210 Canadian horseweed, Canadian fleabane
212 Purple loosestrife

$\mathcal{E}$arthsmoke, or **few-flowered fumitory** (*Fumaria vaillantii*), with its small, reddish, bulging blossoms, is found in the root-crop fields on the Moosberg (a mountain near Bad Wörishofen) from May to October. This relative of the poppy has a blackish-red corolla tip. The genus name *Fumaria* is derived from the Latin word fumus, for "smoke"; like the mustard and the horseradish, it stimulates the development of tears, as does smoke. The chervil-like, pedunculated, deciduous leaves are twice pinnate with flat tips. The species pictured here is named after the French botanist Sébastien Vaillant, who described the flower in 1727 in Paris. A related species, the common fumitory (*Fumaria officinalis*), has been used to treat liver and gallbladder problems, although excessive amounts are known to cause stomachaches.

Growing to a height of only 15 to 45 centimeters (½ to 1½ feet), the **dwarf nettle, or small nettle** (*Urtica urens*), has light-green, ovate, sharp-toothed leaves and horizontally positioned, paniculate blossoms. In contrast to the common, or stinging, nettle (*Urtica dioica*), this nettle is monoecious, meaning that each plant has both male and female flowers. Its leaves contain vitamins, minerals, carotinoids, histamine, chlorophyll, and formic acid. These substances penetrate into the hand through the tip of the nettle when the brittle tip is broken off, leading to the characteristic burning sensation. Among other effects, the histamine brings about the development of wheals. A tea made from the stinging nettle has a diuretic effect and provides relief from prostatic complaints. Used externally, stinging nettle stimulates circulation—for example, when applied in a lotion for the scalp. Young plants are used as a wild vegetable and in salads during the spring. But uncooked, old plants should be avoided, as they can produce dangerous side effects. In the past, the seeds of the stinging nettle were used to make love potions. Today, extracts from the seeds are recommended as a tonic. However, stinging nettle should not be used in cases of congestion or during edema resulting from cardiac or renal insufficiency. Medicinally, the dwarf nettle has demonstrated similar effects.

The **sea buckthorn** (*Hippophae rhamnoides*) is often seen growing on ocean dunes and in regions near the mountains supplied by runoff water. As with most of the thorny plants, which Darwin had characterized as being among the smart plants, the thorns on the dark-gray branches of the sea buckthorn are found only up to a height where livestock are likely to reach. However, the berries from this shrub contain more than 500 milligrams of vitamin C (more than 800 percent of the U.S. RDA) in 100 grams (about 3 ounces) of berries, and are used to make excellent stewed fruit and a tart-tangy juice. Because of its high concentration of vitamin C, sea buckthorn has also been used as a tonic for colds in folk medicine. This shrub reaches a height of up to 3 meters (about 10 feet) and has willowlike leaves. The tiny blossoms appear in April together with the leaves.

Hops (*Humulus lupulus*) is a perennial plant that is seen climbing up poles and cables (usually clockwise) in Bavaria. This member of the hop, or hempwort, family is cultivated primarily for the production of beer. The cone-forming, whitish vine reproduces by means of underground runners. The golden-yellow, bitter hop meal found in the cones contains bitter principles, flavonoids, and essential oil. These active substances not only provide beer with its aroma, durability, and stable foam, but hop glands and their extracts also stimulate digestion. But their main effect is a calming one on the nervous system. Hops are thus administered in combination with valerian, lemon balm, and common Saint-John's-wort. They are also used externally in bath additives to relieve aching muscles and promote restful sleep. Hops are even used in pillows as a method for overcoming insomnia.

213
Earthsmoke, or **few-flowered fumitory** (*Fumaria vaillantii*)
Poppy family (Papaveraceae)
V–X
Herbage of common fumitory
(*Fumaria officinalis* L.)
Alkaloids, fumarine, bitter principles
(M) Spasmodic disturbances of the biliary system
Overdose may lead to stomachaches.

214
Dwarf nettle, or **small nettle**
(*Urtica urens*)
Nettle family (Urticaceae)
Herbage, roots, fruit (seeds)
Tea, plant juice, plant tablets
Sterols, phenylpropane, lignans
(M) For complaints during urination, benign prostatic hyperplasia, diuretic, metabolic stimulant, for rheumatism, gout, disturbances of the biliary system
Not to be used in cases of congestion, or during edema stemming from cardiac or renal insufficiency

215
Sea buckthorn (*Hippophae rhamnoides*)
Sea-buckthorn family (Elaeagnaceae)
VI
Ripe berries
Vitamin C, A, B, E, minerals, fruit acids, sugar
Plant juice, stewed fruit
(F) Restorative tonic for colds

216
Hops (*Humulus lupulus* L.)
Hop, or hempwort, family
(Cannabaceae)
V
Female flowers, glandular scales
Tea, tablets, bath additives
Essential oil (myrcene, humulene), bitter principles, resins (humulone, lupulone), flavonoids
(M) Calming, soporific

213 Earthsmoke, few-flowered fumitory
215 Sea buckthorn

214 Dwarf nettle, small nettle
216 Hops

The oldest-known oak in Germany stands in the town of Erl, in North Rhine–Westphalia and is about 1,500 years old. The **English oak, or pedunculate oak** (*Quercus robur*), can reach an age of up to 2,000 years and can attain a trunk circumference of 15 meters (more than 45 feet). As with all members of the beech family, oaks have separate, unisexùal flowers: male catkins and female blossoms that multiply on the same peduncle. In many myths about the oaks, it is claimed that they have been blessed by the gods. The effects of their bark, with its high concentration of bitter principles, in curbing diarrhea and in arresting bleeding have been known since antiquity.

European mistletoe (*Viscum album*) is another plant often found in myths. In ancient mythology, mistletoe was considered to be a golden, magic rod. This parasitic evergreen plant was also known to be cut from trees by priests using golden sickles to be used as a cure-all. The propagation of mistletoe, which lives on both deciduous trees and conifers, is primarily carried out by thrushes and other birds. Typical of this plant are the greenish-brown and forked branches, the leathery and ligulate leaves with their thick edges, and the yellowish-green springtime flowers. In the summer, the female flowers develop into sticky, white berries, which are dangerous to eat, especially for children. Mistletoe's use as a medicinal plant originated with Hippocrates. Mistletoe preparations help to reduce blood pressure and to strengthen the immune system, and are used in tumor therapy. However, mistletoe should be prepared only with cold water and needs to steep for a number of hours. Sprigs of this plant are used decoratively during the Christmas season. The custom of kissing under mistletoe may be related to it having been a symbol of fertility.

Although it has been cultivated for more than 7,000 years, **common flax, or linseed** (*Linum usitatissimum*), has lovely, blue or violet-blue flowers that are familiar to few of us. However, linseeds, either whole or coarsely ground, are commonly known and, taken with an ample amount of water, have proven to be an effective and harmless laxative. As a result of their extensive swelling, these smooth, flat, shiny, light-brown seeds exercise a stretching stimulus on the intestines. They also serve as a lubricant because of their high concentration of mucilage. Used externally, they have a softening effect on ulcerations. In addition, flaxseed eye pillows are used to soothe tired, sore eyes. As far back as the Stone Age, linen cloth has been produced from the fibers derived from the stems of this plant. Sebastian Kneipp used linen frequently to pack certain substances, and the threads made from this plant have been used by surgeons. Linseed oil is a highly valued kitchen oil because of its high concentration of unsaturated fatty acids. Technically, it is used in the production of paints, varnishes, paper, and leather. Even though blooming flax fields, giving the appearance of a bluish lake, are a sight of the past, relatives of the flax crossed with geranium species when planted in herb gardens conjure up memories of this lovely blue flower.

Common duckweed (*Lemna minor*), with its opposite, light-green leaves, forms a carpet over the moist biotope during the summer. Gaps on the upper surface of the leaves promote the evaporation of water, resulting in a lowering of the temperature of the surrounding air. The inflorescences can hardly be recognized, and the male blossom has a single stamen. Waterfowl are fond of this plant, earning it the name duckweed.

217
English oak, or **pedunculate oak**
(*Quercus robur* L.)
Beech family (Fagaceae)
IV–V
Bark, young sprouts
Tea, extraction by boiling, bath additive
Catechin tannin
(M) Astringent, anti-inflammatory in the event of infections of the skin, mucous membranes, gingiva; used internally for diarrhea

218
European mistletoe (*Viscum album* L.)
Mistletoe family (Loranthaceae)
III–V
Herbage; berries should not be eaten
Tea, plant juice, extract as an injection
Lectins, viscotoxins, flavonoids, lignans
As a supportive treatment for high blood pressure, heart complaints, follow-up treatment subsequent to cancer to strengthen the powers of resistance

219
Common flax, or **linseed** (*Linum usitatissimum* L.)
Flax family (Linaceae)
VI–VIII
Seeds, fatty oil, fibers (linen)
Seeds either whole or coarsely ground, oil, infusion, poultice with paste
Mucilage, fatty oil, glycoside linusitamarine, phosphatides
(M) Mild laxative, lubricant, for inflammations of the mouth, throat, gingiva, and gastrointestinal tract; used externally to soften ulcerations

220
Common duckweed (*Lemna minor* L.)
Duckweed family (Lemnaceae)
V–VI

217 English oak, pedunculate oak
219 Common flax, linseed

218 European mistletoe
220 Common duckweed

*F*lowers associated with hay (*Flores graminis*), or **"Heubloama" ("hay flowers")**, as they are called in the Algau, are used in the form of "hay sacks," bath extracts, and oils, especially for the treatment of rheumatic disorders and colicky pains. The hay sack (or hay pack) is one of the best-known and most appreciated methods among the Kneipp cures. A linen or fleece sack is loosely filled with "hay flowers" and heated to about 40°C (104°F), using steam or by soaking in hot water. This sack is then placed onto the painful part of the body, covered with a cloth, and kept there for a minimum of a half hour.

Historically, hay flowers have been the sediments or deposits from hay that collect on the floor of a barn—that is, the flowers, fruit, seeds, small leaves, and parts of stalks from various grasses and meadow flowers. The hay flowers collected in this manner are naturally only as good as the varied plants that grow in the fields. In and around Bad Wörishofen, the best quality is found in mountain meadows and unfertilized pastures. If possible, they should be mowed only once, before or during blossoming. Aside from grasses and flowers containing essential oil, coumarin-containing plants like sweet vernal-grass (*Anthoxanthum odoratum*), bedstraw, and melilot grow in these fields. During the process of drying, the coumarin glycosides are split fermentatively, and the coumarin that is released provides the wonderful, sweet-scented bedstraw aroma of hay.

Although the comforting and curative effects of the hay sack are primarily due to the long-term and pleasant application of heat, the coumarin resorbed by the skin is described as having a calming effect as well. This is supported further by the other contents of hay flowers, such as sugar, proteins, starches, minerals, trace elements, flavonoids, and essential oils. Extracts from these hay flowers, as well as a pure form of their components, are suitable as ingredients in bath additives and for strengthening the effects of dressings and packs. The hot hay sack is frequently employed clinically today in conjunction with a heating aid in order to provide long-term, uniform warmth.

On its own, the Kneipp hay sack, with its controlled and standardized hay flowers, can be very effective for use at home. Among other effects, it has been shown to stimulate circulation, increase the metabolism of the tissues and the elasticity of the connective tissue, as well as alleviate pain. However, hay sacks should not be applied to open wounds or used during acute rheumatic episodes or inflammations.

221–224
"Heubloama" ("hay flowers")
(*Flores graminis*)
A mixture of grasses, flowers, herbs
V–VIII
Cut leaves, stalks, herbs, blossoms, seeds
"Hay sacks" (steamed), bath additives, wet compresses
Essential oil, furanocoumarins, flavonoids, tannins
(M) Local heat therapy in the event of degenerative rheumatic illnesses, anti-inflammatory, pain-relieving, soothing, relaxing, antispasmodic
Not to be used on open wounds or during acute rheumatic episodes or inflammations

221 "Heubloama" ("hay flowers")
223 "Heumandl" (hay truss)

222 Hay harvest
224 Summer meadow

$\mathcal{I}$t's been said that garlic makes for a long life, but a lonely one as well! This is because, along with its benefits, you inherit its smell. Native to Central Asia, **garlic** (*Allium sativum*) is widely cultivated for its use as a popular kitchen herb. But garlic also has a range of medicinal uses, as the bulbs are effective against bacteria and fungi, reduce the level of fat and cholesterol in the blood, and protect against the development of arteriosclerosis by hindering the conglomeration of the platelets and thus improving the flow of blood. These effects, however, can be achieved only by regularly eating an adequate dose of garlic. Unfortunately, consuming an adequate dose is noticed by others in the surroundings, as the unpleasant odor of the sulfur-containing contents is discharged in the breath and through the skin. Garlic has a long tradition as a highly valued herb. It was even found as a gift in the tombs of the pharaohs. The ancient soldiers, the builders of the pyramids, and the athletes of ancient Greece took this nutrient, which was commonly eaten by the populace, in order to increase their physical powers. Because of its antibacterial and antiseptic effects, this species of leek was not only consumed during the plague in the Middle Ages, but it also received the name "Russian penicillin." This member of the lily family is one of the first cultivated plants and was thought to be a means of protection from evil and magic. Garlic is a perennial plant with a simple, smooth stem that gives rise to long, flat leaves and a rounded umbel of small, white flowers, among which grow numerous small bulbs. These bulbs are made up of individual bulbs, or cloves, enclosed in a papery, white skin.

The **eastern teaberry, wintergreen,** or **checkerberry** (*Gaultheria procumbens*), is an evergreen shrub bearing red, berrylike fruit. Because of its leathery, dark-green leaves, this plant, found in herb gardens, is reminiscent of the bog blueberry, a member of the heath family. The volatile wintergreen oil, which is attained from the leaves through steam distillation, contains more than 95 percent methyl salicylate. This component is an ingredient of many rheumatic bath additives and ointments.

A perennial plant generally growing in mountainous regions, **mountain arnica** (*Arnica montana*) had been found in large numbers in the Alps but now is an endangered species whose collection is strictly prohibited. Typical characteristics of the arnica plants that are planted along the nature trail near the spa here are their two opposite leaves and their yellow, daisylike terminal blossoms, arising from a 40- to 50-centimeter (16- to 20-inch) stalk. Sebastian Kneipp praised the healing effects of arnica, saying, "I consider it to be the first preparation to be used for injuries and I cannot recommend it any higher." Today, many people are aware of the use of an arnica tincture for inflammations of the skin and mucous membranes, as well as for injuries, muscle and joint pain, insect stings, and varicose veins. Arnica is also used in the form of ointments and bath products. Its soothing effects have earned it other names such as "wound weed," "angel's weed," and "strength herb." The easily cultivated North American meadow arnica (*Arnica chamissoris*) contains the same bitter principles, flavonoids, and essential oil.

One of the oldest medicinal plants, the decorative **castor bean,** or **castor-oil plant** (*Ricinus communis*), is primarily cultivated in temperate climates. The stout stem bears typically broad leaves and a terminal raceme of flowers that bloom in late summer. The oil pressed from the fruit's seeds is widely known for its purgative effect, which occurs dramatically 2 to 4 hours after the oil is taken. Nevertheless, castor bean oil should not be used in cases of chronic, severe constipation or bowel obstructions. Although the oil is safe, the entire plant, including the seeds, is poisonous. This oil is also used externally for hair care and technically as a lubricant for motors.

225
Garlic (*Allium sativum* L.)
Lily family (Liliaceae)
VII–VIII
Bulblets (garlic cloves)
Plant tablets, oil capsules, plant juice
Sulfur compounds (alliin), ferment allinase, choline
In cases of infection, bacteria and fungi, elevated lipid levels, a prophylactic agent against arteriosclerosis

226
Eastern teaberry, wintergreen, or **checkerberry** (*Gaultheria procumbens* L.) Wintergreen, or pyrola, family (Pyrolaceae)
VI–VIII
Herbage
Bath additives, tea
Arbutin, ursone, methyl salicylic acid and its esters
Externally, stimulates blood flow, muscle relaxant

227
Mountain arnica (*Arnica montana* L.) Composite, or daisy, family (Compositae)
VI–VIII (endangered and therefore protected!)
Blossoms
Ointment, tincture, gel, oil
Sesquiterpene lactones, flavonoids, essential oil
(M) Externally for bruises, contusions, injuries, muscle and joint pains, venous complaints

228
Castor bean, or **castor-oil plant** (*Ricinus communis* L.)
Spurge, or wolf's milk, family (Euphorbiaceae)
VI–VIII
Oil (seeds are poisonous!)
Oil or oil capsules
Laxative

225 Garlic
227 Mountain arnica

226 Eastern teaberry, wintergreen, checkerberry
228 Castor bean, castor-oil plant

A perennial shrub often found in clusters in sunny sites, the **dwarf elder** (*Sambucus ebulus*) can be seen blossoming on the Moosberg (a mountain near Bad Wörishofen) in July. The white flowers, tinged with reddish purple, grow in cymes. As the seeds are distributed by birds, they are frequently found where people congregate. Because of its disagreeable smell, the dwarf elder supposedly drives away mice and bugs. The root has been used medicinally for its mild laxative, diuretic, and diaphoretic (sweat-inducing) effects. The berries, which are used to dye leather and yarn blue, are slightly poisonous and may cause vomiting or diarrhea if eaten.

Here, at the edge of the forest, near the airport, it's not unusual to come upon the **bloodtwig dogwood** (*Cornus sanguinea*). Its white umbels appear in spring, and its round, unpalatable, blackish berries with their white spots emerge during late summer. The upright woody branches take on a blood-red color in the fall and winter, hence the species name *sanguinea,* which in Latin means "blood-red." The whitish sapwood (alburnum) is suitable for wood turning.

A deciduous tree, the **European mountain ash, or rowan** (*Sorbus aucuparia*), is common to the region around Bad Wörishofen. Reaching a height of up to 15 meters (almost 50 feet), the tree can be seen along the roadside and in gardens. In some places, the European mountain ash is also known as the "false ash," as the pinnate leaves of this member of the rose family are similar to those found on the true ash tree. The Latin species name *aucuparia* means "to catch birds," indicating the attraction of birds to the tree's berrylike fruit. The red, pea-sized fruit develop from numerous small white flowers and ripen in the fall. Somewhat bitter, the fruit contain sorbitol and are eaten by thrushes. Because of the concentration of tannin and sorbic acid in the fruit, a tea made from it is effective against diarrhea and intestinal disorders. Carpenters and cabinetmakers are very fond of the wood.

The **maidenhair tree,** or **ginkgo** (*Ginkgo biloba*), grows in the park of the spa here and is also encountered along the roadside in Hahnenfeldstrasse. It is one of the oldest plants on earth and was probably the most common tree in Europe about 150 million years ago. Ginkgo trees have survived primarily in Southeast Asia and Japan, as they were cultivated there by the priests as temple trees. For Buddhist monks, the characteristic form of the leathery, drooping, two-lobed leaves has served as a symbol for "unity from duality" (the Latin species name *biloba* means "two-lobed"). Botanically, this dioecious tree, which stands as high as 30 meters (almost 100 feet), is closely related to the conifers. In contrast, however, it loses its leaves during the fall. Ginkgo leaves are not suitable for brewing tea. But an extract from the fresh leaves, known as GBE (Ginkgo biloba extract), in the form of drops or tablets, has proven to be very effective for treating diminished blood flow to the brain as well as severe cramping and pain in the legs from exercise. Because it is beneficial for overall cardiovascular health, it enhances general health and well-being. Lately GBE is being used increasingly by the elderly for such conditions as memory loss and depression. The myth of the ginkgo tree as a "tree of life" is further supported by the fact that the ginkgo was the first tree to sprout after the explosion of the atom bomb in Hiroshima.

229
Dwarf elder (*Sambucus ebulus* L.)
Honeysuckle family (Caprifoliaceae)
VI–VIII
Root
Tea
Bitter principles, iridoids, tannins
(F) Diuretic and diaphoretic (sweat-inducing)
Berries are slightly poisonous and may cause vomiting or diarrhea!

230
Bloodtwig dogwood (*Cornus sanguinea* L.)
Dogwood family (Cornaceae)
V–VI

231
European mountain ash, or **rowan** (*Sorbus aucuparia* L.)
Rose family (Rosaceae)
V–VII
Ripe fruit
Stewed fruit, fruit, tea
Vitamin C, fruit acids, bitter principles, sorbitol
(F) For lack of appetite, stomach disorders

232
maidenhair tree, or **ginkgo** (*Ginkgo biloba* L.)
Ginkgo, or maidenhair tree, family (Ginkgoaceae)
Cultivated
Extract from the leaves (GBE)
Standardized tablets and drops
Trilactonic diterpenes (ginkgolides), sesquiterpenes (bilabolids), flavonoids, procyanidins
Dilation of the blood vessels and increased circulation, especially in the region of the brain
Increasingly being taken by the elderly for memory loss and depression

229 Dwarf elder
231 European mountain ash, rowan

230 Bloodtwig dogwood
232 Maidenhair tree, ginkgo

In fields and on barren land, the **stinking Willie,** or **common ragwort** (*Senecio jacobaea*), blossoms a conspicuous yellow. The genus name *Senecio* comes from the Latin word *senex* for "old man" and is a reference to the plant's grayish, downy hair. The disks of this yellow composite flower are tubular, whereas the lateral florets are ligulate. The achenes that ripen from the disk flowers are crinose (hairy), and those from the lateral florets are bare.

During the summer, we frequently encounter the common weed known as **charlock mustard** (*Sinapsis arvensis*). This plant has a cluster of yellow blossoms with four-fold florets at the end of the stalk. The sepals are positioned horizontally, in contrast to those of the similar hedge mustard, in which they stand vertically. Charlock mustard is very similar to cultivated white mustard, the seeds of which are mixed with various components and then ground to produce mustard, a spice that serves to stimulate the gastric juices.

In the forests near the Hartenthal (a valley in this region), it's possible to catch sight of the rare, white-blossoming **golden chervil** (*Chaerophyllum aureum*), a member of the parsley, or carrot, family. Calves supposedly are fond of eating this aromatic, nutritious herb. When rubbed between the fingers, the plant exudes a carrotlike aroma. Golden chervil is easily confused with cow parsley; however, what differentiates it from that plant is its unspotted stalks, shorter and broader bracts, and hardly noticeable, crenated leaves without a narrow flap or lobe. Its fruit is smooth and entirely without ribs.

From the confusing multitude of plants that are members of the parsley, or carrot, family, **Queen Anne's lace** (*Daucus carota*), with its lacy, white flowers in a concave umbel, is easy to identify. Below the umbels, which appear to nod while they are in the younger stages, are large, springlike bracts. The pinnatifid, lacerated leaves have hair-fine tips. The turnip-shaped root is orange like that of the cultivated carrot, although it is woody. This valuable root vegetable, which is rich in vitamins, is cultivated as the "wild carrot" and helps to supply our bodies with the essential provitamin A, which is especially important for proper vision. It is easy to digest and, apart from mother's milk, one of the first nutrients for infants. Grated carrots are helpful in combating illnesses associated with diarrhea and are suitable for salads and uncooked vegetable platters. Carrot juice is recommended after a fatty meal, or should contain a bit of fat itself, so that the fat-soluble vitamins can be resorbed by the body better. In addition, carrot juice reduces stomach acidity and heartburn. At high doses, especially in infants, carotene is deposited in the outer layers of the skin, causing it to turn the typical orange-brown color. Carotene is therefore frequently a component of suntan lotions and preparations used to protect the skin from damaging UV radiation.

233
Stinking Willie, or **common ragwort** (*Senecio jacobaea* L.)
Composite, or daisy, family (Compositae)
VI–X
234
Charlock mustard (*Sinapsis arvensis* L.)
Mustard, or cabbage, family (Cruciferae)
VI–IX
235
Golden chervil (*Chaerophyllum aureum* L.)
Parsley, or carrot, family (Umbelliferae)
VI–VI
236
Queen Anne's lace (*Daucus carota* L.)
Parsley, or carrot, family (Umbelliferae)
V–VII
Root, herbage
Juice of the root
Provitamin A, vitamin B, C, flavonoids, essential oil
Nutritional disorders in children, vitamin A deficiency, mildly diuretic

233 Stinking Willie, common ragwort
235 Golden chervil

234 Charlock mustard
236 Queen Anne's lace

nother member of the parsley, or carrot, family that is found in the upper mountain areas of the Palatinate is **wild parsnip** (*Pastinaca sativa*). The botanical name for this plant is derived from the Latin *pastus* (meaning "meadow," "feed," or "nutrition") and *sativus* (meaning "cultivated"). Wild parsnip tends to prefer abundant meadows and nutrient-rich soils. It can easily be differentiated from the other members of its family growing in the fields through its small, yellow, as many as ten-rayed flowerets. With this species, the angular stalk can reach a height of up to 1 meter (more than 3 feet). Wild parsnip smells something like carrots. The leaves are suitable as a seasoning, and the long roots can be used as a vegetable. Whereas the roots of cultivated parsnip have a sweet taste, especially following a frost, the wild strain is apt to attain a bitter aftertaste and easily becomes woody. Medicinally, wild parsnip is good for gastrointestinal disorders.

Although most people are aware of the blue gentian, the magnificent **yellow gentian** (*Gentiana lutea*) is hardly known at all. This perennial plant has a simple, erect stem bearing large, opposite leaves and bright-yellow blossoms that grow in whorls toward the top. Native to the Alps and the Black Forest, the yellow gentian is an endangered plant, and thus protected, but it is also cultivated so that the species can be maintained. "Gentian is the most magnificent agent for treating the stomach," said Sebastian Kneipp of this stately plant, which is appreciated in herb gardens as well. The thick roots, which reach a length of up to 1 meter (more than 3 feet), are used medicinally. They contain an extremely bitter substance called amarogentin, which even retains its bitter flavor when highly diluted. As the root contains various types of sugar aside from the bitter principles, it is not only used in appetite-stimulating tinctures, teas, bitters, and aperitifs, but can also be mashed and fermented. The mash is then distilled to produce gentian schnapps. Along with its use as a bitter, the yellow gentian is considered to be one of the plants that can help to strengthen the immune system. Nevertheless, it should not be used in cases of gastric or intestinal ulcers or by pregnant women.

Many parts of the forest floor on the Moosberg (a mountain near Bad Wörishofen) are covered with a dark-green lawn of **polytrichum moss** (*Polytrichum commune*). This plant is also known in some places as "star moss," as the pointed leaves stand in spirals above the erect stalks and therefore look like stars when viewed from above. In July, 10-centimeter (about 4-inch) long, pedunculated, square capsules grow from the tips of these moss stalks. Because of their tomentous (feltlike) hairs, these capsules are sometimes called "felt hats." The capsules are actually spore cases. The moss plant is the first sexual generation. It has red male and green, inclined, terminal, female leaflets. The fertilization occurs by means of the male cells' swimming over to the female part of the plant. The spore cases then develop as the second generation, which consequently forms spores in a nonsexual manner, and new moss plants develop from them. In the Tyrol, when picked 30 days after Assumption, this moss is considered to be a cure-all and to ward off death, hence, its German epithet *Widerton,* from *widder den Tod,* which means "against death."

Like mosses, mushrooms, and horsetails, ferns multiply by way of spores. Impressive examples of **common ladyfern** (*Athyrium filix-femina*) can be spotted in the forests on the Moosberg. Filix-femina, the "female fern," with its large rosettes and delicate fronds, is very similar to the shield fern. This robust filix-mas, or "fern male," is also very common in our forests. The pale-green pinnae are pointed terminally. The longer sori (clusters of sporangia) are shaped like a horseshoe. In their sensitive, youthful stages, the ferns protect themselves from evaporating water by rolling up their fronds like a snail. As sporophytes, the ferns do not blossom, but instead sprout inconspicuous spore cases.

237
Wild parsnip (*Pastinaca sativa* L.)
Parsley, or carrot, family
(Umbelliferae)
VII–VIII
Root, fruit
Herb
Essential oil, fatty oil
Gastrointestinal disorders
238
Yellow gentian (*Gentiana lutea* L.)
Gentian family (Gentianaceae)
VI–VIII (Endangered and therefore protected!)
Root
Tea, tincture, tablets, bitters
Bitter principles (gentiopricroside, amarogentin), essential oil
(M) Stimulates the appetite, reduces secretion of gastric juices, flatulence
Not to be used in cases of gastric or intestinal ulceration or by pregnant women
239
Polytrichum moss (*Polytrichum commune*)
Haircap mosses (Polytrichaceae)
III–V
240
Common ladyfern (*Athyrium filix-femina* L.)
Polypodiaceous ferns (Polypodiaceae)
VII–IX

237 Wild parsnip
239 Polytrichum moss

238 Yellow gentian
240 Common ladyfern

The luminous, yellow blossoms of the **common evening primrose** (*Oenothera biennis*), found here on rocky slopes near the airport, usually open only during the evening hours or when the weather is overcast. This blooming occurs in a matter of seconds. The high, lovely, blossoming spikes, which are often feared as weeds, also thrive on railway embankments, in meadows, and along the roadside. The conspicuous, four-fold blossom stands with the pulled-back tips of the calyx on a cylindrical, rounded fruit capsule that resembles a stalk. The stem is covered with nodes and is hairy. During the seventeenth century, the evening primrose was brought from North America to Europe as a salad green. The carrotlike root can be used to make a vegetable similar to black salsify (the edible root of a European herb). The oil extracted from the plant's seeds has been found to have a number of medicinal effects. The oil contains Omega 6 fatty acids, which are essential for the healthy functioning of the immune, hormonal, and nervous systems. It also contains gamma linoleic acid, making it very helpful for a range of conditions, from menstrual problems, allergies, and arthritis to hyperactivity in children. Applied externally, evening primrose oil has a soothing effect on such skin afflictions as psoriasis and neurodermatitis.

With its lemonlike aroma, **common balm,** or **lemon balm** (*Melissa officinalis*), is cultivated mainly as a culinary herb; however, it has a long tradition as a curative herb and is also an excellent honey-producing plant (in Greek, *melissa* means "bee"). This perennial member of the mint family was brought to Europe by the Arabs during the tenth century. It spread from the monastery gardens of the Benedictines to farmers' gardens and further on to fields, hedges, fences, and the edges of forests. The upright, hairy, four-sided, branched stem gives rise to slightly hairy, opposite, ovate leaves and clusters of two-lipped blossoms. The effects of the common balm were praised by Dioscorides and Paracelsus, as well as by Hildegard von Bingen. The barefoot Carmelite monks developed Eau de Carmes ("Carmelite spirits") from the plant in 1611 as a secret substance, and medicinal spirits were recorded as a cure-all in early pharmaceutical books. Common balm has a soothing effect on nervous agitation and is helpful for insomnia, but at the same time is restoring and lifts the spirits. Because of its carminative effect (against flatulence), it is effective in cases of nervous disorders of the gastrointestinal tract. Balm oils are used in tablets, teas, plant juices, and bath additives, as well as in aromatherapy. The mintlike tannin found in the leaves of the plant (rosmarinic acid), as a component of ointments, has proven to have an antiviral effect on fever blisters of the lips and herpes. The leaves from the plant are suitable in themselves as a seasoning for salads, vegetables, and fish, and as a flavoring for desserts and mixed drinks.

A member of the pea family, the **white sweet clover,** or **melilot** (*Melilotus albus*), can be glimpsed on the roadside near Kirchdorf. A short time after the white blossoms are picked, the oxidative transformation of coumarin that is released during drying leads to the typical aroma of hay. This fragrance plays an important role in "hay flowers." A linen sack filled with white sweet clover should keep closets free of moths. Coumarin and the flavones in the plant serve to dilate the blood vessels, reduce blood vessel permeability, and improve the transportation of blood through the veins, in the form of a standardized pharmaceutical. Yet headaches may eventually develop following the administration of higher doses.

The papilionaceous (butterfly-shaped) flowers of the **meadow peavine,** or **yellow vetchling** (*Lathyrus pratensis*), stand out in impressive yellow clusters. Another member of the pea family, the meadow peavine is a good feed plant and is found blossoming in fields during July. This plant is covered with soft hairs, and its rootstock has no tubers.

241
Common evening primrose
(*Oenothera biennis* L.)
Evening-primrose, or willow-herb, family (Onagraceae)
VI–IX
Leaves, root, fatty oil from the seeds
Oil, skin and bath oil, capsules
Unsaturated fatty acids (gamma-linolenic acid), tannins
Neurodermatitis, psoriasis
Menstrual problems, arthritis, allergies, hyperactivity in children

242
Common balm, or **lemon balm**
(*Melissa officinalis* L.)
Mint family (Labiatae)
VI–VIII
Leaves, essential oil
Tea, plant juices, plant tablets, bath additives, ointment, aromatherapy
Essential oil (citronellal, citral, caryophyllene), tannin (rosmarinic acid), bitter principles, minerals
(M) For nervous agitation, disturbed sleep, nervous stomach and intestinal disturbances, herpes of the lips

243
White sweet clover, or **melilot**
(*Melilotus albus*)
Pea family (Papilionaceae)
V–VIII
Herbage, especially of the yellow sweet clover (*Melilotus officinalis*)
Tea, drops, in "hay flowers," ointments, herbal pillows
Melilotine, coumarin, saponins, tannins
(M) Venous disorders, tired legs, cramps in the calf, swelling, external contusions, sprains
Higher doses may lead to headaches.

244
Meadow peavine, or **yellow vetchling** (*Lathyrus pratensis* L.)
Pea family (Papilionaceae)
VI–VII

241 Common evening primrose
243 White sweet clover, melilot

242 Common balm, lemon balm
244 Meadow peavine, yellow vetchling

ecause of the thickness of its flowers, the **brown knapweed** (*Centaurea jacea*) is also known as "fat head" or "trouser button" and, because of its violet-red involucre, also as "meat flower." This tall meadow flower is very similar to a large garden cornflower. It has an angular, stiffly branched, and hard stalk, which has also earned it the name "iron herbage." All of the blossoms in the flower head are five-tipped and tubular. The inner blossoms carry nectar, whereas the outer ones merely attract insects. Depending on the humidity of the plant's habitat, the leaves change their form from lanceolate with a continuous margin to pinnatisect and sinuate. In some places, the plant is also called "tufted flower," as white tufts of hair are observed while the plant is young. Still another name, "fear flower," signifies the supposed power of this plant in helping pregnant women who are frightened.

Whereas the ***black mullein,*** or **dark mullein** (*Verbascum nigrum*), is not employed medicinally, modern science has verified the curative effects that can be achieved using the flowers of a related species, the **dense-flower mullein** (*Verbascum thapsiforme*). Sebastian Kneipp described the blossoms as "producing an effective tea against throat maladies, catarrhs, congestion of the chest, and shortness of breath." The blossoms contain a great deal of mucilage and sugar. This mucilage has an antitussive effect, dilutes the secretions, and protects the mucous membranes. At the same time, the essential oil and saponins have an expectorant effect. The light-yellow, five-lobed blossoms are representative of the basic form of the figwort, or snapdragon, family. However, only a rosette of leaves appears during the plant's first year of life. The round, tomentous (feltlike) flower stalk develops in the second year. The Greeks named the two-year-old, woolly plant, whose 1½ meter (almost 5 foot) flower stalk could be used as a torch after dipping it into pitch, candella regia ("King's candle"). Thus, the plant, which is frequently found in sandy and fallow soil, on rocky slopes, and in sunny meadows, is also known as "torch weed" in some areas. A crack in a wall is often enough to allow for the growth of a magnificent example of this species.

The **yellow spring bedstraw, lady's bedstraw, curdwort,** or **yellow bedstraw** (*Galium verum*), blossoms on the Moosberg (a mountain near Bad Wörishofen) about a month after the white bedstraw, from June to October, with panicles full of small, lemon-yellow, star-shaped flowers. According to legend, Mary and Joseph rested on a layer of ferns and galium when they arrived in Bethlehem. Thus, the plant is also known in some places as "Mary's bedstraw" and "Our Lady's straw" and presented in many images of the Virgin Mary from the Middle Ages. This member of the bedstraw, or madder, family, with its delicate aroma of honey, is a good honey-producing plant. Yellow spring bedstraw is more effective in curdling milk than the white forms of this family, especially because of the rennin found in it. Medicinally, it is mainly applied externally for skin problems and wounds. Internally, it has been used for "blood purification," as a diuretic, and as a supportive agent for inflammations of the kidneys and bladder.

245
Brown knapweed (*Centaurea jacea* L.)
Composite, or daisy, family (Compositae)
VI–X
246
Black mullein or **dark mullein** (*Verbascum nigrum* L.)
Figwort, or snapdragon, family (Scrophulariaceae)
V–IX
247
Dense-flower mullein (*Verbascum thapsiforme* L.)
Figwort, or snapdragon, family (Scrophulariaceae)
VII–VIII
Flowers
Tea, oily extract
Mucilage, saponins, flavonoids, iridoids, sterols
(M) For catarrhs of the upper respiratory tract, contrastimulant, mucolytic
248
Yellow spring bedstraw, lady's bedstraw, curdwort, or **yellow bedstraw** (*Galium verum* L.)
Bedstraw, or madder, family (Rubiaceae)
V–IX
Herbage
Tea
Salicylic acid, tannins, glycosides, organic acids
Externally, for skin problems and wounds; internally, for "blood purification," as a diuretic, as a supportive agent for inflammations of the kidneys and bladder

245 Brown knapweed
247 Dense-flower mullein

246 Black mullein, dark mullein
248 Yellow spring bedstraw, lady's bedstraw, curdwort, yellow bedstraw

The **purple coneflower, hedgehog coneflower,** or **rudbeckia** (*Rudbeckia lacinata*), is an ornamental plant with large, red heads that blossoms in the garden of the Dominican monastery here. The genus of the coneflowers includes forty-five different species, the most famous of which is *Rudbeckia purpurea*, also known as *Echinacea purpurea*, which is native to North America. The alternative name, *Echinacea*, is derived from the hedgehog shape of the flower head and comes from the Greek word *echinos*, for "hedgehog." This species has blossoms with purple, narrow, ligulate petals that are folded back and 4 to 6 centimeters (1½ to 2½ inches) in length. The indigenous people of North America used this flower for the treatment of poorly healing wounds and against snakebites. Today, it is known that extracts from the purple coneflower or compounds isolated from this plant have an immunostimulatory effect. Like bitter principles, they stimulate the body's own defensive powers in the healing of wounds and have a prophylactic effect against infectious illnesses. They are also known to be effective in treating such ailments as rheumatoid arthritis, chronic respiratory tract infections, skin problems, and the flu.

The most spirited-looking summer flower here is undoubtedly the one-year-old **common sunflower** (*Helianthus annuus*). In the summertime, it is often seen in many of the gardens and parks around Bad Wörishofen. Probably originating in Mexico, the plant has a nodding umbel, with a diameter of up to 50 centimeters (about 1½ feet), at the end of a pith-filled stalk. This spongelike stalk serves as a replacement for corks in Russia and is used in the production of paper in China. The genus name *Helianthus* comes from the Greek word *helios*, for "sun," and *anthos*, for "flower," as the flower heads always turn toward direct sunlight (heliotropism). The flower disks are brown and androgynous, and surrounded by golden-yellow rays. Sunflower seeds are known to be highly nutritious and to have diuretic properties. When pressed, they produce a light-yellow, clear oil that, like olive oil, is rich in polyunsaturated fats. In addition to its use as a kitchen oil, sunflower oil, which has a long shelf life, has been used externally as a rub for rheumatic disorders and arthritis.

The blossoms of the **elecampane** (*Inula helenium*), seen in many herb gardens, are like small sunflowers. The stout, coarse, and woolly stem gives rise to large, alternate, ovate leaves and yellow flowers that appear in clusters and by themselves. Containing bitter principles, the fibrous root is used in folk medicine as an antiseptically effective expectorant to be administered in cases of bronchial catarrh and whooping cough. The root supposedly also has a strengthening effect on the curative effects of other herbs that function as diuretics, stomach tonics, and biliary stimulants. However, elecampane may cause adverse effects such as vomiting and allergies, so caution should be taken. The genus name *Inula* is an indication of the vegetable starch inulin found in the plant; inulin is a substance derived from fructose. According to ancient oracles, this very old, cultivated plant protects one from the "evil eye."

The **common borage** (*Borago officinalis*) is cultivated and also grows wild on fallow land and waste places with a high concentration of nitrogen. The hollow, bristly, branched stem bears bristly, aromatic leaves and blue or purplish, star-shaped flowers. These lovely flowers were supposedly the raw material for the fine blue varnishes in Asia. In folk medicine, common borage is used for atopic eczema, neurodermatitis, throat illnesses, and coughs. Borage is also known to be good for lowering a fever and restoring strength while recovering from an illness. In addition, the seeds and leaves have been used to stimulate the production of milk in nursing mothers.

249
Purple coneflower, hedgehog coneflower, or **rudbeckia**
(*Rudbeckia lacinata* L.)
Composite, or daisy, family
(Compositae)
VII–X
Plant extracts from the *Rudbeckia purpurea*, or *Echinacea purpurea*, species
Tablets, drops, tea, ointment
Alkylamides (echinacine), polyynes, caffeic acid, quinic acid
(M) Defense against colds, infectious diseases
Treatment of various ailments
250
Common sunflower (*Helianthus annuus* L.)
Composite, or daisy, family
(Compositae)
VII–X
Tincture, tea, oil for massage
Anthocyan glycosides, flavone glycosides, choline, betaine
251
Elecampane (*Inula helenium* L.)
Composite, or daisy, family
(Compositae)
VII–IX
Tea
Essential oil (helenin), bitter principles, starch (inulin)
Coughs
252
Common borage (*Borago officinalis* L.)
Borage, or forget-me-not, family
(Boraginaceae)
V–IX
Herb, tea, oil capsules
Unsaturated fatty acids (gammalinolenic acid), mucilage, tannins, saponins, flavonoids

249 Purple coneflower, hedgehog coneflower, rudbeckia
251 Elecampane

250 Common sunflower
252 Common borage

As a typical member of the figwort, or snapdragon, family, **butter-and-eggs,** or **common toadflax** (*Linaria vulgaris*), has also aptly been called "small lion jaws." The genus name *Linaria* means "hair-formed" and has to do with the hairlike leaves, which are protected from drying out by a layer of wax. This plant blossoms from July to October. The sulfur-yellow, spurred flowers are ordered not unlike roofing tiles in a long cluster. Only strong bumblebees are able to open the five-lobed corolla with its bisected upper and trisected lower lips, so that they can draw the rich honey into their throats. In order to attain sufficient water from the often very dry habitats where it grows, the butter-and-eggs has a root that extends as far as 1 meter (more than 3 feet) into the ground. Records of it use date back to the Middle Ages, when an extract of this herb with alum served as a starch for the wash. Today, butter-and-eggs is used medicinally as a diuretic and a laxative. It is also applied externally for skin problems and hemorrhoids.

Preferring shady habitats, the **herb bennet,** or **wood avens** (*Geum urbanum*), can be caught sight of growing in the forests on the Moosberg (a mountain near Bad Wörishofen). The plant's plain, yellow, pedunculate flowers demonstrate the five-lobed corolla characteristic of the rose family. Herb bennet is sometimes called "carnation herb," as the odor of its root is similar to that of a carnation. Also known in some places as "blessed herb," it has a long tradition as a medicinal plant. Its essential oil, bitter principles, and tannins supposedly function to strengthen the nerves, curb diarrhea, and aid in the production of milk for nursing mothers. As a gargle, it can be helpful for gum problems.

The **sticky ragwort,** or **sticky groundsel** (*Senecio viscosus*), is found in the Hartenthal (a valley in this region) as a common weed and blossoms from spring through fall. During the time of ripening in summer, the inflorescences form flowers that look like the familiar puffballs that suc-

ceed dandelion flowers. As these fine-hair tufts resemble the silver hair of a very old man, the genus name *Senecio* arose; *Senecio* is derived from *senex,* Latin for "old."

The **common hedge nettle, wood betony,** or **betony** (*Stachys officinalis*), is also known in some places as "healing hedgenettle," as it has a long history in folk medicine as an important medicinal plant. The species name *officinalis* is also an indication of its curative effects, as it is derived from the Latin word *offizin,* meaning "pharmacist." However, the stomach-strengthening, carminative (against flatulence), calming, and wound-healing effects for which it is known have not been verified. The genus name *Stachys* means "spike" and refers to the plant's lovely, purplish-red flower spikes, which are often seen by hikers in forest clearings on the Moosberg. This member of the mint, or dead-nettle, family is also cultivated in gardens.

253
Butter-and-eggs, or **common toadflax** (*Linaria vulgaris*)
Figwort, or snapdragon, family (Scrophulariaceae)
VI–IX
Herbage
Flavonoids, choline, alkaloid (vasicine [peganine])
Diuretic, laxative, also applied externally for skin problems, hemorrhoids
254
Herb bennet, or **wood avens** (*Geum urbanum* L.)
Rose family (Rosaceae)
V–X
Root, herbage
Essential oil (eugenol), bitter principles, tannins
Tea, gargle, dressings
Against diarrhea, for infections of the mouth and throat, hemorrhoids (externally)
255
Sticky ragwort, or **sticky groundsel** (*Senecio viscosus* L.)
Composite, or daisy, family (Compositae)
VI–IX
256
Common hedge nettle, wood betony, or **betony** (*Stachys officinalis* L.)
Mint, or dead-nettle, family (Labiatae)
VII–VIII
Herbage without the root
Tannins, bitter principles
Previously for diarrhea, bronchitis

253 Butter-and-eggs, common toadflax
255 Sticky ragwort, sticky groundsel

254 Herb bennet, wood avens
256 Common hedge nettle, wood betony, betony

The **common peppermint** (*Mentha piperita*) is a hybrid that is the result of crossing the water mint with the spearmint. It is primarily cultivated but also grows wild in moist meadows, along the banks of streams, and in ditches, and propagates only by means of offshoots. The erect, branching, reddish-purple-tinged stem gives rise to opposite, dark-green leaves and terminal spikes of small, purple blossoms. The genus name *Mentha*, to which the long-leafed **European horsemint** (*Mentha longifolia*) also belongs, can be traced back to the nymph Menthe, who, according to legend, was changed into this plant by Persephone, the queen of the underworld. The peppermint is rightfully one of the best-known and most popular of the medicinal plants. As an agent for the treatment of gastrointestinal disturbances, it has few rivals. Sebastian Kneipp also praised the "gastric strengthening effect" of this plant. With menthol as its primary active component, the zesty, fresh essential oil has disinfectant, spasmolytic, cooling, blood-flow stimulating, carminative (against flatulence), and cholagogue (bile-flow stimulating) effects. Peppermint tea is therefore helpful for disorders of the abdominal region. The decorative leaves are also used to season salads, soups, and sauces and to flavor mixed drinks and desserts. Used externally, mint oils, also under the names of Chinese and Japanese balms, are helpful as anti-inflammatory liniments for the treatment of muscle and joint pains. In addition, a drop rubbed into the temple often reduces the complaints associated with migraines, and a drop on the tongue or under the nose frees the respiratory tract. However, babies and small children should not be treated with cold balms containing menthol, because this substance can have a damaging effect on them merely by being inhaled.

According to legend, Achilles discovered the **yarrow, milfoil,** or **common yarrow** (*Achillea millefolium*), and used it during the Trojan War to heal King Telephus. The bitter principles and essential oil in this plant are similar to those found in chamomile. Therefore, like chamomile, yarrow has anti-inflammatory and spasmolytic effects on illnesses of the gastrointestinal tract and also stimulates the appetite. Sheep are especially fond of yarrow, which grows in pastures and meadows, as well as along the roadside. The species name *millefolium*, meaning "thousand little leaves" in Latin, indicates the plant's numerous, alternate leaflets, which are suitable as a seasoning. The large number of composite flowers, consisting of yellow disks with white rays, offer insects a treat and a hiding place. Recent literature surprisingly praises yarrow extracts for their antiseptic, anti-inflammatory, and even antibiotic effects. Yet the soothing effects of yarrow for female disorders, including painful menstruation, are no surprise, as the following verse implies:

> Yarrow in the system
> is good for every woman.

Native to southern Mediterranean countries, **garden thyme** (*Thymus vulgaris*) is extensively cultivated in Europe and the United States mainly for its culinary use. The plant has woody stems, clusters of little, bluish-purple, two-lipped flowers, and small, downy, opposite, aromatic leaves. It is the pungent-smelling leaves that are used as a seasoning for such foods as sausage, meat, and fish. The main component of its essential oil is thymol, a substance with a very strong antibacterial effect. For this reason, thyme is used as an ingredient in pectoral and bronchial teas. When employed as a bath additive, the essential oil, with its intensive, disinfectant effects, provides substantial relief from colds. Sebastian Kneipp said that extracts from thyme serve to "clear the chest." The essential oil is used in aromatherapy too, where it has been shown to stimulate circulation as well as mental and physical energy. Thyme is also taken in the form of cough syrup, drops, and lozenges; however, excessive internal use has been known to cause symptoms of poisoning and an overstimulation of the thyroid gland.

257
Common peppermint (*Mentha piperita* L.)
Mint family (Labiatae)
VII–IX
Leaves, essential oil
Tea, oil, in ointments, tablets, herb
Essential oil (menthol), flavonoids, bitter principles, tannins
(M) Gastrointestinal and biliary disturbances
May not be suitable for long-term use or for infants

258
Yarrow, milfoil, or **common yarrow** (*Achillea millefolium* L.)
Composite, or daisy, family (Compositae)
VI–X
Herbage
Tea, plant juices, plant tablets, tincture, seasoning
Essential oil (chamazulene), bitter principles, minerals
(M) Disturbances of the gastrointestinal and the biliary systems, lack of appetite, female disorders

259
Garden thyme (*Thymus vulgaris* L.)
Mint family (Labiatae)
V–X
Herbage, essential oil
Tea, cough syrup, drops, lozenges, bath additive, aromatherapy, seasoning
Essential oil (thymol, carvacrol, borneol), tannins, flavonoids
(M) Bronchitis, whooping cough, catarrhs of the upper respiratory tract, lack of appetite, stomach disorders

260
European horsemint (*Mentha longifolia* L.)
Mint family (Labiatae)
VII–IX

257 Common peppermint

259 Garden thyme

258 Yarrow, milfoil, common yarrow

260 European horsemint

The **bog chickweed,** or **bog stitch-wort** (*Stellaria uliginosa*), with its small, unassuming flowers, is found growing individually in the damp meadows of the Moosberg (a mountain near Bad Wörishofen). The genus name comes from *stella* ("star") and is a reference to the star-shaped flower of this member of the pink, or campion, family. Bog chickweed has bare stalks and few branches. The leaves are long, pointed, and opposite, and the flowers grow in a forked, apparent cyme (single terminal flower). Its fruit are capsules. This lazily climbing herb breaks easily at the joints.

The **grasslike starwort** (*Stellaria gra-minea*), with its highly branched, somewhat creeping stalks, on the other hand, spreads itself over the grassy edges of fields and meadows. The blossoms of this plant create a slack, many-branched, umbelliferous cluster. The number and size of the blossoms differ quite a bit. These five-fold, star-shaped blossoms have petals that are separate down to the base. The blossoms close at night or during cooler weather, possibly leading to self-pollination.

A hardy plant that is particularly fond of moist meadows, **spotted lady's thumb,** or **redleg** (*Polygonum persicaria*), has a four-sided stalk, as is common to the group of plants to which it belongs. This annual plant can easily be recognized through its dense, cylindrical spikes of pink or magenta flowers. Because of its long, pointed, broad leaves, it is also known in some places as "peach-leafed knotgrass." In folk medicine, it has been used for a number of conditions, including arthritis, jaundice, diarrhea, and eczema.

Native to South America, the **potato, Irish potato,** or **white potato** (*Solanum tubero-sum*), is a perennial plant that can be cultivated in nearly every type of climate and soil. The potato was introduced into Europe in the middle of the sixteenth century, when the Spaniards brought back soil that contained samples of the potato after their conquest of Peru. From Europe, it made its way to North America. Like the tomato, the paprika, and the eggplant, this plant is a member of the tomato, or nightshade, family. The potatoes that we eat are tubers at the end of underground runners. As storage organs, they are filled with reserve substances such as starches, proteins, vitamins, minerals, and trace elements. The potato's significance as an economical, basic food not only has to do with its wide cultivation but also with its easy storage and neutral taste. Potatoes eaten with their skins still on are especially rich in vitamins (primarily vitamin C) and minerals. Aside from the cultivated potato, there are about 200 wild types of potato known in North and South America.

261
Bog chickweed, or **bog stitch-wort** (*Stellaria uliginosa*)
Pink, or campion, family
(Caryophyllaceae)
V–VI

262
Spotted lady's thumb, or **redleg**
(*Polygonum persicaria* L.)
Milkwort family (Polygonaceae)
VII–IX
(F) Arthritis, jaundice, diarrhea, eczema

263
potato, Irish potato, or **white potato** (*Solanum tuberosum* L.)
Tomato, or nightshade, family
(Solanaceae)
VI–VIII
Starches
Polysaccharide
Auxiliary substances in powders and ointments

264
Grasslike starwort (*Stellaria graminea* L.)
Pink, or campion, family
(Caryophyllaceae)
V–VII

261 Bog chickweed, bog stitchwort
263 Potato, Irish potato, white potato

262 Spotted lady's thumb, redleg
264 Grasslike starwort

*L*ike the cotton bush and the cocoa tree, the **common marshmallow** (*Althaea officinalis*), with its delicate, light-pink blossoms, is a member of the mallow family. This perennial shrub grows wild in moist habitats and is also cultivated in herb gardens, preferring a saline soil. It has tomentose (densely matted) hairs and develops a horizontally creeping rootstock. Also known in some places as "healing root," it has been considered an exceptional mucilaginous drug since the dawn of history. As such, common marshmallow is especially helpful in soothing irritated tissue. It has been used to soften ulcers, relieve itching and insect stings, and treat gastrointestinal disorders as well as bronchitis and colds. Common marshmallow is employed in different forms—for instance, as a poultice, a gargle (from the leaves and blossoms), and a tea. The cut roots that are used as a mucilloid (mucilaginous drug), however, should be mixed only in a cold solution, as boiling water would cause this mucilage to curdle.

The **woodland angelica**, or **wild angelica** (*Angelica sylvestris*), is easily recognized in damp parts of forests because of its height and large, white umbels. As a result of its curative effects on disturbances of the chest, it is also known in some places as "chest root." Typical of this plant are the large, bulbous, leaf sheaths surrounding the round, hollow stalk. Like the garden angelica, the wild plant has essential oil in all of its parts. Its roots also contain tannins and resins. A tea made from the seeds, leaves, or root has diuretic and diaphoretic (sweat-inducing) effects, and helps to strengthen the stomach. Yet woodland angelica needs to be used with caution, as excessive amounts can paralyze the central nervous system and cause sensitivity to sunlight, irritating the skin.

Growing wild along fences and paths, **common motherwort** (*Leonurus cardiaca*) has been cultivated as a medicinal plant as well. Since the Middle Ages, it has been used for nervous heart problems and for stomach cramps and flatulence.

Today, it is also taken for menopausal problems, congestion, and shortness of breath. However, consuming too much can lead to such side effects as vomiting, abdominal pain, and thirst. This plant is also called "lion's tail" in some places because of the form of its reddish-purple false whorls. A member of the mint family, the common motherwort blossoms only in July and August, and has an unpleasant odor.

Primarily cultivated, the **feverfew** (*Chrysanthemum parthenium*) is a perennial plant that grows in the garden of the Dominican monastery here. Its blossoms are not only similar to those of chamomile but also contain similar substances that are effective in healing wounds and stimulating the menstrual cycle. Feverfew has a long tradition as a medicinal plant. In the Middle Ages, it was frequently mixed with wine or honey and taken as an agent against dizziness or depression. When applied as a poultice, the boiled flower heads are supposedly effective in treating bruises and skin irritations. Nevertheless, some people have been known to be allergic to feverfew, and it should not be used by pregnant women.

265
Common marshmallow (*Althaea officinalis* L.)
Mallow family (Malvaceae)
VII–IX
Root; less frequently leaves and blossoms
Mucilage, starch, sugar
(M) Reduces the stimuli associated with inflammations of the mouth, throat, gingiva; also for stomach pains, gastrointestinal disorders, diarrhea

266
Woodland angelica, or **wild angelica** (*Angelica sylvestris* L.)
Parsley, or carrot, family (Umbelliferae)
VII–IX
Essential oil, tannins, resins, tea, wine
(F) Mild, cramplike disturbances of the gastrointestinal tract
Avoid overdose.

267
Common motherwort (*Leonurus cardiaca* L.)
Mint family (Labiatae)
VI–IX
Blossoming herbage
Tea
Bitter principles, essential oil, cardioactive glycosides
(F) Heart problems
Avoid overdose.

268
Feverfew (*Chrysanthemum parthenium* L.)
Composite, or daisy, family (Compositae)
VI–VIII
Leaves, fresh or dried
Powder
Essential oil
Menstrual problems, bruises, skin irritations
Use caution, as allergies can develop; not to be used by pregnant women!

144

265 Common marshmallow
267 Common motherwort

266 Woodland angelica, wild angelica
268 Feverfew

Fall

The **American red raspberry, or garden raspberry** (*Rubus idaeus*), is found growing wild in forests and is also cultivated extensively for its fruit. The red berries (*rubus* means "red") from this member of the rose family are used to make jams and juices, as well as form the basis of the aromatic, white raspberry brandy. This plant begins blossoming in May, and the berries ripen in June, to be harvested in the fall. In contrast to the leaves of the common blackberry, raspberry leaves are lighter, have fleecelike hairs on the back, and are three- to five-fold pinnate with a single terminal leaf. But like the leaves of the blackberry and the strawberry, raspberry leaves, with their concentration of tannin, are suitable for neutral, aromatic teas and as a mild agent against diarrhea. In folk medicine, the leaves have also been used for infections of the mouth, throat, and mucous membranes. The juicy berries contain citric acid and pectins. Fresh raspberry juice, with a little honey, has been taken to bring down a fever, and, made into a syrup, may be beneficial for the heart.

The **dwarf honeysuckle** (*Lonicera xylosteum*) is named after the author of a book on herbs who died in 1586, A. Lonicer. This plant's leaves are rounded with a short tip, its flowers are short, white, and shaped like a funnel, and its fruit are red. The strong branches are made of a very hard wood (*xylos* means "wood"), valued for wood turning. In contrast to the goat's beard, the dwarf honeysuckle does not climb. (The name goat's beard has to do with the fact that sheep and goats are fond of its leaves.)

An exotic plant in the inclement Algau region, the climbing **domestic grape** (*Vitis vinifera*) grows along the wall of the Dominican monastery here. However, in Bad Wörishofen it is more of a decorative plant, as the local beer is more famous and better liked than the wines of this Kneipp town. Nevertheless, it's important to remember that Sebastian Kneipp highly recommended medicinal wines—that is, the mixture of medicinal herbs and fruit with wines, and their subsequent use as a tonic.

The **vervain mallow, or European mallow** (*Malva alcea*), with its purplish-pink blossoms, is a perennial weed commonly seen in dry, roadside areas. The leaf form and the hairiness of this species are quite variable. As a plant that is fond of nitrogenous habitats, it has become quite disseminated. The vervain mallow also has a long history of being cultivated in herb gardens, as it has been used as a mucilaginous drug, as have the common marshmallow and the mallow. In the Middle Ages, it was believed that this plant protected one from accidents, and it was carried as an amulet around the neck to help strengthen the eyes.

269
American red raspberry, or garden raspberry (*Rubus idaeus* L.)
Rose family (Rosaceae)
V–VI
Leaves, fruit juice
Tea, syrup
Tannins (leaves), vitamins A, B, minerals (fruit)
(F) Leaves for infections of the mouth, throat, and mucous membranes
Agent against diarrhea, additive to teas (in fermented form), juice to possibly lower a fever

270
Dwarf honeysuckle (*Lonicera xylosteum* L.)
Honeysuckle family (Caprifoliaceae)
V–VI

271
Domestic grape (*Vitis vinifera* L.)
Grape family (Vitaceae)
VI–VIII
Berries
Medicinal wines, tonic
Exhilarating, restoring

272
Vervain mallow, or European mallow (*Malva alcea* L.)
Mallow family (Malvaceae)
VI–IX
Mucilaginous drug

269 American red raspberry, garden raspberry
271 Domestic grape

270 Dwarf honeysuckle
272 Vervain mallow, European mallow

The purplish-red flower clusters of the nearly man-high **fireweed, or small-flowered willow herb** (*Epilobium angustifolium*), stand out in forest clearings on the Moosberg (a mountain near Bad Wörishofen) and in the Hartenthal (a valley in this region). The fireweed belongs to the evening primrose, or willow herb, family. Like dandelions, the fireweed and other willow herbs, as weeds, are difficult to fight and disseminate by way of flying seeds. The Latin genus name *Epilobium* comes from *epi* ("over") and *lobos* ("pod"), as the blossom stands above the pod. The small leaves are similar to those of the willow. The roots of this plant were formerly eaten as a substitute for asparagus. The use of fireweed tea to relieve complaints associated with the prostate has recently grown in popularity. This effect was previously attributed only to the hoary willow herb (*Epilobium parviflorum*), which contains a substance called sitosterol that has long been used to treat prostate complaints. Yet sitosterol has been discovered in the more economical, small-leafed fireweed as well.

In the past, the **garden cornflower** (*Centaurea cyanus*), together with the corn poppy, created a scattering of color in grain fields (*cyanus* means "blue"). However, because of the use of herbicides and fertilization, this species is hardly seen anymore. The example found in Bad Wörishofen thus originated from a seed mixture of field flowers. The garden cornflower is native to Asia and has accompanied grains since ancient times, having not found a habitat with any other group of plants. The garden cornflower has thin, branched stems that give rise to narrow, lanceolate leaves and large, blue blossoms. A tea made from the blossoms is considered by some to promote menstruation. Usually, however, the intensive blue flowers are mixed in teas for their visual effect.

Cultivated for its use as a spice (oregano), **wild marjoram** (*Origanum vulgare*) also grows wild and can be found blooming during the late summer into the fall in the dry fields and along the paths on the Moosberg. A pungent-smelling plant, it has a creeping rootstock, a round, reddish stalk covered with hair, and pedunculated spikes of brownish-red, two-lipped flowers. This flowering herb is an excellent honey plant and is rich in essential oils. Because of its fragrance, wild marjoram has been used for its mood-elevating effects since the Middle Ages. Today, it is often employed as a part of the filling of herb pillows that provide relaxation by means of aromatherapy. Marjoram has also been used to treat stomach problems, respiratory ailments, and headaches. Nevertheless, excessive internal usage should be avoided, especially by pregnant women.

A member of the bluebell, or bellflower, family, **Dane's blood** (*Campanula glomerulata*) can be glimpsed growing along the paths on the Moosberg. The plant's lovely, violet-blue blossoms almost look like a type of gentian. Dane's blood is one of the 250 species of this enchanting genus.

273
Fireweed, or small-flowered willow herb (*Epilobium angustifolium* L.)
evening primrose, or willow herb, family (Onagraceae)
VI–VIII
Herbage (primarily from *Epibobium parviflorum*)
Tea
Beta-sitosterol, flavonoids, quercetin glycosides
Prostate complaints

274
Garden cornflower (*Centaurea cyanus* L.)
Composite, or daisy, family (Compositae)
VI–IX
Blossoms
Tea
Coloring agent, tannins, bitter principles, mucilage

275
Wild marjoram (*Origanum vulgare* L.)
Mint family (Labiatae)
VII–IX
Herbage
Tea, seasoning (oregano)
Essential oil, tannins, bitter principles
Disturbances of the gastrointestinal tract, diarrhea, coughs
Excessive internal usage should be avoided, particularly by pregnant women.

276
Dane's blood (*Campanula glomerulata* L.)
Bluebell, or bellflower, family (Campanulaceae)
VI–IX

273 Fireweed, small-flowered willow-herb

275 Wild marjoram

274 Garden cornflower

276 Dane's blood

In contrast to the meadow cranesbill, the **marsh cranesbill** (*Geranium palustre*) is fond of damp meadows and forests. Its large, purplish-red flowers are conspicuous on the Moosberg (a mountain near Bad Wörishofen). Typical of this plant are the almost angular leaves that are shaped like a hand and divided into seven segments. The dehiscent fruit has five flaps and a form similar to that of a stork's bill, which is a characteristic feature of the members of this family.

On the way to the reservoir of Bad Wörishofen, it's easy to recognize the **church steeple,** or **common agrimony** (*Agrimonia eupatoria*), from its spike full of small, yellow, almost roselike flowerets. According to a superstition of the past, the harvest time was revealed depending on whether these flowerets were thickest at the top, in the middle, or at the bottom of the spike. The church steeple can be identified as a member of the rose family through its unpaired, pinnate, and toothed leaves, which exude a pleasant aroma when rubbed between the fingers. The thorned fruit that sticks to clothing like a bur is also typical. Its genus name *Agrimonia* means "living in the fields" in Latin, and this perennial plant does live in fields as well in forests and along the roadside. It is also called "liverwort" in some places, reflecting its use as a medicinal plant. Taken internally, common agrimony has been used to treat liver, kidney, and spleen disorders. Because of its concentration of tannins, bitter principles, and essential oil, it is also used as a tea for stomach ailments and as a gargle for inflammations of the mouth and throat. Externally, it can be applied for superficial skin inflammations.

Clustered dock (*Rumex conglomeratus*), with its greenish glomerate flowers, can be seen blossoming along rocky slopes in the Zillertal (a valley in the Austrian Alps). This member of the milkwort family has an erect, reddish stalk with leaves up to its tip. The lowest leaves are cordate and ovate in form, becoming lanceolate in the middle. Its androgynous blossoms are arranged in clusters of false whorls, and its dark-brown nuts have small warts.

The **astrantia** (*Astrantia major*), which can reach a height of up to ½ a meter (about 1 ½ feet), is not immediately recognized as a member of the carrot, or parsley, family. Its light-pink, glomerate heads are frequently spotted in the meadowlands of the Hartenthal (a valley in this region). Typical are the hand-shaped leaves that are separated into "five fingers" with toothed margins. The small umbels are enclosed by a cuff of green bracts. It's easy to see the connection of the astrantia to the queen of the meadow, or meadowsweet.

277
Marsh cranesbill (*Geranium palustre* L.)
Geranium, or cranesbill, family (Geraniaceae)
VI–IX
278
Church steeple, or **common agrimony** (*Agrimonia eupatoria* L.)
Rose family (Rosaceae)
VI–VIII
Blossoming herb
Tea, poultices
Tannins, triterpenes, essential oil, salicylic acid
(M) Nonspecific, acute diarrhea, inflammations of the mucous membranes in the mouth and throat, externally for superficial skin inflammations
279
Clustered dock (*Rumex conglomeratus*)
Milkwort family (Polygonaceae)
VII–IX
280
Astrantia (*Astrantia major* L.)
Parsley, or carrot, family (Umbelliferae)
VI–VIII

277 Marsh cranesbill
279 Clustered dock

278 Church steeple, common agrimony
280 Astrantia

A perennial plant native to America, the **monkey flower** (*Minulus guttatus*) grows wild in many areas and has acclimatized itself especially along the banks of streams. Because of this preferred habitat, it is also known in some places as "yellow stream-side flower." Although this member of the figwort, or snapdragon, family is not observed very often, it has found a home by the stream in the Zillertal (a valley in the Austrian Alps). Its yellow blossoms occasionally have red spots. Reminding some people of the wounds of Christ, they have led to the plant's also being called "five-wound floweret" in Switzerland.

A thistle species frequently seen in Bad Wörishofen is the **cabbage thistle** (*Cirsium oleraceum*), a plant that, because of its preferred habitat, has also been called "meadow thistle" in some places. The cabbage thistle is often regarded as an aggravating weed, although it can be used as a pig feed. In contrast to many other types of thistle, this species has light-yellow blossoms. As a result of the notch in its leaves that resembles a plowshare, it is also known in certain areas as "share weed" or just "plowshare." It characteristically inhabits damp meadows and usually blossoms after the first hay harvest. It flees soil with high acidity and tends to be fond of such fellow inhabitants as the queen of the meadow, or meadowsweet, the meadow peavine, the marsh cranesbill, and the eltrot, masterwort, or hogweed. At one time, the cabbage thistle was used medicinally to treat rheumatism and gout, but this is no longer recommended because of its mildly poisonous side effects.

The genus of the Saint-John's-wort family includes 200 different species, differentiated further into eighteen subspecies based on the structure of their blossoms. The best known is the common Saint-John's-wort, rose of Sharon, or Klamath weed (*Hypericum perforatum*), which is administered internally to strengthen the nerves and applied externally to heal wounds. The **imperforate Saint-John's-wort** (*Hypericum maculatum*) is a species that can be seen blossoming in July in the moist pastures and ditches on the Moosberg (a mountain near Bad Wörishofen). This plant reaches a height of 20 to 40 centimeters (about 8 to 16 inches), and its bare stalks have branches only in the upper portions. The yellow flowers have black spots, as do the stalks. The blossoms appear in clusters at the end of the black, glandular peduncles.

About a month after the white flowers of the false baby's breath, or hedge bedstraw, bloom, the yellow flowers of the **yellow spring bedstraw, lady's bedstraw, curdwort,** or **yellow bedstraw** (*Galium verum*), follow in June. Its spikes are covered with tiny, light-yellow, star-shaped flowers that have a delicate aroma like that of honey. Aside from glycosides and essential oil, this species contains a great deal of rennin, making it good for curdling milk. Yellow spring bedstraw has been used medicinally for "blood purification," as a diuretic, and as a supportive agent for inflammations of the kidneys or bladder. A tea made with the herb has a calming effect and is even recommended for epilepsy. The old Germanic peoples dedicated this plant to Freya, the goddess of love, beauty, and fecundity. That adoration was later transferred to the Virgin Mary, so images of yellow spring bedstraw are frequently seen in many of the Madonna portraits in the panel paintings of the Middle Ages.

281
Monkey flower (*Minulus guttatus*)
Figwort, or snapdragon, family (Scrophulariaceae)
VI–X

282
Cabbage thistle (*Cirsium oleraceum* L.)
Composite, or daisy, family (Compositae)
VI–IX
Herbage, leaves, root
Extracts as a decoction
Tannins, alkaloids, glycosides, essential oil
Formerly for rheumatism and gout, but no longer used because of its mildly poisonous effects

283
Imperforate Saint-John's-wort (*Hypericum maculatum*)
Saint-John's-wort family (Guttiferae)
VI–IX
The common Saint-John's-wort, rose of Sharon, or Klamath weed (*Hypericum perforatum*), is prescribed medicinally.
Essential oil, flavonoids, resins, tannins

284
Yellow spring bedstraw, lady's bedstraw, curdwort, or **yellow bedstraw** (*Galium verum* L.)
Bedstraw, or madder, family (Rubiaceae)
V–IX
Herbage
Tea
Salicylic acid, tannins, glycosides, organic acids
"Blood purification," diuretic effect, supportive agent for inflammations of the kidneys or bladder

281 Monkey flower
283 Imperforate Saint-John's-wort

282 Cabbage thistle
284 Yellow spring bedstraw, lady's bedstraw, curdwort,
yellow bedstraw

As a type of clover, **yellow sweet clover,** or **ribbed melilot** (*Melilotus officinalis*), has the typical, three-leafed cloverleaf, although the glomerate flower heads are lacking. Here, along the bicycle path to the reservoir, this fairly tall plant, with its lengthy clusters of yellow, papilionaceous flowers, begins blossoming in June. Preferring pebbly roadsides and rocky slopes, it is also known in some places as "stone clover." The Latin genus name *Melilotus* is made up of the word *meli* ("honey") and lotus ("fragrant"), leading to the plant's also being called "honey clover" in certain areas. Typical of the yellow sweet clover species is its coumarin content, giving it the strong aroma of sweet-scented bedstraw. In addition, this blossoming herb contains mucilage and choline. Like a related species, the white sweet clover, it is a component of high-quality "hay flowers." These hay flowers are often used in the stuffing of herb pillows. Furthermore, yellow sweet clover is used as a tea and in ointments, and has been employed to treat a number of ailments, from stomach problems and bronchitis to leg cramps and venous disorders to hemorrhoids and contusions. However, drinking the tea occasionally leads to headaches.

Whereas the **Venus' chariot,** or **monk's-hood** (*Aconitum napellus*), is generally cultivated in gardens here, the **wolfsbane,** or **aconite** (*Aconitum vulparia*), is often spotted in the forest clearings of the Zillertal (a valley in the Austrian Alps). These members of the buttercup, or crowfoot, family are also known as "helmet" and "fool's cap" in some places because of the form of their blossoms. The Venus' chariot, or monk's-hood, also grows wild in pastures and alpine meadows, as well as areas around watering places for cattle. According to legend, this plant, which is poisonous throughout its parts, provided protection against wild animals. People living in the mountains used the black, meaty root as rat bait, and an extract derived from the root was used to control pests. Today, in the hands of physicians, the aconitine

alkaloids are employed homeopathically for the treatment of rheumatic complaints. But as little as 3 to 6 milligrams may constitute a fatal dose for an adult. Therefore, children must be warned about the Venus' chariot, grown as an ornamental flower in many gardens. The yellow-blossoming wolfsbane species comes from China and is quite common in the Himalayas. This plant is also poisonous in all of its parts.

Although the corn poppy, or corn rose, is frequently seen here growing profusely on rocky slopes and in fields, the **opium poppy** (*Papaver somniferum*) keeps somewhat hidden behind the walls of the Dominican monastery. This type of poppy, which is native to Asia, has lovely blossoms that can be red, whitish, or violet in color. The opium poppy is one of the most important medicinal plants we have and grows primarily in strictly controlled fields. The thickened, milky sap that exudes from the unripe, scarified poppy head is known as "raw opium." The alkaloids contained in this substance are misused throughout the world as components of addictive, narcotic drugs. But when extracted, standardized, and then prescribed in precise, small doses, these alkaloids have proven to be indispensable in the hands of physicians: Morphine is a beneficial, highly effective painkiller; papaverine is a spasmolytic agent against attacks of colic; and codeine is often the agent of choice in the event of dry, hacking coughs. Morphine was the first plant component to be isolated in its pure form by the pharmacist Sertürner in 1804. All parts of the opium poppy plant, except for the seeds, are poisonous. These seeds have a fat concentration of up to 50 percent and are a popular ingredient in baking, as in poppyseed cake. The figure of speech "to rest in the arms of Morpheus" refers to the primary active agent in the opium poppy. The Greeks considered a good sleep to be a gift of the gods. Opium poppies were therefore dedicated to Hypnos, the god of sleep, and his son Morpheus, the god of dreams.

285
Yellow sweet clover, or **ribbed melilot** (*Melilotus officinalis* L.)
Pea family (Papilionaceae)
V–IX
Herbage
Tea, ointments, herb pillow
Coumarin, melilotoside, saponins
(M) Venous disorders, tired legs, cramps in the calf, itching, swelling, hemorrhoids
Contusions
Tea occasionally causes headaches.

286
Wolfsbane, or **aconite** (*Aconitum vulparia*)
Buttercup, or crowfoot, family (Ranunculaceae)
VI–VIII
Extremely poisonous!
Not suitable for self-medication; in the event of poisoning (burning mouth, tingling sensation, profuse sweating), a physician should be consulted immediately!

287
Venus' chariot, or **monk's-hood** (*Aconitum napellus* L.)
Buttercup, or crowfoot, family (Ranunculaceae)
III–V
Poisonous!
Mucilage, flavonoids, allantoin

288
Opium poppy (*Papaver somniferum* L.)
Poppy family (Papaveraceae)
VI–VIII
Highly poisonous!
Prescribed by physicians in the form of tablets, drops, injections
Alkaloids (morphine, codeine, papaverine)
Severe pain (tumor patients)
Not suitable for self-treatment, highly habit-forming!

285 Yellow sweet clover, ribbed melilot
287 Venus' chariot, monk's-hood

286 Wolfsbane, aconite
288 Opium poppy

The **horse chestnut** (*Aesculus hippocastanum*) is a magnificent tree that can reach an age of up to 200 years. It successively bears silver-haired, hand-shaped leaves; red, yellow, or white candlelike flowers; and then prickly, green fruit, containing shiny, brown seeds. In contrast to the edible chestnut, the fruit of the horse chestnut, which appears in late summer, is very rich in starch, tastes bitter, and can be eaten only as a fattening or winter feed. Aside from flavonoids, the seeds contain up to 4 percent escin. The extract is thus effective in tablets, drops, and ointments for the treatment of impaired blood-vessel vitality, varicose veins, hematomas, and hemorrhoids. The escin found in the bark is a component in cosmetics and serves to provide protection from sunburn. In addition, the bark has been used for diarrhea and the fruit for bronchitis and respiratory problems.

Because of the size of the infructescence (ears) and its grains (kernels), **corn** (*Zea mays*) can be considered a "giant grass." In the production of grains throughout the world, corn occupies the second position behind wheat. Columbus discovered corn in 1492 during his trip to America. Already by 1525, fields of corn were being cultivated in southern Spain. In 1543, an initial diagram of the corn plant appeared in an herb book by Leonhard Fuchs, a physician from Tübingen. Medicinally, corn has been used to soothe irritated tissue, especially mucus membranes, and employed as a diuretic.

As fitting with its name, the **hedge false bindweed,** or **hedge bindweed** (*Convolvulus sepium*), is a vine often found in habitats shared with bushes and hedges. The twining stalks favor fences and can reach a length of up to 3 meters (more than 9 feet). The leaves are characteristically shaped like arrows. If the funnel-shaped flowers remain closed in the morning, this is supposedly an indication of rain. Pliny compared the hedge false bindweed with the lily, saying, "Because of their white color, they are very similar, as if Mother Nature had learned from this plant how to make a true lily." In folk medicine,

the hedge false bindweed was used as a laxative, but it is no longer recommended because of its irritating effects on the intestines.

In contrast to chamomile, which it is sometimes mistaken for, **scentless mayweed** (*Matricaria inodora*) is not used medicinally. Even though this plant more closely resembles the ox-eye daisy, it is also called the "false chamomile." Its receptacle is filled with pith, however, whereas that of the true chamomile, with its high concentration of effective components, is characteristically hollow. As indicated by the Latin species name *inodora,* meaning "scentless," the typical aroma of the essential oils is lacking in this species.

289
horse chestnut (*Aesculus hippocastanum* L.)
horse-chestnut family (Hippocastanaceae)
V–VI
Seeds, leaves, bark
Tincture, tablets, ointments
Triterpene saponins (escin), flavonoids, coumarin
Chronic venous complaints, mobilization of fluids, anti-inflammatory

290
Corn (*Zea mays* L.)
Grass family (Gramineae)
VII–IX
Tea, powder, and as a basis for tablets
Fatty oil, saponins, tannins, minerals, starches
(F) Diuretic

291
Hedge false bindweed, or **hedge bindweed** (*Convolvulus sepium* L.)
Morning-glory family (Convolvulaceae)
VI–IX
Resins, tannins
(F) Laxative, today obsolete
Found to have irritating effects on the intestines

292
Scentless mayweed (*Matricaria inodora*)
Composite, or daisy, family (Compositae)
VII–X
Only the true chamomile (*Matricaria chamomilla*) is used medicinally.

289 horse chestnut
291 Hedge false bindweed, hedge bindweed

290 Corn
292 Scentless mayweed

$\mathscr{A}$bsinth **sagewort,** or **common wormwood** (*Artemisia absinthium*), is native to the steppe regions of Eastern Europe and Central Asia and cultivated mainly in the Mediterranean region. The Greek word *absinthion* ("displeasure"), from which the species name is derived, is a warning that this plant, although aromatic, has an unpleasant fragrance. A tea made from the absinth sagewort is also not very appetizing, as it still tastes bitter even at a dilution of one to 15,000. Because of its bitter principles, essential oil, and high concentration of potassium, this plant is extremely medicinal, stimulating the secretion of the salivary and gastrointestinal glands, and increasing the rate of peristalsis in the stomach and intestines. As a bitter plant, absinth sagewort, administered in the form of a tea, a tonic wine, or drops, is excellent for treating a lack of appetite, colicky disorders of the gastrointestinal and biliary systems, and general conditions of weakness. In his works, Sebastian Kneipp praised this plant for its therapeutic effects no less than seventeen times. However, as absinth sagewort contains a substance called thujone, prolonged use can lead to nerve damage. And it should not be used at all in cases of gastric or intestinal ulcers, or by pregnant women. In addition to its therapeutic applications, wormwood is used to flavor and aromatize aperitifs and vermouths.

The **European white birch** (*Betula pendula*) can be identified easily because of its typically whitish-gray, cracked bark. This tree's young branches have resinous glands that exude a "birch camphor." In Russia, this substance is distilled to make a product for aromatizing leather goods. The sap obtained from the trunk is used to make lotions for the scalp and mild alcoholic beverages. Birch leaves contain flavonoids, essential oil, vitamin C, and tannins, and they have a diuretic effect without stimulating the kidneys. Thus, they are suitable for diuretic and "blood-purifying" teas, to be used especially in the treatment of gout and rheumatic

disorders. The avenues of birches around Bad Wörishofen, with their wonderful, balsamic fragrance, are a joy to hikers.

Fond of moist meadows and forest clearings, **centaury** (*Erythraea centaurium*) is an inconspicuous member of the gentian family that can be glimpsed along the forest paths leading to the Hartenthal (a valley in this region). Growing in cymes, its rose-colored flowers bloom from June through September. The species name *centaurium* is derived from the Greek messenger of the gods, Chiron, a mythical centaur. This is the first medicinal plant with which Sebastian Kneipp became familiar through his mother. He later expressed his high regard for it, saying, "The centaury should receive top marks as a medicinal agent for stomach ailments." This plant still tastes bitter at a dilution of one to 2,000, and thus helps to increase the secretion of gastric juices, as well as the appetite. An unsweetened tea should be taken as a gastric tonic a half hour before meals. In some places, this tonic is also recommended as a cure for hangovers. However, centaury should not be taken in cases of gastric or intestinal ulcers.

The **autumn crocus,** or **meadow saffron** (*Colchicum autumnale*), is unusual in that it brings forth its narrow, basal leaves and fruit capsules in the spring and its lilac-colored blossoms in the fall. This strange cycle was therefore described with the phrase "filius ante patrem" ("the son comes before the father"). The lovely flowers of this member of the lily family seem to shoot out of the ground overnight, unmistakably heralding winter. Because of its leafless, crocuslike blossoms, this plant is also known in some places as "naked lady." Animals avoid the autumn crocus, and people should as well, as all of its parts are poisonous. Colchicine, a strong cellular poison, is especially concentrated in the blossoms and the seeds. But when administered by physicians in a standardized form and at a precise dosage, it continues to be the most effective agent we have in treating extremely painful, acute attacks of gout and arthritis.

293
Absinth sagewort, or **common wormwood** (*Artemisia absinthium* L.)
Composite, or daisy, family (Compositae)
VII–IX
Tea, tincture, wine, seasoning
Bitter principles (absinthin, artabsin)
(M) Gastrointestinal and biliary disturbances, lack of appetite
(F) Tonic, strengthening the powers of resistance
Not to be used in cases of gastric or intestinal ulcers, or by pregnant women

294
European white birch (*Betula pendula*)
Birch family (Betulaceae)
IV–V
Leaves, tar, sap
Plant juice, plant tablets, tea
Flavonoids, essential oil, bitter principles
(M) Increases urine, prevents the development of urinary gravel and uric acid calculi, "purifies blood"

295
Centaury (*Erythraea centaurium*)
Gentian family (Gentianaceae)
VII–IX
Tea, wine
Bitter principles (amarogentian, gentiopicrin), flavonoids, sterols
(M) Gastric disturbances arising from inadequate gastric juices
Not to be used in cases of gastric or intestinal ulcers

296
Autumn crocus, or **meadow saffron** (*Colchicum autumnale* L.)
Lily family (Liliaceae)
VII–XI
Alkaloids (colchicine)
Contents are poisonous, not suitable for self-medication!

293 Absinth sagewort, common wormwood
295 Centaury

294 European white birch
296 Autumn crocus, meadow saffron

*W*hereas the lovely, white flowers of the **hawthorn,** or **whitethorn** (*Crataegus oxyacantha, Crataegus laevigata,* and *Crataegus monogyna* species), are a joy to hikers around Bad Wörishofen in the spring, the red berries, which can be used like the leaves and the blossoms for making a medicinal tea, are seen to sparkle during the fall. Whitethorn tea normalizes blood pressure by regulating the heart. The tea should be taken for a period of at least four to six weeks. Whitethorn is also employed in the form of tablets and drops, and its continued use is often recommended for older patients whose hearts show signs of being weakened by age.

Native to America, the **pumpkin,** or **summer squash** (*Cucurbita pepo*), is cultivated extensively for its fruit. This creeping plant has a long stem with branched tendrils, large, triangular leaves, and yellow, funnel-shaped flowers. Its fruit, of course, is the familiar, large, orange pumpkin, which contains numerous seeds. On Halloween, children hollow out pumpkins and carve distorted faces in them so that they can be used as jack-o'-lanterns. The fruit is rich in vitamins and trace elements. In America, Thanksgiving wouldn't be complete without pumpkin pie for dessert. But the fruit is also used in soups, bread, puddings, and cake. The medicinal part of the plant, however, is its seeds, which contain cucurbitin, vitamin E, phytosterol, and selenium. Men with prostate problems have been known to get relief by ingesting pumpkin seeds. Yet relatively large amounts of pumpkin seeds, either whole or roughly ground, must be taken in order to treat a nervous bladder or benign prostate hyperplasia. A husk-free, special strain, or extracts from these seeds in capsule form, has eliminated the bothersome task of shelling the seeds and thus proven to be easier to take. Applied externally, pumpkin-seed oil is used for healing wounds.

Rose hips, high in vitamin C, are the fruit of the pleasant-smelling **dog rose,** or **brier rose** (*Rosa canina*), glimpsed in fields and along the roadside.

Ripening in the fall, rose hips are used to prepare mildly purgative juices and a somewhat sour-tasting tea. Sebastian Kneipp recommended dog rose tea or a tea made from only the seed kernels, because "it can provide relief for, and clean out, the kidneys and the bladder." Because of its high content of vitamin C, the tea is also good for strengthening the defense mechanisms. In addition, the dog-rose shrub has proven to be a very suitable plant for grafting precious roses. But unfortunately improper farmland consolidation has led to the endangerment of this previously so prevalent species.

A member of the cypress family, **common juniper** (*Juniperus communis*) can be found in many gardens in Bad Wörishofen and the surrounding areas. Also favoring dry, rocky habitats, this evergreen shrub has needle-shaped leaves and either yellow or green flowers. Because it is dioecious (having male flowers on one plant and female on another), its fruit is rarely seen. Aside from essential oil, the berrylike cone contains flavone gylcosides and tannins. Juniper "berries" are used in distilleries in the production of gin. As a spice, they not only enhance the flavor of food but also stimulate the appetite and counteract flatulence. Medicinally, they are often taken in the form of a tea that is especially helpful for digestive problems and water retention. Sebastian Kneipp included a juniper berry cure in his medicinal treasures. His instructions—in which he prescribed a small initial dose that is gradually increased to an optimal amount and then slowly decreased back to the initial dose—took into account the damage to the kidneys that can occur when the dose is too high or the therapy too long. Nevertheless, juniper berries should not be used by people with kidney problems or by pregnant women. This plant also has external applications. The distilled essential oil isolated from the wood serves as an effective bath additive for rheumatic pains and, in the form of a liniment, can be used to help promote the flow of blood and relieve muscle tension.

297
Hawthorn, or **whitethorn**
(*Crataegus oxyacantha* L.,
Crataegus laevigata L., and
Crataegus monogyna L.)
Rose family (Rosaceae)
V–VI
Flowers, leaves, fruit
Tea, plant juice, coated tablets, drops
Proanthocyanidin, flavone gylcosides
(rutin, hyperoside, vitexin, etc.)
(M) Reduced physical powers, heart problems

298
Pumpkin, or **summer squash**
(*Cucurbita pepo* L.)
Cucumber, or gourd, family
(Cucurbitaceae)
VI–IX
Seeds, oil
Seeds, granular powder, capsules
Fatty oil, essential oil, protein
(M) Bladder problems
Externally, oil for wounds

299
Dog rose, or **brier rose** (*Rosa canina* L.)
Rose family (Rosaceae)
VI
Fruit (rose hips)
Tea, marmalade
Vitamin C, minerals, fruit acids, sugar
To strengthen the defense mechanisms, mild purgative, mild diuretic

300
Common juniper (*Juniperus communis* L.)
Cypress family (Cupressaceae)
IV–V
Fruit, essential oil
Tea, plant juices, seasoning, bath additive
(M) For indigestion
(F) For water retention

297 Hawthorn, whitethorn
299 Dog rose, brier rose

298 Pumpkin, summer squash
300 Common juniper

SCHUTZMARKE

Following in the tradition established by Sebastian Kneipp, with his master-piece *How to Live* and his naturopathic therapy, the KNEIPP-WERKE, with its KNEIPP health products and KNEIPP pharmaceuticals, continues its efforts to keep ahead of its time.

As with the Kneipp cures, the general application of further developments combined with modern knowledge are part of today's contemporary treasury of Kneipp agents.

The historical cooperation (since 1891) between Sebastian Kneipp and his friend the pharmacist Leonhard Oberhäußer, which led to the founding of the KNEIPP-WERKE, carries over to today, fulfilling the basic premise of Sebastian Kneipp that we can use our intellect in order to discover riches and ultimately employ them against the many evils known to threaten life.

MEDICINAL TEAS
Composition, Preparation, and Applications

Originally, herbal cures were taken as pressed juices from fresh plants. However, as these juices had to be used immediately after harvesting, it was soon discovered that the plants could be preserved and used more easily by drying them and then reconstituting them with a liquid. This method has since been used for thousands of years. The parts of the plant to be used—whether blossoms, leaves, herbage, root, bark, fruit, or seeds—are dried carefully and then ground and stored. These herbs must be protected from light and the atmosphere, which is why you'll often see herbs and teas kept in tin boxes.

The simplest herbal cure is obtained by extracting the important components with a reconstituting solution. If you use water to perform this extraction, then you are left with a tea. If you use alcohol, you have made a tincture. If fatty oils are employed, the result is a medicinal oil.

Preparation of Herbal Teas

Depending on the part of the plant and its components, three different methods are used for preparing the tea.

1. Brewing (infusion) for leaves, herbage, blossoms, and seeds:

Pour 1 cup of simmering water over 1 to 2 teaspoons of the individual tea or tea mixture, and leave to steep in a covered container for 5 to 10 minutes. Strain into a cup. The condensation on the cover should be rinsed into the cup as well. This method of preparation is especially suitable for plants with essential oils, bitter principles, and saponins.

2. Decoction for wood, roots, and bark:

Pour 1 cup of water over 1 to 2 teaspoons of the plant parts, and then boil the mixture on the burner for 10 to 15 minutes. Strain out the herbs after they have cooled. This method is appropriate for plants rich in tannin such as oak bark or tormentil roots. It is not suitable, however, for plants containing bitter principles or mucilaginous agents.

3. Cold water extraction (cold infusion):

Pour 1 cup of cold water over 1 to 2 teaspoons of the plant parts, and leave to steep for a period of about 8 hours, much as you would when making sun tea. After straining, boil the extract for a short time in order to reduce the concentration of bacteria. This method of preparation is ideal for mucilaginous drug extractions such as those from the common marshmallow or linseed. A tea from mistletoe or from senna leaves can also be prepared this way.

Tea Mixtures

Although chemical pharmaceuticals are increasingly being prepared with single active ingredients (mono-preparations) in order to prevent undesirable interactions and adverse effects, tea extracts actually benefit from a variety of different active substances (such as alkaloids, essential oils, and bitter principles) and accompanying substances (like natural enzymes, vitamins, emulsifiers, and sugars). Therefore, a useful tea mixture could include the following:

❖ *A cardinal drug, or the main active ingredient,* which determines the principal effect of the tea and its indications (for example, valerian in a nerve tea or mint in a tea to soothe the stomach)

❖ *Supplementary drugs,* which support the primary active ingredient and have their own mild effect (for example, common balm leaves)

❖ *Auxiliary drugs,* which improve the taste and aroma, making the tea more pleasant to take and therefore more likely to be taken (for example, peppermint leaves in a bitter gallbladder-liver tea)

❖ *Refining agents,* which serve to make the tea more pleasant to the eye, thus increasing the likelihood of its being used (say, blue blossoms from the garden cornflower)

Let's take a look at the ingredients of a pectoral tea (for chest ailments), for example, to see how the components of a tea mixture serve to support one another in their effects:

❖ Cowslip blossoms, as a saponin drug, have both mucolytic and expectorant effects.

❖ Thyme herbage, containing thymol, not only has an

antibacterial effect, but also a mild spasmolytic effect on the bronchial tissues, which is especially helpful for a dry cough.

❖ The mucilage of mallow plants coats the irritated mucous membranes of the respiratory tract, thereby relieving the stimulus to cough (antitussive effect).

❖ Fennel fruit improves the taste of the tea mixture, as well as increases the rate of movement of the cilia in the respiratory tract.

As with many tea mixtures, the totality of the mixture is more effective than the sum of the effects from all of the individual extracts. This is why it is important to balance teas with a variety of extracts rather than relying on only a single one.

How Herbal Teas Are Taken

The best way to take medicinal teas is to drink 2 to 3 cups of moderately warm tea in small sips between meals, either unsweetened or sweetened with honey. Sebastian Kneipp recommended how tea should be taken and warned against drinking it fast: "This has an effect like a cloudburst and can disturb more than it helps. Like all medications, it [the tea] should be taken slowly one spoon or one swallow after another."

Wild versus Cultivated Medicinal Plants

If you want to try collecting the herbs yourself, it's necessary to follow a few important rules:

❖ Evaluate the habitat of the plants critically, looking for signs of pesticides, trash, and other unclean conditions (stay away from such places as railway embankments, roadsides, and dumps). You can't always remove residues by simply washing the plants, so it's best to avoid them altogether.

❖ If possible, harvest only that part of the plant that is to be used medicinally.

❖ Leaves should be harvested while young, herbs during the beginning of the flowering season, and fruit and seeds when they ripen.

❖ Never harvest the plants in damp weather, rain, or fog, as the parts collected could easily spoil or grow mold, which can lead to the development of dangerous aflatoxins.

❖ Whatever you harvest should be dried quickly in fresh air, but avoid high temperatures and direct sunlight.

Although it's rewarding to collect wild plants yourself, there are many advantages to using herbs cultivated under controlled conditions:

❖ As a result of uniform seed quality, few if any impurities are introduced, and you are left with almost the pure form of the seed type.

❖ The climate, habitat, soil preparation, crop rotation, sowing and harvesting times, harvesting technology, and drying are designed specifically for the particular plant.

❖ The harvested plants are examined for heavy metals, insecticides, pesticides, aflatoxins, radioactive contamination, and bacterial count. As a result of quality control and residue analysis, only medicinal herbs that are flawless and rich in active ingredients come to the consumer.

❖ Herb cultivators generally follow regulations concerning wildlife conservation and continue to improve agricultural structures. Therefore, there are additional benefits to supporting the cultivated-herb industry.

Tea Quality

Whereas tea that is used mainly as a beverage needs to meet only food-quality standards, tea that is employed for medicinal purposes must comply with pharmacological quality standards as stipulated by the International Pharmacopoeia. Most food-quality teas do not ever reach these standards in terms of their specific concentrations of active ingredients. A careful look at the labels of prepared teas will usually provide a clue to their quality. For example, on the label of a food-quality chamomile tea, you might find a description such as "wholesome." On the other hand, the label for chamomile of pharmacological quality may say something like "for the relief of gastrointestinal disorders and irritations of the mucous membrane of the mouth and throat."

When it comes to using loose tea or tea bags, it's mainly a matter of personal preference, as many tea bags contain ground and mixed leaves that are at least as high in quality as loose tea. The grinding and bagging merely allow for easier extraction (2 grams of a finely cut tea provide the same amount of extract as 5 grams of a coarsely cut leaf). In addition, the tea bags help keep the tea fresher, so the active ingredients remain effective longer than those in loose teas. Of course, tea bags are practical and economical as well. The following statement by Sebastian Kneipp also applies to tea from tea bags: "Through a tea, a fire is set aglow in the stomach that serves to warm the entire disposition."

Primary Components of Medicinal Plants

Essential oils: Volatile oils that give plants their distinctive odors, with anti-inflammatory, spasmolytic, digestion-stimulating, and mucolytic effects

Alkaloids: Complex, bitter plant components containing nitrogen, with pain-relieving and spasmolytic effects

Bitter principles: Components with a bitter taste that effect the mucous membranes of the mouth and stomach, with appetite- and digestion-stimulating effects

Saponins: Various primarily toxic glucosides that produce a soapy lather, with diuretic effects

Mucilaginous substances: Components distinguished by a gummy or gelatinous consistency, with protective, enveloping, and soothing effects

Tannins: Various soluble, astringent substances, with contracting and antibacterial effects

Minerals, vitamins, and trace elements: Important for metabolic processes

PURIFYING THE BODY AND REVIVING THE SPIRIT
Medicinal Herbs for a "Spring Cure"

*D*uring the winter, most of us tend to eat too much, drink too much, and get too little exercise. So, by the time spring arrives, we're ready for a "spring cleaning," a time to lose some weight and get off to a fresh start. The "spring cure" is an old tradition (thought to be based on Lent, because it often involves a period of fasting) that helps to purify the body after a long winter. The fasting serves to eliminate poisons, prevent illness, and increase the body's overall powers of resistance. Medicinal herbs—especially in the form of plant juices that "wash out" the body and "blood-purifying" teas—have also proven to be extremely helpful for these purposes.

Although we still use the term "blood purifying," it is technically inaccurate, as there is no blood exchange or actual filtering out of pollutants, but rather a diuretic and overall purifying effect. Sebastian Kneipp clearly defined the effects of "blood purification," as based on the actions of a tea made from the **European black elder, or European elder** (157): "This most simple blood-purification tea helps to clean the machine of the human body in a superb manner [diuretic effect!] and provides the poor with a substitute for the pills, alpine herbs, and other things that are frequently making the rounds today in fine boxes and little cartons, and which often have quite unusual effects."

It's important to make sure that any "blood-purification" substance you use contains diuretics for the most part and no strong laxatives, or else you run the risk of building an immunity to these purgatives. This is a side effect that is overlooked by many people.

Purifying Herbs

A specially concocted tea mixture or a well-selected plant juice can work as the perfect "purifying cure." Try out some of these herbs to create your own:

❖ Dandelions, European white birch, or stinging nettles, which serve as diuretics to remove fluids

❖ Bitter centaury, gentian root, or absinth sagewort, which help to stimulate the digestive tract

❖ Chamomile, peppermint, caraway, or fennel, which induce spasmolysis of the stomach or intestinal region

❖ Hibiscus or rose hips, which offer invigorating vitamins

Long ago, Sebastian Kneipp described a cure with berries from the **common juniper** (300) because of their outstanding diuretic effect. Juniper berries are botanically unique, as they are made up of three meaty carpels grown together to form a false, globular berry. He said to begin the cure by chewing four berries on the first day, five berries on the second day, and six berries on the third day, and to continue this way until reaching a total of twelve days with fifteen berries. Then he said to reduce the intake of berries by one each day until four berries are reached again.

Kneipp's recommendation has since been supported by scientific research, as it was found that the reliable fluid removal that these berries achieve has to do with their renal-stimulating components. Because of these components, however, juniper berries should not be taken by people who have suffered kidney damage. For the same reason, this herbal cure should never exceed six weeks.

For mild fluid removal and overall purification, parsley herbage, dandelion root and herbage, European white birch leaves, stinging nettle leaves, watercress, and rose-hip skins are also helpful. All are recommended for a period of three to four weeks at specific dosages in different forms:

❖ As a tea, 2 to 3 cups are taken daily

❖ The fresh plant juice is taken after meals. Adults take 1 tablespoon two to three times a day, and children 1 teaspoon two to three times a day.

❖ One or two plant tablets are taken three times a day before meals with water, herbal tea, or fruit juice.

Or try this herbal tea mixture:

Juniper berries (crushed)	20 g
Peppermint leaves	60 g
European white birch leaves	20 g

One to 2 cups of the brewed tea are taken three times a day.

Most herbal cures are effective if carried out for an extended period of time. Nature demands patience.

Kneipp Cures

To increase the benefits of the herbal cures, consider extending your spring cleaning (which can be carried out in the fall as well) to include a whole day or more of a number of sensible, mild Kneipp cures. This would involve drinking a purifying, invigorating herbal tea, instead of perhaps the usual beer. The aperitif before meals is a vegetable-juice cocktail, containing plenty of vitamins. Well-seasoned whole-grain foods are the primary components of the reduced meals. Not only women but also men should take care of their skin and hair, as well as pamper themselves in general. In the evening, after a relaxing bath with common balm or lavender, you may reach for the book you have always wanted to read when you had some peace and quiet. After a day like this, you will feel fresh and restored, and probably come to the realization that you could well become used to this feeling.

Supportive Measures

If you can't set aside a "cure day," think about at least incorporating some of the following supportive measures into your daily life:

❖ Immerse yourself in a full bath with hayseed oil or "hayflower" bath additives a few times a week.

❖ Try a combination of ablutions, affusions, and wraps.

❖ Be active. Perspiration, especially when it flows profusely, helps remove toxins from the body.

❖ Eat a diet high in vitamins and dietary fibers.

❖ Drink vegetable and fruit juices, for both their nutritional aspects and their benefits as liquids in removing toxins.

WHEN COLD SEASON HITS
Medicinal Herbs for Head Colds, Coughs, and Hoarseness

*A*lthough there is really no cure for the common cold, we can effectively relieve some of the nagging symptoms with a variety of medicinal herbs. Synthetic medicines found at drugstores are generally composed of mono-preparations (with only one active ingredient) in order to reduce the possibility of interactions and adverse effects. Herbal therapies, on the other hand, greatly benefit from the mild effects and the interactions of a number of different ingredients. Even within one herb, various components are employed. For example, only the full extraction of chamomile brings about its soothing and curative effects, and not the sum of the individual flavones, minerals, and mucilaginous substances.

A Pectoral Tea with Multiple Ingredients

It's often best to make a tea from a number of medicinal herbs, to take advantage of their complementary effects. Let's look at the ingredients of a pectoral tea, for example:

❖ The essential oil of the **fennel** (67) fruit, with its terpenes, is highly bactericidal.

❖ The essential oil of **garden thyme** (259) is twenty-five times as strong as the disinfectant phenol.

❖ The **anise** fruit relieves convulsive coughs.

❖ The **narrow-leaf plantain** (34), with its mucilage and salicylic acid, decreases the swelling and soothes the inflammation of the mucous membranes, making the cough less irritating. Like the **cowslip** (6), it also induces the cough stimulus, which is important for cleansing the respiratory tract.

❖ In order for the mucus to be brought upward and coughed out, it must be diluted with mucilaginous drugs like those found in the blossoms of the **dense-flower mullein** (247) ("wool-herb blossoms") or the **high mallow** (84), or in the roots of the **common marshmallow** (265). By drinking a lot of fluids, you will further dilute the mucus.

❖ The thick mucus becomes more liquid as a result of the active components of the **licorice root,** which help to reduce the surface tension.

The combination of all these tea ingredients also activates the cilia (microscopic hairs) in the trachea that help to move the mucous up and out. Coughing is actually a protective reflex of the body, and the mixture of these herbs supports this reflex. The comforting warmth of the tea is an added bonus.

Controlling a Cough

Although the cough reflex is helpful in recovering from a cold, there are times when we want to control it, such as when we lie down in bed at night. Basically, coughing should be blocked only to avoid interruptions during sleep. Codeine, which is prescribed all too often for coughs, is also a strong, effective plant component. It is derived from the dried, milky sap of the unripe, scarified heads of the **opium poppy** (288). Aside from sugar or honey, cough drops and lozenges often contain essential oils (such as eucalyptus, anise, fennel, and thyme), soluble vegetable jellies, mucilage, and glycerine. They coat the mucous membranes of the respiratory tract with a film, keeping it moist, and, as a result of your sucking action, stimulate the production of saliva. The mucilaginous lichens Iceland moss and Irish moss, with their antibacterial lichenin, are also helpful for coughs. Spasmodic whooping coughs are best soothed using a mixture of thyme extracts with a small component of sundew and ivy extracts.

External Applications and Gargles

The external application of medicinal herbs plays an especially important role in the treatment of colds. In addition to sweat baths and footbaths, bronchial balms rubbed into the chest have proven to be very effective. Chest rubs not only allow the essential oils from such herbs as peppermint, eucalyptus, mountain pine, and thyme to be continuously inhaled, but they also help to strengthen the localized circulation and promote the production of fluids by the bronchi. However, babies and small children should not be treated with cold balms containing menthol, as this substance can have a damaging effect on them merely by being inhaled.

For respiratory infections in general, but especially for a runny nose, maintaining high humidity in the room is very helpful. Try using a vaporizer or a humidifier or even hanging up wet towels. But it's very important to carry out everything hygienically and to change the water daily to prevent the growth of bacteria. You might want to add a few drops of thyme, mint, or mountain pine oil to the humidifier, because this not only smells good but also has a disinfectant action.

If you are suffering from chronic respiratory problems, the cause may be allergic or possibly just environmental. An adult breaths in about 1,500 gallons of air a day and with it large amounts of dust, smoke, pollutants, and microorganisms. Normally, the natural bacteria present in the mouth and throat remain in a physical equilibrium, but the pollutants breathed in each day may disturb this balance so that a sore throat, hoarseness, and difficulties in swallowing can develop.

Medicinal plants may help such conditions in the form of gargles, rinsing solutions, lozenges, or inhalants. (For inhalation, brew the herbs until steaming and then inhale the steam with a towel draped over the head.) In addition to extracts from chamomile blossoms and thyme, try using gargles or rinses from the **kitchen sage,** or **garden sage** (118). This plant is native to the Mediterranean region and has been used medicinally since ancient times. Sebastian Kneipp said, "Whoever has a small garden at home will not regret it if he adds a sage shoot there; it is a lovely, decorative plant. I have often seen how passers-by take a leaf and rub their darkened teeth with it. This shows what a cleansing effect sage has."

As sage contains essential oils with cineole, thujone, and camphor, it has destructive and inhibitory effects on bacteria, fungi, and viruses. Tenacious gargling with sage tea not only helps to combat a developing cold, but it is also a reliable method for curing hoarseness or difficulties in swallowing. Used as a rinse, sage tea even kills bacteria in dental plaque, relieves pressure sores caused by dental prostheses, eliminates bleeding from the gums, and reduces swelling and inflammations of the gums and mucous membranes. In drops and oral ointments, sage is often supplemented with other ingredients such as anti-inflammatory cinnamon and clove oil, thymol, menthol, chamomile extract, and refreshing peppermint and eucalyptus oil. In addition, when taken internally as a beverage, large doses of sage tea have proven to be the only effective agent to inhibit sweating. But this tea should not be taken for too long or in too concentrated a form, otherwise it could cause gastric complaints. The components effective in combating perspiration are actually taken more comfortably in the form of fluid extracts or tablets.

More Herbal Remedies

For relief of the irritation associated with acute and chronic bronchitis and dry, hacking coughs, try the following:

❖ Prepare a tea as a cold water extraction using either the root of the common marshmallow, Iceland moss, or blossoms of the dense-flower mullein.

❖ Prepare an infusion (or brewed tea) from either high mallow blossoms or leaves, narrow-leaf plantain, or thyme.

In addition, a cough syrup made from the common marshmallow and narrow-leaf plantain can be helpful. Take 1 to 2 teaspoons three times a day. Another option is Iceland moss lozenges. Suck one of these lozenges every 2 to 3 hours.

For relief from a productive cough and for a disinfectant, prepare an infusion (or brewed tea) either from thyme, fennel fruit, blossoms of dense-flower mullein, blossoms of cowslip, or narrow-leaf plantain. Drink 3 to 5 cups daily. Extracts from sundew or ivy leaves in the form of drops or juice are also recommended. Take 20 drops, or 2 teaspoons, three times a day. In addition, thyme tea and thyme oil are very suitable for inhalants and gargles. However, chamomile tea, chamomile extracts, and lime-blossom teas, used in the form of inhalants, are milder.

For a pectoral and bronchial tea, mix the following ingredients:

Fennel fruit	15 g
Cowslip blossoms	15 g
Thyme	35 g
Narrow-leaf plantain	35 g

Most adults suffer from colds caused by a viral infection about three or four times a year; children as often as twelve times a year.

For a cold with a runny nose and a mild fever, a tea mixture with elderberry blossoms, lime blossoms, queen of the meadow blossoms, and rose hip peels can be helpful.

However, in cases of a fever or if your symptoms last more than three days, it's best to contact your physician. Always consult a physician if a child develops a fever, but especially in conjunction with a throat infection, as there may be a possibility of scarlet fever or tonsillitis. Such conditions need to be treated with appropriate medications in order to prevent chronic damage.

For a sore throat or hoarseness, these methods are recommended:

❖ Make a tea from the root of the common marshmallow or from Iceland moss for drinking and irrigation.

❖ Create a gargle or inhalant with sage, thyme, or chamomile tea.

❖ Suck on Iceland moss lozenges or on caramels with anise, sage, menthol, or honey.

Supportive Measures

To realize the full effects of many of these herbal cures, the following supportive measures can be helpful:

❖ Soak in a warm thyme or eucalyptus bath (37°C, or 98.6°F) for 10 minutes at night before going to sleep.

❖ For a cold, rub a balm with mountain pine, thyme, eucalyptus, and rosemary oil into the chest and apply below the nose a number of times each day.

❖ Take a footbath or an arm bath with increasingly warmer water (starting at 33°C, or 91.4°F, and increasing to about 39°C, or 102.2°F) over the course of 15 minutes before you go to sleep.

❖ If you have a fever, wrap a cold, wet compress around your calves (rewet the compress when no longer cool).

❖ For hoarseness and a sore throat, wrap cold compresses around your neck.

❖ Be sure to get a great deal of bed rest in a well-ventilated room with high humidity.

❖ Drink a lot of fluids, especially herbal teas and fruit juices.

❖ Eat a light, nutritious diet with plenty of fruit.

WHEN INFLUENZA IS RAMPANT!

Medicinal Herbs for the Flu and as a Prophylactic Measure

The capability of our bodies to ward off specific infectious agents, which we have developed through natural contact or by means of inoculations, is known as immunity. As influenza does not result in lasting immunity however, influenza epidemics occur repeatedly. How widespread these illnesses become and their degree of severity can be reduced through influenza vaccines. In most cases, however, the flu is not caused by influenza viruses, but is rather a type of "grippal infection." There are about 300 different strains of virus, generally characterized by sudden onset, fever, severe aches and pains, a sore throat, a runny nose, and a cough. These symptoms can be alleviated with chemical or plant agents. Over the last few years, the use of immunostimulants has gained increasing recognition. These are generally plant substances that are able to stimulate defensive reactions within the body against nonspecific pathogens.

The "five pillars" of Kneipp therapy are all outstanding for strengthening the immune system: a toning-up cure by means of applying hot and cold water, sports and movement in the fresh air, repeated saunas, and healthy nutrition, as well as a well-balanced state of mind. In addition, plant alterants are used to help strengthen the body so that it can help itself without any adverse effects.

Herbs That Stimulate an Immune Response

Synthetic immunostimulants have to be administered very soon after the outbreak of an infection, and they frequently result in a fever and are tolerated poorly. Vegetable immunostimulants are given short-term. They are also recommended as a prophylactic measure for lowered resistance due to stress—for example, while traveling or before an operation.

In addition to bitter drugs (such as absinth sagewort, gentian, and centaury), various pharmaceutical plants are used for a stimulation therapy and are considered to have a similar tonicizing effect. For instance, a combination of extracts from different species of the **coneflowers** (249) (*Echinacea purpurea* and *Echinacea angustifolia*), the **thuja** or **eastern arbor vitae** (*Thuja occidentalis*), **wild indigo** (*Baptista tinctoria*), and different **thoroughwort** species (*Eupatorium cannabinum* and *Eupatorium perfoliatum*), usually taken in the form of drops administered immediately after the first signs of symptoms, helps to shorten the duration of the illness and are quite effective as prophylactic agents as well. Likewise, the red coloring agent in the **beet root** is attributed to having a stimulating effect on the defensive reactions within the body. Admittedly, to be effective, this plant juice has to be drunk in such quantities that the urine and even the stool turn red.

Herbs High in Vitamin C

During flu epidemics, an optimal supply of vitamin C is considered to provide a certain amount of protection, as vitamin C strengthens the body's defense mechanisms. Aside from eating fruit such as grapefruit and oranges with a high concentration of vitamin C and vegetables like tomatoes that additionally have the provitamins necessary for absorption into the body, a tea made from rose hips has proven to be quite suitable as well. Rose hips are the fruit of the **dog rose,** or **brier rose** (299). Drunk cold, rose-hip tea is also effective in quenching the thirst associated with a fever.

Sebastian Kneipp said this of the dog rose: "The mother who also takes her house apothecary into consideration not only picks the lovely roses from the dog rose shrub but also collects the so-called rose hips and not alone for sauces but also for therapeutic effects." However, Kneipp was primarily impressed with the rose hips' mild diuretic effect.

As rose hips hardly cause the tea water to be colored red, and as patients frequently expect this reddish color, **hibiscus blossoms** are often added to the tea. Hibiscus blossoms, which are often mistaken for red mallow flowers, not only add color but also improve the taste as well as the concentration of vitamins.

Other excellent sources of vitamins are the stewed fruit or juice from the **sea buckthorn** (215) and from the **European black currant** (43), in which 1 kilogram of the fruit (2.2 pounds) contains 2 grams of vitamin C.

Plants That Promote Perspiration to Bring Down a Fever

As a fever is a natural defensive reaction of the body, it should be suppressed only when the temperature goes above 39°C (102.2°F) or if there is a danger of adverse effects developing, as in the elderly or in children. A proven method for lowering a fever involves wrapping cold, wet compresses around the calves. An increasing temperature accompanied by attacks of shivers can be treated with a sweat cure (hydrosudotherapy).

One method entails rapidly drinking 1 to 2 cups of strong, hot tea made from the **European black elder** (157)—also known as "lilac tea" in some places—or from the **small-leafed lime,** or **little-leaf linden** (112), and then going to bed immediately afterward. If you are also experiencing cold symptoms, it is recommended to make a tea mixture with the blossoms, in equal amounts, of European black elder, small-leafed lime, and chamomile, as chamomile blossoms eliminate the toxic bacteria and thus improve one's overall state of health. The blossoms of European black elder are especially helpful in curing the inflamed nasal mucous membranes and paranasal sinuses.

None of these sweat-inducing teas should be boiled, but instead left to steep for 10 minutes after mixing the herb with simmering water. To improve the taste, honey can be added as a sweetener.

The effect of such teas in causing sweating can be increased further by taking a hot footbath or a hot full bath (at 40°C, or 104°F) afterward. The essential oils from **thyme** (259), **eucalyptus leaves,** and **spruce** and **mountain pine needles** are effective as bath oils. Not only are these oils absorbed through the skin, but they also evaporate in the steam, whereby they are inhaled and thus soothe and disinfect the mucous membranes. A few minutes after the bath, you should get into bed, where, under the warm covers, you will sweat for a further half hour. Then, after taking a warm shower, you'll be set for a good night's sleep. A stable circulatory system, however, is a prerequisite for such a sweat cure.

Further Herbal Remedies

To strengthen the body's defense mechanisms against infections, take Echinacea tablets or drops. Suck one tablet or take 40 drops three or four times a day for no longer than eight weeks. A similar effect can be achieved by taking a mixture of extracts from the purple coneflower, the tips of the thuja, and the roots of the yellow indigo (rattle weed).

Absinth sagewort tea, gentian-root tea, or tea made from the centaury, as drugs containing bitter principles, also have an immunostimulatory effect. Drink 1 cup of the brewed, unsweetened tea slowly, one sip after another, three times a day.

As a local disinfectant for the mucous membranes in the mouth and for the respiratory tract, gargle or rinse with sage-leaf tea or thyme tea (brewed with simmering water) or 10 to 20 drops of thyme or mint oil stirred in half a glass of warm water. In addition, sage, eucalyptus, peppermint, cinnamon, clove, fennel, and anise oils make a good mixture for drops.

Teas made from thyme, chamomile blossoms, or small-leafed lime blossoms are effective in anti-inflammatory head steam baths. (Brew the herbs until steaming, and then inhale the steam with a towel draped over the head.) However, an easier method is to add 20 drops of thyme oil or 2 to 3 tablespoons of concentrated chamomile to 1 liter, or quart, of boiling water.

For cold symptoms, this tea mixture is helpful:

Blossoms from the European black elder	30.0 g
Blossoms from the small-leafed lime	30.0 g
Queen of the meadow	20.0 g
Rose-hip skins	20.0 g

In addition, thyme, willow bark, fennel fruit, creeping thyme, or mallow can be effective. Drink 1 to 2 cups of the brewed hot tea three times a day.

As a sweat cure, similar to the sweat cures described above, brew a tea made from the blossoms of the small-leafed lime or the European black elder. Then mix this tea with the juice of half a lemon and sweeten, if desired, with 2 teaspoons of honey. Quickly drink 1 to 2 cups of this tea mixture at a temperature as hot as possible. Follow this with a footbath or an arm bath with an increasing temperature (from 33°C to 38°C, or 91.4°F to 100.4°F) or, better still, and only if you have a stable circulatory system, a hot full bath (at 38°C, or 91.4°F), with oil of thyme, eucalyptus, or spruce needles, for 3 to 5 minutes. Get into bed, where you will sweat for a half hour more. Take a warm shower, and then go to sleep.

Supportive Measures

❖ Wrap cold, wet compresses around the calves (rewet when no longer cool).

❖ Drink vitamin-rich plant juices from sea buckthorn fruit, the European black currant, or European black elder berries (juices also can be taken hot).

❖ In general, eat plenty of fruit and drink a lot of fluids in the form of fruit juices and herbal teas.

JOINT OR MUSCLE PAIN?
Medicinal Herbs for the Relief of Rheumatic Complaints

*I*f you suffer from a sensation of pulling and pinching in your lower back, most likely you have a condition commonly known as "rheumatism." However, rheumatism is very complex and can manifest differently from person to person, as Sebastian Kneipp already pointed out: "One person suffers from headaches, another from pains in the toes, still another from pains in the arms, and others have pains in the legs, the back, or the chest." Following an initial diagnosis, the physician today differentiates among a number of rheumatic disorders.

Arthritis: A lack of synovial fluid and the subsequent, painful inflammation

Arthrosis: The pathological attrition of the cartilaginous and bony structures of the joints

Gout: The accumulation of uric acid in the form of nodes especially in and around the joints

Multiple degenerative joint disease: Metabolic disturbances in the joints

Nonarticular rheumatism: Inflammation in the muscles, tendons, and tissues

Osteoporosis: Attrition of the intervertebral disks with muscular contraction and painful constriction of nerves, with development as far as the luxation of a disk and the decalcification of the bones

Rheumatoid arthritis: Inflammation, pain, stiffness, and sometimes destruction of the joints

Sciatica: Attrition of the intervertebral disks with muscular contraction and painful constriction of nerves

What is common to all of these conditions is the pain. Rheumatism can be inherited or can be the result of infection and inflammation, inadequate or no exercise, poor nutrition, or the development of attrition over time. For the treatment of the approximately 400 different, painful disorders of the joints or muscles within this category, highly effective "antirheumatics" must be administered as a basic therapy to alleviate the inflammations (antiphlogistics) and to lessen the pain (analgesics). Especially in severe cases, even antibi-

otics or cortisone are taken by patients in order to obtain some control over the basic condition. In addition to exercise and changes in diet, medicinal herbs are used to strengthen the defense mechanisms, eventually reducing the dosages of these powerful medications. Herbs are also employed to support traditional therapies, which are still far from ideal today, providing relief from pain.

With rheumatism, the supply of blood to the muscles needs to be improved, the muscles need to relax, the disturbed balance in heat needs to be regulated, and the metabolism should be stimulated. Although the supportive therapy for rheumatism is centered around the external application of medicinal herbs, a number of herbs are also used in teas for internal treatment. Topping the list of tea ingredients are the roots and herbage of the dandelion, European white birch leaves, the stinging nettle, and the field horsetail, with their purifying, dehydrating, and fluid-mobilizing effects. These herbs, as well as others that are effective for rheumatism, are discussed below.

Herbs Recommended for Rheumatic Disorders

Dandelions (55) stimulate the overall activity of the cells, have a positive effect on the connective tissues, and promote the circulation. Patients who suffer from chronic arthritis have reported noticeable improvements following a dandelion-tea or dandelion-juice cure carried out over a period of six weeks during the spring or the fall.

Leaves from the **European white birch** (294) help to mobilize the flow of fluids without being a strain on the kidneys. This process, along with a low uric acid diet and no alcohol, is especially effective for relieving the symptoms of gout. A similar stimulation of the metabolism as that brought about by the European white birch is observed with the herbage of the **stinging nettle** (120). For the treatment of an acute attack of gout, a proper dosage of the **autumn crocus,** or **meadow saffron** (296), with the alkaloid colchicine, is still considered to be a superior agent. This highly effective preparation, however, must be administered by a physician.

As the herbage of the **field horsetail** (86) contains salicylic acid, which has strengthening effects on the connective tissues, it is a valuable ingredient in teas against rheumatism. The diuretic effect of this herb, however, is rather low.

Berries from the **common juniper** (300), in either extracts or tablets, are highly effective against rheumatic symptoms. Its essential oil has both diuretic and antiseptic properties. Yet there is the possibility of renal disturbances following long-term internal administration. When applied externally, the essential oil serves as an effective bath additive for rheumatic pains and, in the form of a liniment, can be used to help promote the flow of blood and relieve muscle tension.

The principal component found in the bark of the willow is salicylic acid, the model for and precursor of aspirin (acetylsalicylic acid). Since ancient times, this bark has been used as an agent for relieving pain and reducing fever. The bark of the willow also contains a high concentration of tannins, so it is said to have a protective effect against irritations of the mucous membranes. As the moderately strong healing drug in the bark releases its contents gradually, it is more suitable for the treatment of rheumatic disorders and colds than for the relief of severe pain.

Queen of the meadow, or **meadowsweet** (64), also has salicylic compounds, which can be isolated from the ground blossoms. The essential oil contains salicylaldehyde and salicylic acid methyl ester, which smells similar to chewing gum. The latter, which promotes the flow of blood (hyperemic) and can irritate the skin, is often mixed in ointments for rheumatism. Its effects can be increased substantially through the addition of the pungent substances found in the **paprika fruit** (such as capsaicin). These active agents stimulate the warmth and pain receptors when applied to the skin, thus bringing about an increase in local circulation. This external effect, which can be achieved not only with ointments but also with plasters, can be strengthened even further and rounded off through the use of various essential oils such as camphor, mountain pine, and menthol.

Antirheumatic plasters are especially effective if you have lumbago, which often develops after making an incorrect movement when the muscles of the back are cold from a draft. These plasters furnish warmth, increase the circulation, and alleviate the cramping. In addition, the plasters provide support and help to prevent a new attack of lumbago from developing as a result of faulty movements. Aside from the circulatory-stimulating effects from the paprika extracts, the plasters often have anticramping effects thanks to their extracts of **belladonna** (101); many also contain the effective agents found in **mountain arnica** (227) that relieve muscle and joint pain.

Tips for External Applications

Patients with rheumatism who take advantage of the external applications often experience a spontaneous relief from pain with fewer adverse effects. Two basic principles need to be considered when it comes to applying herbs externally for rheumatic disorders:

❖ Acute, inflammatory complaints involving the nerves (arthritis, sports injuries, sprains, and strains, for example) should always be treated with cold methods, such as loam poultices, curd wraps, cool compresses, cooling sprays, mint oils, rubbing alcohol, or cold water.

❖ Chronic, degenerative complaints (like arthrosis and soft-tissue rheumatism) should be treated with warmth, using baths, embrocations, ointments, warming layers and wraps, "hay-flower sacks," clay baths, paraffin fomentation, or potato packs.

The baths should not be taken for longer than 10 to 15 minutes. Juniper, spruce, and mountain pine oils, mineral salts, or **"hay-flower"** extracts are suitable as bath additives. With the term "hay flower" (221–224), we now come to the key component of one of the best-known applications of heat among the Kneipp cures: the "hay sack" (or "hay pack"). Modeled somewhat after a large tea bag, this sack is made of linen or fleece and filled loosely with hay flowers (*Flores graminis*).

The already-prepared, single-use hay packs, which come in various sizes, offer an easy way of performing a home treatment: Heat the hay pack to about 40°C (104°F), using steam or by soaking in hot water. Then place it onto the painful part of the body (the back, shoulder, or knee, for example), cover it with a cloth, and keep it there for a minimum of a half hour. When the temperature of the hay pack has cooled down to around body temperature, remove it and relax for a while.

These hay-flower sacks are highly valued for two reasons:

In contrast to other methods of applying warmth (such as electric heating pads, hot-water bottles, and clay), these sacks don't transfer a compact warmth, but rather a gentle, moist warmth that is both mild and continuous. Therefore, they are excellent for the treatment of rheumatic pains and for colics.

The components (essential oils and coumarin) affect the skin directly, stimulating the blood flow, relieving pain, and alleviating cramps. In addition, the inhalation of their vapors has a comforting and relaxing effect.

Sebastian Kneipp, who used hay flowers only as an additive to baths, said, "The coffee-brown water opens the pores and relieves the body of congestion."

More Specifics

The following purifying plant parts *mobilize the removal of fluids, alleviating the complaints of gout and rheumatism:* dandelion roots and herbage, leaves of the European white birch, leaves of the stinging nettle, herbage from the field horsetail, and roots of the spiny restharrow.

❖ Drink 2 to 3 cups of a brewed tea daily between meals for three to four weeks.

❖ Adults take 1 tablespoon of the plant juices two or three times a day; children 1 teaspoon two or three times a day after meals.

A cure with juniper berries has a similar effect. Sebastian Kneipp recommended beginning the cure by chewing four berries on the first day, five berries on the second day, and continuing in this manner until reaching a total of twelve days with fifteen berries. This dose is then reduced by one berry a day until the initial dose of four berries is reached again. However, this cure is easier in the form of a plant juice from the common juniper: Take 1 tablespoon two or three times a day after meals.

A number of pain-relieving and anti-inflammatory medicinal plants are used for *treating rheumatic and neuralgic complaints,* such as blossoms from the common juniper, linden blossoms, queen of the meadow blossoms, and willow bark, mixed and brewed as a tea. Drink 2 to 3 cups of this tea, at a moderately warm temperature, slowly, one sip after another, for a period of three to four weeks.

The following two tea mixtures are also helpful for rheumatic complaints:

❖ Bittersweet stalk, willow bark, elderberry leaves, and common juniper berries

❖ Elder blossoms, common juniper berries, stinging nettle leaves, European white birch leaves, and dandelion root with herbage

With both, drink 2 to 3 cups daily over a period of three to four weeks.

Various herbal remedies are *applied externally to relieve pain and cramping:*

❖ Rheumatism ointment with extracts from cayenne, or red pepper

❖ Baths for relief from rheumatism using juniper and wintergreen oils

❖ Antirheumatic plaster with extracts from the mountain arnica and cayenne, or red pepper

❖ Hay pack: Pour boiling water over an already-prepared hay pack until it is just covered, and let steep for 5 minutes. Drain off the water, and press the hay pack with a cold washcloth (so your hands are protected) to get rid of any excess water. Better still, steam the hay pack in a large pot for about an hour. Once it has aired and cooled down to about 50°C, or 122°F, place the hay pack on the part of the body to be treated and cover it with a cloth. After removing it about an hour later, relax for a further half an hour.

Certain herbs are helpful in the event of *ischiatitis and neuralgia:*

❖ Rub mint oil into the painful sites.

❖ Use cooling ointments with mint oil, menthol, rosemary oil, and camphor.

❖ Also try arnica gel, arnica tincture, Saint-John's-wort oil, and mountain pine oil (as well as rubbing alcohol).

Supportive Measures

❖ Cool the painful area with ice, a loam or curd wrap, ablutions, or lukewarm partial baths; the more inflamed the complaint, the colder the treatment.

❖ Do various forms of exercise, including isometric stretching.

❖ Physiotherapy, back training, swimming, and bicycling are all recommended.

❖ Refrain from standing or sitting for too long.

OH, MY ACHING STOMACH!
Medicinal Herbs for Acute Stomach Problems

When we eat something that doesn't agree with us, our stomachs rebel and we experience such symptoms as nausea, retching, a feeling of pressure, and mild cramping. Sometimes it even feels like a there's a heavy stone lying in the stomach. Everyone has had an upset stomach, a common remedy for which is a cup of chamomile or peppermint tea. It's not without good reason that these teas are so popular. However, with stomach complaints, it is always a good idea to visit a physician in order to investigate the deeper causes. A basis for such problems could be an ulcer, for example.

Nevertheless, these complaints involving the gastrointestinal system represent a special field in herbal therapy. Along with changes in diet (less sugar and more roughage, for example), habits (smoking and drinking less or not at all), and lifestyle (less stress!), certain herbs are known to bring about an improvement. Even for acute stomach problems, a therapy in the form of a tea, simple tinctures, plant juices, or tablets alone may be helpful.

The Most Effective Herbs

Three herbs in particular have proven to be especially effective for stomach troubles: chamomile, peppermint, and common balm.

German, or **wild, chamomile** (105) is an excellent illustration of the premise that the whole is more beneficial than the sum of the parts. Only the entire effective complex of the essential oils from the dried blossom, with chamazulene, matricin, and bisabolol, provides the full "chamomile effect." The water-soluble flavonoids give the teas and inhalants their excellent anti-inflammatory and spasmolytic results. It has been shown that chamomile also inhibits bacteria and fungi. Yet an adequate concentration of the herb is required for it to be effective as a cure, and its administration must be carried out resolutely and for a relatively long period of time (anywhere from two weeks to a number of months, depending on the severity of the condition). In cases where the mucous membranes of the stomach are inflamed, the use of strong chamomile tea or concentrated chamomile in the form of a "roll cure" (in which the body is rolled along the longitudinal axis after drinking the chamomile extract, so that the entire stomach is covered with a layer of the drug) has proven to be effective. Chamomile tea is frequently combined with lactose (milk sugar) to retune the effects from an intestinal obstruction and to restore the intestinal flora.

Common peppermint (257) has a long tradition as a medicinal plant, and it's just about as popular as chamomile for stomach problems. Sebastian Kneipp considered mint to be "one of the most important agents for strengthening the stomach and promoting digestion." He further said that its refreshing aroma "is an indication that this herb occupies an important position with regard to its healing powers." Peppermint should be administered especially in cases where the symptoms of nausea or retching are prevalent, during disturbances in the biliary system, or in the event of fermentation in the intestinal tract. It demonstrates less of an anti-inflammatory effect and is more spasmolytic as well as mildly analgesic. It also relieves flatulence and has a mild disinfectant effect on the decomposed contents of the stomach. Mint oil is particularly effective in promoting the secretion of the gallbladder and increases the production of bile.

Common balm, or **lemon balm** (242), used internally in the form of a tea, juice, or tablets, and externally as an additive in a lukewarm bath, has a relaxing and comforting effect even at lose doses. The area in which it is most effective is the treatment of nervous disturbances of the stomach. Spirit of carmelite, a distillate of balm with other drugs found in orange peels, ginger, cloves, and cinnamon, is also frequently used. This substance, however, is 70 percent alcohol. As with the bath additives, spirit of carmelite not only contains the essential oil found at a low concentration in the common balm but also a similar oil derived from the lemon grass, a plant common in Sri Lanka and Japan.

WHEN HEARTBURN IS A WAY OF LIFE
Medicinal Herbs for Chronic Gastric Disorders

*M*edicinal herbs are valuable in the treatment of chronic stomach disturbances, because they improve the psychovegetative alterations associated with a weak or nervous stomach. Such stomach complaints are frequently due to psychological issues that trouble us so much they make us sick. But they can also develop as a result of taking certain medications, from a reduced action of the stomach, or through a pressure in the gallbladder.

Bitter Principles for Promoting Digestion

In plants, along with mucus-forming agents, bitter principles are effective in stimulating the production of digestive juices, protecting the inflamed mucous membranes, relieving spasms and flatulence, and strengthening the stomach in general. Bitter principles are substances used in bitters and bitter tonics, as well as in teas, tinctures, plant juices, and tablets. It's important for bitter principles to be taken before meals, and teas with these substances generally should be drunk cold and unsweetened. Should you have an acute gastritis attack following a rich meal, it is sometimes helpful to fast for one or two days and drink weak peppermint tea, containing bitter principles. Bitters stimulate the appetite and improve the general sense of well-being at the same time. In recent years, they have been found to also substantially improve the defense mechanisms. Their reflexive stimulation of the pancreas and their production of gastric juices is recognized scientifically. The tonicizing effect of bitters, however, is created only with long-term applications.

Although the upset stomach experienced by children can frequently be relieved with chamomile or peppermint tea, that observed in adults is treated best with stomachics or bitter tonics. Symptoms that are noted include heartburn, stomach pains or cramps, nausea and vomiting, and occasionally diarrhea. If the home remedies mentioned here help, these symptoms can be considered harmless. But if no relief is achieved after a few hours, it's wise to consult a physician.

Plants Containing Bitter Principles

Bitter principles are found in such plants native to Germany as **centaury** (295), **yellow gentian** (238), and **common buckbean** (76), all members of the gentian family. According to Sebastian Kneipp, a tea made from centaury "relieves the stomach winds [flatulence], removes the useless and unhealthy acids, supports and improves the gastric juices, and has a favorable effect on the kidneys and liver. It is the best agent for the treatment of heartburn or, as the country folk say, against the boiling waters of the stomach." The one-year-old plant still tastes bitter when diluted one to 3,500 (the "bitter value"). Its bitter principles not only increase the secretion of gastric juices but also the stomach's activity.

The root of the yellow gentian is the part of the plant used pharmaceutically. All of the gentian species have become endangered and are therefore protected, so the yellow gentian is now being cultivated in order to preserve this species. Because of the high concentration of sugar in the root, it is distilled to produce a schnapps as well. The root of the yellow gentian contains no tannin; therefore, it can be used in a tonic without stimulating the stomach or having an astringent effect. Sebastian Kneipp said, "Gentian tea, cooked briefly, and taken before meals, serves to stimulate the appetite. Taken after meals, it relieves the pressure of the stomach and the feeling of fullness."

The common buckbean is also known as "bitter swamp clover" in some places because of its large quantity of bitter principles. Kneipp recommended it especially for a weak stomach and flatulence.

The root of the very showy **angelica,** or **angel's wort** (159), which is a member of the parsley, or carrot, family, also contains bitter principles. It is highly valued as a component in liqueurs and in teas partially because of its spicy flavor. Kneipp said, "The angelica is rightfully recommended as an excellent home remedy. People should collect a large amount of this plant throughout the year from the meadows and forests, hang it in the air to dry, and then store it in a dry place. As the stomach often demonstrates an uncomfortable sense of cold, a cup of tea made from such roots brings the stomach a renewed warmth."

Bitter principle drugs like those derived from **cinchona,** or **condurango,** bark—which were formerly very popular—are today nearly all taken in the form of tonic wines. Aside from bitter principles, the aromatic tonics contain essential oils that are spasmolytic, eliminate flatulence, and stimulate the gallbladder.

The peel of the **Seville,** or **bitter, orange** is used in aromatic tinctures and stomach-strengthening drops. Its sharp, bitter substances, like those found in the **ginger** root, for example, are especially suitable for reducing stomach acidity, although they are frequently tolerated poorly by people with sensitive stomachs.

Whereas mild cramping can be alleviated using peppermint or chamomile, the active ingredients of **deadly nightshade,** or **belladonna** (101), still remain the agent of choice for severe cramps in the gastrointestinal tract. Belladonna is a classical, highly effective medicinal plant whose components, such as atropine or papaverine, provide the ideal requirements for the pure substances demanded of medicinal plants. Isolated, standardized, and then prescribed in precise, small doses, the pharmaceutical agents have proven to be highly effective in the hands of physicians. But consuming only a few of the berries from this plant may be deadly, so its use is by no means suitable for self-treatment.

Herbal Remedies

For a sensation of pressure, heartburn, hyperacidity, and mild inflammations of the stomach's mucous membranes:
❖ Use chamomile blossoms brewed as a tea or chamomile extract in a "roll cure" (see page 179 for a description of this cure).
❖ Drink a large cup of lukewarm chamomile tea after getting out of bed in the morning.
❖ Take a cold infusion made from mucilaginous linseeds or the root of the common marshmallow.
❖ Lie relaxed for 5 minutes on your back, 5 minutes on your left side, 5 minutes on your stomach, and then 5 minutes on your right side in order to rinse the inner walls of the stomach from all sides.

A gastrointestinal tea made up of the following ingredients is also helpful:

Chamomile blossoms	30.0 g
Peppermint leaves	30.0 g
Common, or lemon, balm leaves	30.0 g

Drink 1 to 2 cups three times a day.

For nervous gastric disorders, indigestion, and nausea, a calming and relaxing tea with these ingredients is recommended:

Chamomile blossoms	20.0 g
Peppermint leaves	10.0 g
Common balm leaves	10.0 g
Fruit of the hops	5.0 g

Drink 1 to 2 cups three times a day slowly.

You might also try drinking a warm cup of milk mixed with chamomile tea (in equal amounts) before going to sleep.

For a weak stomach or a sense of pressure following meals, these remedies are effective:
❖ Absinth sagewort, mugwort, sweet basil, marjoram, and thyme, taken as an herb
❖ Absinth sagewort and thyme, taken as a brewed tea
❖ Gentian tincture: 20 drops taken before meals

To promote the secretion of gastric juices and to stimulate the appetite:
❖ Take bitter drops, consisting of alcohol extractions from the angelica root, chamomile blossoms, caraway, blessed milk thistle, leaves of the common balm, peppermint leaves, greater celandine herbage, and licorice root. The dosage is 20 drops three times a day, for a few days if you have a chronic condition, and for just one day otherwise.
❖ Drink a single-substance tea made from gentian root or centaury.

This tea mixture works well too:

Gentian root	20.0 g
Peel of the Seville, or bitter, orange	20.0 g
Centaury herbage	25.0 g
Absinth sagewort herbage	25.0 g
Dandelion herbage	10.0 g

Drink 1 to 2 cups of the unsweetened tea three times a day.

Supportive Measures

❖ A wet wrap or a "hay sack"
❖ A footbath of increasing temperature (starting at 33°C, or 91.4°F, and increasing to about 39°C, or 102.2°F, over the course of 15 to 20 minutes)
❖ Regular meals eaten slowly
❖ Better management of stress (eventually including drinking a tea made from the common Saint-John's-wort)

FOR THAT UNCOMFORTABLE BLOATED FEELING
Medicinal Herbs to Reduce Flatulence and a Feeling of Fullness

Everyone is familiar with the sensation of feeling blown up like a balloon. Excessive gas in the upper abdomen can result from an inadequate resorption of the gas that develops in the intestines by means of fermentation, or it can be due to functional disturbances in the biliary system. If the release of gas from the gastrointestinal tract is hindered by cramps at the inlet of the stomach or cramping of the intestines, colicky pains and belching can ensue. The unpleasant feeling of being bloated not only puts pressure on the heart but also influences the mood, appetite, and sleep. Eating such gas-forming foods as cabbage, beans, and fresh whole-grain bread further intensifies these complaints.

Ironically, people often suffer from colicky pains and a feeling of fullness when they start to eat more healthfully. Motivated by newspaper articles and aroused by a bad conscience following rich holiday meals, they decide to strike sugary desserts and white bread from their diets. Keeping an eye on proper nutrition, these eager, well-meaning individuals search for whole-grain foods and dietary fibers. They add crunchy raw vegetables and whole grains to their diet, finding they taste surprisingly good. Enjoying whole wheat rolls, they discover that the toast they were accustomed to now tastes like cardboard. However, this extreme change in nutrition puts demands on the gastrointestinal tract that are hard to handle. In changing your diet, it is therefore vital to add these new nutrients gradually.

Herbs as Carminative Agents

The fruit from a number of plants in the parsley, or carrot, family are known to provide exceptional relief from flatulence, and are collectively grouped under the heading of "carminatives" (agents used to expel gas from the intestines). Foremost among these plants are **caraway** (40), **fennel** (67), and anise, as well as coriander. Carminatives contain essential oils that have a spasmolytic effect, are antifermentative, and promote digestion throughout the entire gastrointestinal tract. Therefore, they also aid in the removal of gas from the stomach.

We are aware of this beneficial effect from the fennel tea that is often given to babies to relieve them of their tummy aches. Although fennel has been used in folk medicine to promote milk secretion in nursing mothers and tear production in cases of tired eyes, its spasmolytic and mildly narcotic effects are in the forefront today. Fennel is also made use of as a flavoring in teas as well as in breads and other baked goods, and as an aromatic agent in liqueurs. Sebastian Kneipp was aware of its effects, having said, "Fennel powder as a seasoning eliminates the gasses from the stomach and the lower regions."

An even stronger gas-eliminating effect is observed from the ripe dehiscent fruit of the caraway, which also stimulates the appetite and promotes the secretion of gastric juices. Caraway is not only used as a tea and a seasoning, but it is also regarded highly as an agent with stomach-strengthening effects in the form of a liqueur. In addition, well-informed cooks use caraway to season foods that cause flatulence. In this instance, we can easily recognize the transition from a seasoning agent to a mild medicinal herb.

Fennel and caraway are often combined in drops and tablets with extracts or herbal powders from the spasmolytic peppermint or gentian root, with its stimulatory effects on the gastric juices. Two of these herbal tablets taken before meals demonstrate a noticeable relief.

The milk powder given to young children who are bottle-fed can easily be mixed with diluted fennel tea. Or a teaspoon of anise and fennel oils in honey can be added to the bottle. What is not recommended is dipping the child's pacifier in fennel honey—not only because of the teeth, but it can also lead to diarrhea. The "wind ointments" with marjoram or caraway, which were formerly very common, are worth an attempt in the case of babies who suffer from flatulence, perhaps also supported by an electric heating pad that is not too hot.

If you have heartburn as well, the combination of caraway with coriander is recommended. Anise fruit is a good carminative but an even better flavoring agent. Consider the pleasant taste of an anise loaf; anise is also used in a number of aperitifs.

Here are a few practical tips regarding the preparation of teas using these herbs. It's important for the fruit to be used always when freshly ground; this way, the effective essential oils are liberated better from the broken oil glands. As the essential oils are volatile in steam, the tea mixtures should not be boiled but instead brewed with simmering water and left to steep for 10 minutes in a covered container. The drops that condense on the bottom of the cover should also be drained into the tea, for they contain large quantities of the effective agents.

Herbal Remedies

For flatulence, a feeling of fullness in the upper abdomen, and intolerance to certain foods, this tea mixture is helpful:

Anise fruit	15.0 g
Fennel fruit	15.0 g
Caraway fruit	5.0 g
Chamomile blossoms	20.0 g
Peppermint leaves	10.0 g

The fruit must be ground. Have 1 to 2 cups three times a day after meals. This tea mixture is suitable for babies if the peppermint is left out.

Similarly effective are the following:

❖ Taking two flatulence tablets, containing fennel fruit, caraway fruit, peppermint leaves, and gentian root, three times a day after meals

❖ Massaging pure caraway oil or a 10-percent solution into the skin of the abdomen above the stomach

❖ Using the Seville, or bitter, orange peel in the form of a tincture

As heartburn can result from pressure on the heart because of a gas-filled gastrointestinal system, here are a couple of *remedies for heartburn:*

❖ Tea brewed from caraway and coriander fruit: 1 to 2 cups of unsweetened tea three times a day after meals

❖ Peppermint oil, either pure or in the form of a capsule

Supportive Measures

❖ Seasoning foods that cause flatulence using caraway, coriander, fennel, and anise

❖ Movement following meals

❖ "Hay sack" on the stomach or upper abdomen in cases of cramps

❖ Refraining from drinking too much or too quickly during meals

ALTERNATIVES TO TRADITIONAL LAXATIVES
Medicinal Herbs for Constipation and Sluggishness of the Bowels

For people who tend to be constipated, becoming "regular" is one of the greatest joys on earth. Many people suffer from occasional or chronic constipation, associated with abdominal pain, a feeling of fullness, and flatulence. But instead of taking a look at the causes of this uncomfortable condition, they all too readily reach for a laxative. Constipation, however, has a number of clear-cut causes, including the following:

❖ An irregular lifestyle with psychological stress
❖ Inadequate or imbalanced nutrition with little dietary fiber
❖ A lack of fluids (especially in the elderly)
❖ A lack of movement or prolonged sitting, so that the food remains undigested in the body for too long

Metabolic disturbances like a thyroid insufficiency or mechanical obstructions in the intestines (such as bowel occlusion, polyps, or painful hemorrhoids) are rarely the cause. In such cases, however, a physician should definitely be consulted.

So, before running to the drugstore, go to the root of the affliction and attempt to change your habits:

❖ Consciously try to reduce the amount of stress in your life. Consider giving meditation, yoga, or visualizations a chance, and set aside some time during the day just for yourself.
❖ Make a point of eating more whole-grain foods, vegetables, salads, and fruit. Chew thoroughly, and allow enough saliva to develop.
❖ Drink at least 2 liters, or quarts, of fluids a day, perhaps starting with a glass of water or fruit juice early in the morning.
❖ Get sufficient physical exercise. For instance, do gymnastics for your abdomen or ride a stationary bicycle in the morning. Leave your car at home for a change.
❖ It's also helpful to go to the toilet at the same time each day; train your intestines to be punctual.

If these suggestions cannot be carried out, or if they prove to be ineffective, the use of a laxative can then be contemplated. With the short-term, controlled application of a laxative, it is possible to regulate your bowels. Laxatives can be helpful when traveling, beginning a cure, or changing your diet, or for specific types of diets, or if you are confined to a bed. They are recommended especially following surgery and for patients with painful anal afflictions who suffer doubly with constipation.

Laxatives are available in various forms, including dietary fibers, bulk-forming agents, lubricants, saline cathartics, and contact cathartics that stimulate the large intestine. However, for an acute case of constipation or if the stool must be loosened temporarily (say, for a medical procedure), herbal laxative teas or tablets have proven to be the method of choice. A tea brewed from senna leaves or husks or from buckthorn bark, for example, can be made weak or strong to suit the individual's needs.

However, used long-term or at high doses, most laxatives can lead to a loss of minerals, along with the loss of liquids, and to the production of overly liquid stools. The loss of potassium in particular can disturb the cardiovascular system, reduce the rate of mental and physical reactions, and intensify the effects of cardioactive medications.

Various Herbal Options

The plant substance caster oil from the **castor bean** (228) promotes a wavelike contraction of the intestines, thus bringing about a further transportation through the intestinal tract. One teaspoon of the oil is taken on an empty stomach. The purgative effect occurs dramatically 2 to 4 hours later. However, as a fatty oil, it is not suitable in the event of biliary disturbances.

Bulk-forming agents, which form a voluminous, indigestible mucilage in the intestines following an adequate amount of water, are both harmless and effective. However, aside from having to drink a lot of water with them, you need to have a great deal of patience, for they usually function only after two to three days. The most popular bulk-forming agent is the **common flax,** or **linseed** (219). It's important to be aware that a dose of linseeds has between 200 and 500 calories (linseed oil!). Yet some of these calories can be eliminated by allowing the seeds to swell in water for 2 hours beforehand.

Perhaps a better choice is psyllium seeds, as they are especially nonirritating, almost free of calories, and highly capable of swelling. These seeds are derived from a type of plantain that is considered to be the "linseed of Italy." In many places, they are available as whole seeds loose or in packages for a single application, or with only the mucilaginous husks of the seeds.

Dietary fibers, which can be obtained from fruit, vegetables, and whole-grain foods such as **oats** (189) and wheat bran from **common wheat** (192), are continuing to be increasingly important to individuals with disturbances in their digestion. Dietary fibers are valuable for the ecological equilibrium of the digestive tract. They increase the weight of the stool and thus bring about a mechanical stimulus on the intestines. They also shorten the duration of the gastrointestinal passage and help to make the stool softer. As a side benefit, and one that is frequently sought, they serve to curb the sensation of hunger. Foods rich in fibers also seem to have a protective effect against the development of diverticulitis and intestinal cancer.

Fortunately, whole-grain foods are now in vogue. Types of grain that had almost been forgotten like the **common spelt,** or **German wheat** (191), which Sebastian Kneipp valued so highly, are being cultivated again. Fruit laxatives such as plums, figs, and a tamarind drink, contain fruit acids and pectins as well as dietary fibers. As with hibiscus blossom tea and sauerkraut, they have a mildly regulating effect, are free of adverse effects, and can be used long-term.

Make use of dietary fibers routinely, and be sure to drink plenty of fluids. Don't let initial cases of flatulence deter you.

Even people who are stressed out from their jobs and eat in fast-food restaurants can easily take fruit-fiber or bran tablets and munch on granola bars today. There's a broad spectrum of choices for this common problem.

Specific Herbal Remedies

For a short-term application for acute cases of constipation and to soften the stool:

❖ Drink a laxative tea from senna fruit, blackthorn blossoms, and peppermint leaves. Have ½ to 1 cup of this tea in the evening before going to bed (defecation should occur within 6 to 8 hours). This tea should not be used in the event of pains in the lower abdomen, because of a danger of intestinal obstruction, or by pregnant or nursing women.

❖ Take laxative tablets containing a dry extract from senna fruit. One to three tablets are recommended with fluids in the evening. These agents should not be taken in the event of intestinal obstructions, acute inflammatory illnesses of the digestive tract, or cases of abdominal pain.

Swelling and bulk-forming agents for stimulating the intestines naturally include the following:

❖ Linseeds: Take 1 tablespoon with a minimum of 2 cups of fluids two or three times daily with meals. Flatulence may occur without sufficient fluids. If you have an inflammatory intestinal illness, the linseeds should be allowed to swell in water before being ingested.

❖ Psyllium seeds (*Plantago psyllium*): Rapidly stir 1 tablespoon in a glass of cold water, tea, or fruit juice, and take immediately, two or three times a day before or after meals. More fluids should be consumed afterward.

❖ Fruit-fiber tablets: Take two to six tablets with one or two glasses of water or herbal tea 20 minutes before each meal.

NATURAL BINDING AGENTS
Medicinal Herbs for Mild Cases of Diarrhea

Illnesses involving diarrhea tend to be more prevalent during the summer. Frequently independent of food intake, they are usually due to a harmless viral infection that becomes acute during the transitional period from colder to warmer weather. Whereas vegetable agents are effective only as supportive measures in the treatment of infectious diarrhea, the mild cases of diarrhea that often occur in the summer can be treated well with medicinal herbs containing tannin.

Sources of Tannin

The **erect cinquefoil, tormentil,** or **bloodroot** (169), is a plant rich in tannins, containing from 15 to 20 percent of these substances. The root, which gradually turns red during storage, is the part used medicinally. A pinch of the dried powder or a decoction from this root helps to counteract diarrhea, especially in the case of particularly odiferous stools. If you are concurrently suffering from flatulence, an equal amount of caraway is recommended as well. The antibacterial effects are attributed to the plant's red coloring agent, which, similar to the synthetic coloring agent aniline, has a disinfectant outcome.

The blue coloring agent of the **bilberry** is credited with having similar antibacterial effects. Yet only the dried fruit, containing 7 percent tannin, is effective against diarrhea. A number of the dried berries should be chewed over the course of a day. However, in sensitive adults and in children, the irritation of the already unsound intestinal mucous membranes is further intensified by the skin and pips of the fruit. This is why bilberry is often taken in the form of a decoction or an extremely concentrated, unsweetened juice, both of which are less irritating. The juice is sometimes mixed with cottage cheese, increasing the binding outcome. When the fruit is mixed with milk and sugar, it has an especially extensive cathartic effect. But remember not to use the fresh fruit.

Sebastian Kneipp said, "No house should be without dried bilberries, which are saved throughout the year. Whoever suffers from diarrhea should chew and swallow a dried, raw bilberry from time to time. This mild agent is frequently adequate. I have seen many guests at large spas who have taken along the 'antidiarrheal pilules' from their experienced and prudent wives in order to avoid an unpleasant surprise during a hike."

In addition to the proven binding home remedies like rice water, taken alternately with a freshly grated apple (pectin), bananas, or dark, bitter chocolate, **black tea** is a popular treatment for diarrhea. This dark tea, which is rich in tannin, should be allowed to steep for at least 10 minutes. Black tea is also suitable for children.

It's often a good idea to add a pinch of salt to the tea. Several cups of this tea not only replace the fluids lost as a result of the frequent, watery stools, but also the vital minerals lacking for the same reason. The loss of both fluids and minerals, especially in children and the elderly, may occasionally lead to a state of weakness that can be so severe that it becomes life-threatening. An alternative to using loose tea or tea bags is making a tea by dissolving a tea tablet, which you can purchase at a drugstore. These tablets are not only very easy to use but also have the advantage of containing magnesium and potassium.

As a proven home remedy, activated charcoal cannot be neglected either, as it counteracts the toxins and bacteria while at the same time having a binding effect if taken in an adequate concentration.

Using the agents noted here, your complaints should be relieved after two to three days; otherwise, a physician should be consulted.

Useful Tea Mixtures

The following tea mixtures can be helpful for mild cases of diarrhea:

Bilberry fruit	20.0 g
Common balm leaves	10.0 g

Chamomile blossoms	10.0 g
or	
Erect cinquefoil root	20.0 g
Peppermint leaves	10.0 g
Chamomile blossoms	10.0 g

Bring 1 to 2 teaspoons of the mixture in 1 cup of water to a simmer, and let steep in an open container for 5 to 10 minutes. Take 3 to 4 cups daily.

WHEN PAINFUL COLICS THREATEN
Medicinal Herbs for Gallbladder and Liver Conditions

*D*isturbances of the biliary system mainly involve the insufficient production or the inadequate secretion of bile. Gallstones, for instance, formed in the gallbladder or the biliary passages, affect many people, although they may not even be aware that they have them. Gallstones are frequently the cause of painful colics or may result in an inflammation of the gallbladder. Should you have gallstones, you have no choice but to visit your physician. Nevertheless, herbal agents also play an important role, especially in the treatment of functional disturbances or as a preventive measure, should such a colic attack appear to be unavoidable. However, in contrast to traditional forms of therapy for the treatment of gallbladder conditions, herbal agents are milder, demonstrate a more compensative and regulatory effect, and generally offer no strong, immediate relief.

Effective Herbal Agents

Absinth sagewort, or **common wormwood** (293), in the form of a tea or drops, has proven to be the most effective medicinal plant for gallbladder conditions. With absinth sagewort, it is important to know the best time for harvesting, because its concentration of the bitter principle absinthin increases twice as much when the plant is in full blossom.

Sebastian Kneipp described the enormous "bitter value" of this plant as follows: "Like a tiny pellet of frankincense glowing on a coal that fills an entire room with its pleasant aroma, a leaf of the absinth sagewort, or common wormwood, 'breathes' a bitter taste into a whole bottle of spirits—a sign of the strength and efficacy of the tincture." Furthermore, he said that travelers who frequently suffer from stomach complaints and nausea should always bring with them "their bottle with a tincture of the absinth sagewort, or common wormwood, as their faithful companion."

In addition to its strictly medicinal applications, wormwood is used in appetite-increasing and digestion-promoting vermouths and aperitifs. Vermouth stimulates the functions of the biliary tract and the stomach, while also providing an overall strengthening effect by heightening the defensive powers of the body.

Should a colic threaten, 30 to 50 drops of a wormwood tincture should be taken in very warm water or a wormwood tea should be drunk while as hot as possible. The gallbladder will then calm itself down. In addition, warm applications of "hay-flower sacks" may provide relief for or shorten the duration of gallbladder colics.

If a tea is to stimulate the gallbladder or the bile production, you need to drink 1 cup after meals for a period of three to four weeks. This tea must be taken unsweetened, as bitter and sweet flavors don't mix well.

Gallbladder and liver teas are usually effective in providing relief from such complaints associated with reduced bile production or secretion as mild constipation, pressure in the region of the gallbladder, a disturbed digestion of fats, and a feeling of fullness with flatulence. Mixtures of herbs containing bitter principles with those that have a spasmolytic and carminative effect (against flatulence) or mixed tinctures (bitter drops) are tolerated very well and generally provide quite rapid relief.

The roots and the herbage of the common **dandelion** (55) contain bitter principles and mineral salts that function choleretically (stimulate bile flow), without having an extremely bitter taste. In France, the tender, springtime leaves are frequently used in salads. In addition to the bitter principle taraxerol, this plant contains enzymatically active substances that stimulate the activity of the liver and kidneys. This component is also said to have an inhibitory effect on the development of gallstones.

A proven agent in the treatment of gallbladder disturbances is the **black salsify,** or **oyster plant.** The juice of the plant, which loses its sharp taste if allowed to stand for a while, has a strengthening effect on the musculature of the biliary tract, enabling the bile to flow better. In addition, there is an improvement in the intestinal flora. Nevertheless, with this agent, a long-term cure is not recommended.

The **artichoke,** known to many as only a vegetable, is a plant from the Mediterranean region that contains a bitter substance (cynaropicrin) and cynarin. The later has an effect on both the liver and the gallbladder. It stimulates the secretion of bile, while having a protective effect on and stimulating the flow of blood in the liver, thus promoting its regeneration. Artichoke juice (1 tablespoon taken three times a day before or during meals) is also claimed to have a lipid-reducing effect on the fat metabolism. This can explain its favorable consequences on the development of gallstones.

Although herbal agents have an effect on the symptoms of pain, pressure, and nausea, as well as on the digestive complaints associated with gallbladder disturbances, they must be used with care when taken for the often recommended indication of liver illnesses. In fact, liver ailments should generally not be handled by means of self-treatment. Fatigue, a lack of appetite, allergic reactions, and constipation may indeed develop during liver illnesses, but are not in themselves enough to justify the claim that they are caused by the liver. When it comes to liver ailments, it is sensible to use medicinal herbs mainly preventively. Still, with certain liver ailments, herbs can provide support and relief when employed in conjunction with a special diet and abstinence from alcohol.

A warming therapy in the form of a "hay-flower sack"—a procedure that improves the blood circulation through the liver cells—has proven to be effective in cases involving a swollen liver. The strengthening effect on the liver cells is attributed to such **"hay flowers"** (221–224) as the root of the dandelion, the mugwort, the peppermint, and the brown knapweed.

The protective effect on the liver brought about by the silybin in the **milk thistle** (82) has been verified scientifically. This well-known medicinal plant from the Mediterranean region is still found in the monastery garden here in Bad Wörishofen. Together with other medications, silybin, a component of silymarin, helps to restore the damaging effects of various hepatic toxins. Even the fatal consequences of consuming certain mushrooms that results in liver destruction can be halted by taking high concentrations of silymarin. In addition, it reduces the formation of sub-

stances in the tissues that may promote an inflammation, supports the biosynthesis of proteins, and accelerates the cell-regeneration processes of the liver. In cases of chronic hepatitis, it substantially improves the gastrointestinal complaints, especially the sense of pressure in the upper abdomen. Unfortunately, it's very difficult to prescribe silymarin as a tea at the proper dosage. In the form of tablets, however, when combined with a special diet, it is suitable for use in the prophylactic therapy of acute jaundice and for the fatty degeneration of the liver.

Greater celandine (31), a member of the poppy family, with a yellow, milky sap, should not be overlooked either. In his *Doctrine of Signatures* Paracelsus stated that the effects of a plant could be "read" through its form and appearance. Therefore, it was believed that this plant's yellow, milky sap which resembles bile, must be effective in the treatment of complaints involving the liver and gallbladder that manifest in a yellow discoloration of the skin. In fact, it has been verified that the components in this sap, which, a mild spasmolytic and calming effect on the gallbladder. Yet a sensible dosage is necessary, as overdoses can lead to stomach pains.

Now a brief word on the pancreas: In addition to the pancreatic juices that help to support the digestive processes in the small intestine, the islets of Langerhans are responsible for the production of insulin and glucagon. Insulin regulates the sugar balance of the body, and a deficiency leads to the development of diabetes mellitus, a widespread illness affecting millions of people. Although medicinal herbs are not suitable directly for the treatment of diabetes, such agents as bean skins, bilberries, stinging nettle, and goldenrod, as well as ginseng, can be employed as supportive measures. However, in no way can they serve as a replacement for the carefully monitored diet and the prescribed medication. Maintaining both while also losing weight, with or without medicinal herbs, is frequently the best advice.

Further Remedies

In cases of a "restless" gallstone and the beginning of colic:

❖ Brew absinth sagewort and brown knapweed as a tea. When needed, 1 to 2 cups of the tea should be taken unsweetened and as hot as possible. Or 30 to 50 drops of a wormwood tincture should be taken in half a glass of very warm water.

❖ Lay a "hay sack" on the painful site.

For colicky complaints in the region of the biliary ducts:

❖ Take pure peppermint oil or peppermint in a capsule diluted with olive oil.

❖ Take greater celandine extract in the form of a capsule.

A liver/gallbladder tea with the following ingredients is also helpful:

Peppermint leaves	40.0 g
Curcuma root (turmeric)	15.0 g
Dandelion herbage with roots	45.0 g

Take 1 cup several times a day for a few weeks.

The following remedies are used *to stimulate the secretion of bile and in the event of digestive disorders:*

❖ Drops with extracts from the greater celandine, the milfoil (or yarrow), herbage from the dandelion, curcuma root, artichoke leaves, and herbage from the absinth sagewort

❖ Plant juice from the artichoke or extracts from artichoke leaves in capsule form

❖ Plant juice from the dandelion or the black salsify (or oyster plant): 1 tablespoon after meals two or three times a day

These herbs are useful *as a prophylactic measure against the development of liver complaints and for strengthening the liver function:*

❖ Dandelion herbage and roots with milk thistle fruit brewed as a tea

❖ Extract from the milk thistle (standardized): an average daily dose of 200 to 400 milligrams of silymarin

Supportive Measures

❖ A footbath with "hay flowers" of increasing temperature, a wet wrap

❖ Fasting with tea, or no between-meal snacks

❖ Improved management of stress

STRENGTHENING YOUR HEART
Medicinal Herbs for Cardiovascular Disorders

*I*llnesses of the cardiovascular system are very diverse, may be congenital or may develop over the course of life, and are occasionally caused by infectious diseases. Risk factors common today—like stress, smoking, insufficient exercise, poor nutrition, alcohol abuse, and being overweight—have led to a huge increase in the pathological constriction of the coronary vessels (arteriosclerosis) and in the development of cardiac arrhythmia. Disturbances in heart sensations or the development of illnesses require the attention of a physician. If the physician is a naturopath or makes use of natural remedies, he or she may prescribe specific dosages of herbal medications containing the active components of **foxglove** (181–184), **squill, European lily of the valley** (121), or **oleander leaves.**

If your physician tells you that everything is in order organically, and you just want to do something that helps preventively or as a supportive measure, a mild medicinal plant that you can use is **whitethorn** (109, 297). Of course, it also helps to eliminate the risk factors mentioned above. The blossoms, leaves, and fruit of this shrub can be used in high doses in the form of a tea, drops, or capsules. Although in the past the "minor heart therapy" associated with the whitethorn was considered to be equivalent to no therapy at all, the following effects of this plant have since been verified scientifically:

❖ The coronary vessels become diluted, and the circulation is improved.

❖ The myocardium is strengthened, the oxygen supply is improved, and the cardiac output is increased.

❖ A mildly irregular pulse (extrasystole, or gallop rhythm) becomes regulated.

A prerequisite for success with this agent is using it long-term and in high doses. Whitethorn preparations don't contain specific pharmaceutical agents for the treatment of acute cardiac illnesses, but are primarily proven prophylactic agents used for a number of indications, such as a reduced cardiac capacity as observed in the elderly, sensations of pressure and constriction in the region of the heart, and mild disturbances in the heart rhythm. People who drink whitethorn tea generally feel more lively. But at the same time, whitethorn preparations are known to have a calming effect, which is why they are especially effective for the treatment of nervous heart ailments.

A Few Words About Blood Pressure
As a result of the rhythmic impulses of the heart, the pressure in the arteries varies. This pressure on the walls of the blood vessels is measured as blood pressure: the systolic pressure during the contraction of the heart muscle, and the low value, the diastolic pressure, while the myocardium is relaxed. Today, a normal value is considered to be 140/90 mmHg. Values that are below 100/70 mmHg over relatively long periods of time are considered to be low blood pressure (or hypotension), whereas those that are continuously 160/95 mmHg or higher are regarded as high blood pressure (or hypertension).

Systolic values between 140 and 160 mmHg need to be controlled, and may eventually be reduced through eating a low-sodium diet. In addition to seasoning your food with herbs instead of salt, magnesium salts may be helpful. High blood pressure is a dangerous risk factor for sclerotic vascular constriction, leading to impairments of the heart, blood vessels, and kidneys, and needs to be treated by a physician. Although individuals with high blood pressure frequently feel quite healthy, they should control their blood pressure regularly.

Treating Hypertension
Unfortunately, there is no mild herbal agent that reliably reduces high blood pressure. **European mistletoe** (218), which lives as a parasite on trees, is recommended in folk medicine for lowering blood pressure, but neither mistletoe tea, capsules, nor drops have yet been verified unequivocally. Its stimulating effects on the defense system and the antitumorigenic effects of diluted solutions used as an injection for the treatment of cancer, on the other hand, have been proven

scientifically. Hypertension, a condition that affects millions of people, along with elevated blood-lipid levels and a conglomeration of the thrombocytes, are the three principal risk factors for arteriosclerosis, popularly known as "hardening of the arteries." This is often the cause of myocardial infarctions, strokes, and occlusive arterial diseases.

However, **garlic** (225) can be used in this context. Garlic has a long tradition as a medicinal herb, and its effects have been verified scientifically, This bulb, employed as a popular kitchen herb, occupies the transitional position between an herb and a medicinal agent. Fresh garlic cloves, garlic extracts, and garlic powder have the following consequences:

❖ They have an anti-infectious effect against bacteria, fungi, and parasites.

❖ They reduce the cholesterol level—that is, the dangerous LDL-cholesterol level—whereas the concentration of HDL-cholesterol, which protects against the development of arteriosclerosis, increases.

❖ The conglomeration of thrombocytes and the subsequent coagulation of the blood is inhibited.

Garlic cloves and garlic preparations primarily function as a result of their sulfur-containing components, which are also responsible for the unpleasant odor. Of course, fresh garlic cloves are the most effective, although many people are deterred from their use because of the odor. Parsley, common juniper berries, cloves, chlorophyll tablets, and chewing gum are said to be good antidotes. But the unpleasant-smelling fission products of allicin are absorbed and then eliminated not only by the lungs but also through the pores in the skin. Therefore, all of the claims made are dubious. Basically, if garlic can't be smelled, it has no effect.

Garlic is available in various forms. The plant juice is closest in function to the natural product. The tablets, which are pressed from the powder and/or extract and then coated, are very effective too. They have the advantage of not only containing fat-soluble but also water-soluble components. However, combination preparations with whitethorn, mistletoe, hops, rutin, or ginseng usually contain such a low dosage of garlic that they must be considered merely "alibi" combinations.

An average daily dose of 4 grams of fresh garlic is recommended. Two to 3 grams should be adequate as a prophylactic dose; this is equivalent to 600 to 1,000 milligrams of the dry extract or, in the usual doses, two tablets taken three times a day.

Garlic preparations should not be given to children. Overdoses in adults also result in stomachaches, vomiting, and changes in the mucous membranes.

Treating Hypotension

It's been claimed that with low blood pressure you may live long but poorly. In contrast to people with high blood pressure, who generally feel good, individuals with low blood pressure tend to be fatigued and generally unenthusiastic. Everything is too much for them, and they complain of having no energy, especially in the morning. Except possibly in risk groups, such as the elderly and children, the feelings of ill-health that are experienced don't necessarily require treatment.

However, if these complaints become more severe, with the development of dizziness, a lack of appetite, poor concentration, ringing in the ears, or circulatory disturbances in the hands and feet, it's wise to take advantage of Sebastian Kneipp's favorite plant, **rosemary** (44). In this case, the needlelike leaves are used because of their high concentration of essential oil. The primary component, the "rosemary camphor," like true camphor, is not only centrally activating and tonicizing on the circulatory system but also causes an elevation in blood pressure. As the pure tea tastes somewhat bitter, it can be mixed with a cardiovascular tea, or rosemary can be taken in the form of a wine. Sebastian Kneipp espoused its use as a wine, saying, "Small portions of rosemary wine have proven to be an effective agent against a weakness of the heart."

Warm, activating rosemary baths in the morning or early afternoon are especially popular. These baths can be used in conjunction with mild, short-term cold stimuli in the form of arm baths, water treading, exercises and sports that tone the muscles and the blood vessels, repeated saunas, or massages. Whereas rosemary spirits (an agent that was previously very popular and made from alcoholic liniment intensified with camphor and menthol) have been forgotten to some extent, the heart balms containing rosemary oil are being used more and more today. These heart balms have a comforting, tonicizing, and relieving effect on mild heart complaints when massaged into the region of the heart a number of times a day.

Ephedrine, an alkaloid found in the ephedra, or desert herb, with its blood-pressure-elevating effect, has frequently been abused and is therefore not prescribed today. Yet the early-morning cup of coffee or even black tea, which should steep for only 2 to 3 minutes, can be recommended as a home remedy. Here, as well, the dose of these agents could make them into harmful stimulants. But sometimes merely the aroma of a morning cup of coffee is enough to bring about the stimulus. The effects of coffee, as with pure caffeine, begin quite rapidly, only to disappear within a relatively short time. With tea, the stimulus develops more gradually and is reduced more gradually as well. Therefore, coffee tends to be more invigorating in the morning, and tea is more effective for individuals who want to put in several hours of work.

Remedies

For a reduced functional capacity of the heart, a sensation of pressure or constriction in the heart region, or a geriatric heart (a heart weakened by age), the following remedies with whitethorn are helpful:

❖ Whitethorn tea made from the leaves and blossoms: Steep the tea for 10 minutes. Drink 1 to 2 cups three times a day.

❖ Plant juice from the whitethorn: Take 1 tablespoon before meals two or three times a day.

❖ Dry extract from whitethorn leaves and blossoms as a solution or as capsules (a daily dose of 45 to 90 milligrams of oligomeric proanthocyadins)

Or try this cardiovascular tea:

Rosemary leaves	35.0 g
Whitethorn leaves	35.0 g
Common motherwort herbage	5.0 g
Common Saint-John's-wort	20.0 g
Green maté	15.0 g

Drink 1 cup before breakfast and in the afternoon.

To stimulate the circulatory system and in the event of low blood pressure, there are a number of options:

❖ Rosemary leaves brewed as a tea: Drink 1 cup in the morning and at noon.

❖ Juice from the rosemary plant: Take 1 tablespoon before meals two or three times a day.

❖ Drops from extracts of whitethorn fruit, camphor, and menthol: Take 5 to 10 drops on sugar or bread as needed.

❖ A hot, full bath with rosemary bath oil or bath salts (at 38°C, or 91.4°F, for 10 to 15 minutes, resting after the bath)

❖ Contrasting-temperature arm baths, footbaths, or affusions

❖ Heart ointment with rosemary oil, menthol, and camphor: Massage in the ointment in the region of the heart and the surrounding area a few times a day.

Although hypertension must be treated by a physician, there are various *supportive measures for high blood pressure* you can employ yourself:

❖ A cold infusion from mistletoe: Mix 1 to 2 heaping teaspoons of mistletoe with cold water, allow to steep for 6 to 8 hours; after straining, bring to a short boil. Take 1 cup three times a day.

❖ Juice from the mistletoe or mistletoe tablets: Take 1 tablespoon of the juice three or four times a day or one or two tablets 1 to 2 hours after meals.

❖ A bath (three-quarters full) with common, or lemon, balm or garden valerian

❖ A dry-brush massage

❖ Cold, wet compresses around the calves

For nervous heart complaints, try this tea mixture:

Whitethorn leaves with blossoms	30.0 g
Common balm leaves	30.0 g
Mistletoe herbage	20.0 g
Common Saint-John's-wort	20.0 g

Take 1 to 2 cups daily.

For circulatory disturbances, dizziness, or a lack of concentration, the dry extract from ginkgo leaves in the form of standardized capsules is known to be effective (daily dose of 30 to 60 milligrams of ginkgo flavone glycosides).

Overall Supportive Measures

❖ Ablutions, water treading

❖ Walking, endurance sports, breathing exercises

❖ Stress management, including autogenic training such as biofeedback

❖ Affusions with contrasting temperatures

INSTEAD OF SLEEPING PILLS AND TRANQUILIZERS
Medicinal Herbs for Insomnia, Nervousness, and Depression

any people don't get enough sleep. But how much sleep do we actually need? The sleep requirement differs according to age. A baby sleeps as much as 16 to 18 hours a day. A six-year-old child requires about 10 hours. In adults, the need for sleep varies from 5 to 9 hours a day, with the average between 7 and 8 hours. It is claimed that the elderly require even fewer hours of sleep; however, their shorter sleep patterns may have more to do with daily habits than with less need for sleep.

Without a routine or a daily rhythm, people who are retired usually get up later. They often interrupt the asleep–awake rhythm of the body by taking intermittent naps, and miss the point when they are bone-tired and should go to bed because they are watching television, for instance. All of this can lead to insomnia or troubled sleep. In addition, as their bodies no longer have to undergo such rigorous demands, the deep-sleep phases of regeneration are now lacking.

If you are able to fall asleep but awaken during the night, it's likely that you are overloaded with problems and stress. In such cases, rather than struggling to get back to sleep or "counting sheep," it's far better to get up and read a book, listen to some soothing music, drink a cup of calming tea, or even wash your feet with cool water. But what is most important is to try to resolve the conflicts causing your distress.

Three Important Calming Agents

Disturbed sleep, nervousness, nervous exhaustion, and stress (from a constantly increasing workload or relationship or money problems, for example) can all cause people to reach for some kind of tablet that functions as "rose-colored glasses for the psyche." Yet sleeping pills, which act as tranquilizers and forcibly induce sleep, are rarely the right solution, and more times than not cause a "hangover" the next morning.

When many people request a milder agent, they are advised to take a preparation containing valerian. However, accustomed to strong medications, they often doubt the effectiveness of a "mere herb," insisting it won't help at all.

Nevertheless, experiments performed in sleep laboratories have clearly proven this opinion to be incorrect. The centrally sedative effects of **garden valerian** (89) have been verified scientifically as well. But these effects cannot be definitely attributed to the essential oil or the so-called volepotriates. The advantage of valerian preparations is that they have a calming and relaxing effect without demonstrating any impairments on concentration.

The root of the valerian is used in the form of a tea, tincture, juice, or extract in herbal tablets. When valerian is not effective, it is usually the result of incorrect preparations or doses that are too low. Tea made from valerian should steep for at least 15 minutes. It's best if you brew your "sleep tea" in the morning and then drink it, eventually sweetened with honey, cold or slightly warmed in the evening about a half hour before going to bed. A few drops of a valerian tincture are not enough to promote sleep. The recommended dosage is rather a teaspoon in half a glass of water. Valerian has also been shown to be useful for other complaints. In the event of nervous heart disturbances, 30 drops of the tincture are taken three times a day. For a nervous stomach, an unsweetened tea made from valerian root and chamomile blossoms has proven to be effective.

In addition, **hops** (216) are calming on the nervous system. Along with essential oil and tannins, hops contain the bitter principles humulone and lupulone. Some people have absolute confidence in hops tea sweetened with honey, and use it to help them sleep or to treat a nervous stomach. Because of its volatile components, however, hops should not be cooked, but instead left to steep for 4 to 5 hours. Two teaspoons are used per cup. The effects are even better if hops are mixed with valerian. This combination is particularly effective for nervous insomnia or as an aid in falling asleep.

For instances of nervous agitation, a mixture of valerian with leaves from **common balm,** or **lemon balm** (242), has been shown to be an effective combination. The primary active components of common, or lemon, balm are citronellal, citrals, and geraniol. The leaves of this herb are the calming agents of choice in cases of stress associated with the stomach, as they not only have calmative but also spasmolytic and carminative (against flatulence) effects.

Other Helpful Herbs

Aside from this classical triumverate of calming agents, a number of other herbs are very good for the treatment of nervousness and disturbed sleep when used in drops, teas, or tablets. **Common oats** (189) are suitable as an aid in falling asleep, especially when used in the form of a tincture or an extract. **Orange blossoms,** with their essential oils, not only provide a lovely aroma for tea mixtures and fragrant sachets, but they are also effective when used in calming teas for children and the elderly. For individuals who have difficulties sleeping and are nervous and have trouble concentrating, the herbage of the beautiful **passion flower** is excellent for teas, especially when mixed with the common balm and hops. The juice of the ripe passion fruit is said to have a calming effect as well.

Another medicinal herb that must be mentioned in this context is the **common Saint-John's-wort** (110). This herb is often recommended for nervous or anxious women during menopause, as well as for elderly individuals who tend to brood over their troubles. It's particularly helpful for nervous restlessness and poor concentration, as well as for those times when everything seems to get on our nerves. However, with Saint-John's-wort, there is often an increased sensitivity to sunlight, especially for people with pale complexions.

External Applications

The essential oils of valerian, hops, and common balm are also suitable in a calming evening bath. When restlessness develops as a result of daily stresses and annoyances, a bath with common balm, which is often combined with an equal amount of cymbopogon grass (*Cymbopogon winterianus*), has shown to be very relaxing. Valerian-oil baths pleasantly scented with rose oil and hops-oil baths are ideal aids for falling asleep. Yet it's important not to dawdle before going to bed or to fall asleep while still in the bathtub. Baths with lavender and oat-straw are balancing, as both have sedating and bracing effects, building up the individual through

relaxation. Be sure that such baths are not too hot. The ideal temperature is 37°C (98.6°F), and the recommended duration is about 10 minutes.

Not only are the active substances absorbed through the skin, but the essential oils pleasantly stimulate the olfactory nerves. The latter, of course, is paramount in aromatherapy. For instance, special aromatherapy "sleep pillows" filled with lavender blossoms, hops strobiles, leaves from common balm, or lemon balm, and herbage from common Saint-John's-wort have proven to be very effective. The addition of valerian is a matter of preference.

Kneipp sleeping aids include ablutions at room temperature, as well as washing the feet or wearing wet socks before going to bed (see below).

Specific Remedies

For nervous restlessness and disturbed sleep, these remedies are helpful:

❖ A tea mixture with valerian root, common balm (or lemon balm) leaves, and hops strobiles: In the evening as well as throughout the day, drink 1 to 2 cups of the warm brewed tea sweetened with honey slowly, one sip after another.

❖ Valerian drops: As a relaxing agent, take half a teaspoon diluted in half a glass of water two or three times a day; for sleep problems, take 1 teaspoon diluted in half a glass of water a half hour before going to bed.

❖ Valerian juice and tablets: Take 1 tablespoon of the juice or four to six tablets in the evening.

❖ Capsules with a combination of dry extracts from valerian root and hops strobiles: To calm your nerves, take one or two capsules with water, herb tea, or fruit juice once or twice over the course of the day; to help you fall asleep, take two capsules with water, herb tea, or fruit juice a half hour before going to bed. Extracts from common balm (or lemon balm) leaves, blossoms from the passion flower, the common Saint-John's-wort, and oat fruit can be used as an alternate combination.

❖ Partial baths in moderately warm water with valerian, common balm (or lemon balm), or hops as bath additives: Baths are taken during the afternoon or evening at 36 to 37°C (96.8 to 98.6°F) for 10 minutes.

❖ A hot drink made of chamomile tea and milk (in equal amounts), sweetened with honey: Drink shortly before going to bed.

❖ An herbal sachet with harmonizing lavender or hops strobiles: Place under the pillow as an aid for sleep.

In addition, this tea mixture is good for the nerves and sleep:

Common, or lemon balm, leaves	55.0g
Valerian root	30.0 g
Sweet orange peel	15.0 g

Drink 1 to 2 cups of the warm tea during the day and the evening.

For mild depression, nervous restlessness, exhaustion, and anxiety, try the following:

❖ A brewed tea made with herbage from the common Saint-John's-wort: Drink 2 to 3 cups daily over a period of at least six weeks. Common balm, or lemon balm, leaves may be added to the tea.

❖ Juice or capsules with common Saint-John's-wort: One tablespoon of the juice taken three to four times a day before meals or one to three tablets taken with fluids

Supportive Measures

❖ Water treading in the bathtub

❖ Ablutions of the calves or the lower half of the body

❖ Washing warm feet briefly with cold water or putting on a pair of wet socks: The latter method, developed by Sebastian Kneipp, involves moistening a pair of cotton socks in cold water and putting them on, followed by a pair of woolen socks, shortly before going to bed.

❖ Evening walks (don't eat too much in the evening)

❖ Resolving troubling issues, managing your stress better, having a bed that is orthopedically sound and the proper pil-

BENEFICIAL "BLADDER AND KIDNEY TEAS"

A Medicinal Herbs for Bladder Disorders and Kidney Ailments

s a filtering organ, the most important tasks of the kidneys is clarifying all substances eliminated with the urine, regulating electrolytes, and maintaining water balance. More than 400 gallons of blood flow through the kidneys daily. This blood is filtered and freed from metabolic waste products in the fine ramifications of the kidneys. Damage to the kidneys can lead to dangerous poisoning, urinary tract infections, renal failure, or kidney stones. The possibilities for self-treatment, however, are limited.

Any sensible self-treatment first calls for a proper diagnosis. For illnesses of the bladder or kidneys, however, the layperson is usually underqualified. If you suffer from colicky pains in the region of the kidneys and are thirsty, tired, exhausted, or have a fever with shivers, you should consult a physician as soon as possible.

Nevertheless, "bladder and kidney teas" are legitimate forms of therapy. As a result of an increased circulation in the kidneys, they bring about a greater elimination of water. By thoroughly rinsing the pelvis of the kidney and the efferent urinary passages, as well as by washing out the urinary gravel, they may hinder the development of stones. These teas also demonstrate antibacterial and spasmolytic effects to some extent. An increase in the production of urine is often desired and sensible, especially in the elderly. But for such a washing-out therapy to work, it is necessary to drink an adequate amount of tea (4 to 5 cups a day). Therefore, it's important for bladder and kidney teas to be palatable.

Herbs for Self-Treatment

Especially the stinging nettle and the leaves of the European white birch, as well as the root and herbage of the **dandelion** (55), bring about this desired increase in renal activity. Although both Sebastian Kneipp and the general public have held the **stinging nettle** (120) in high regard, it plays more of a subordinate role in herbal therapy textbooks. However,

because of its flavonoids, salicylic acid, potassium, and calcium salts, it has proven to be an effective diuretic, allowing an increased elimination of urea and chlorides. Watery extracts or fresh plant juice from the **European white birch** (294) increase the elimination of urine by more than 50 percent when administered at a relatively low dose.

Whereas the increased urination brought about by the stinging nettle and European white birch leaves, as well as goldenrod and **bean skins** (often mixed with chamomile and peppermint to improve the taste) makes these agents very effective for washing out the urinary tract and as prophylactics against the development of stones, **parsley fruit** and **juniper berries** (300) should not be used in cases of urinary tract illnesses. These herbs are mainly effective for the elimination of water and the purification of healthy organs. A tea made with the leaves of the **bearberry** (37) is the best choice for disinfecting the efferent urinary tract. A warming therapy using "hay sacks" or "hay-flower" and horsetail baths can be used in such cases as supportive measures.

Arbutin is the active agent in bearberry leaves. To make use of this substance's very good disinfectant action on the efferent urinary tract, the following must be taken into consideration: In order for the arbutin to be cleaved into the effective agent hydroquinone, the urine must react as an alkali. You can achieve this by eating large quantities of vegetables and dispensing with meats. But an even easier method is adding a pinch of bicarbonate of soda to the bearberry tea.

Even though bearberry leaves are hardy, the tea should not be cooked for a long period of time, as this would cause it to be enriched with too much of the unpleasant-tasting and gastric-irritating tannins. The best means of preparation is a cold infusion, containing about 80 percent arbutin and only a little tannin. Let the infusion stand for 8 to 10 hours. Drink 4 to 6 cups of this tea daily (using 2 teaspoons of the leaves per cup). This way, the necessary concentration of the active substance can reach the urine. A tea mixture made up of disinfectant bearberry leaves with anti-inflammatory chamomile blossoms and spasmolytic peppermint leaves has also proven to be effective. As soon as the complaints disappear, a follow-up treatment with such diuretic drugs as those found in the stinging nettle, leaves of the European white birch, dandelion, or goldenrod can be administered.

A Few Words About Stones

Motionless bladder or kidney stones are frequently discovered only by chance. "Vagrant" stones, on the other hand, often result in colicky pains that are so unbearable that the sufferers are forced to visit a physician. After the acute colic is over, some patients have benefited from what is known as the "hop cure": After drinking about 2 liters, or quarts, of a diuretic tea (some suggest the use of warm beer instead), you're supposed to hop down the stairs, step by step. Occasionally the stone is set free this way and can leave the body in a natural manner. The root and herbage of the dandelion are especially ascribed as having a prophylactic effect against the enlargement and renewed formation of kidney, bladder, and gallbladder stones. But generally, and especially in the case of elderly people, the best preventive measure is to drink a lot of fluids.

Specific Remedies

As a supportive therapy in the event of inflammations of the bladder in order to increase the amount of urine and improve the voiding of the bladder, a bladder-kidney tea with the following ingredients is helpful:

Horsetail herbage	30.0 g
Goldenrod herbage	25.0 g
European white birch leaves	20.0 g
Roots from the spiny, or thorny, restharrow	10.0 g
Skin of rose hips	5.0 g
Peppermint leaves	5.0 g
Marigold blossoms	5.0 g

Drink 1 cup between meals three to four times a day as an irrigation.

For an initial inflammation of the bladder without a fever, drink a tea made from bearberry leaves, either brewed as a decoction or made as a cold infusion: With the first method, add 1 to 2 teaspoons of the herbage to approximately 150 milliliters (about 5 fluid ounces) of water, cook for 15

minutes, and then strain off the herbage. With the second, place the herbage in cold water and let it stand for several hours. Drink 3 to 4 cups daily. By eating large quantities of vegetables and abstaining from meat or by adding a pinch of bicarbonate of soda to each cup, it can be assured that the urine will be alkaline.

As a follow-up therapy for an inflammation of the urinary tract or as a preventive measure against the development of stones, a tea mixture with the following ingredients is useful: dandelion roots and herbage, horsetail, rose hips, European white birch leaves, Java tea, chamomile blossoms, peppermint leaves, and goldenrod herbage. To wash out the kidneys, drink 1 to 2 liters, or quarts, of this herbal tea daily. Tea mixtures with these drugs are also suitable for the elimination of urinary gravel or stones, after consulting with a physician.

To reduce the pain of colics stemming from bladder or kidney stones, try the following:

❖ Chamomile blossom tea: 1 to 2 cups drunk slowly one sip after another while as hot as possible

❖ Spasmolytic tea mixtures made from chamomile blossoms, peppermint leaves, fennel fruit, coriander fruit, common balm (or lemon balm) leaves, and herbage from the milfoil (or yarrow)

❖ A "hay sack" laid on the lower abdomen or a warm "hayflower" bath (at 38°C, or 99.5°F, for about 10 minutes and followed by bed rest)

Note: The urine that forms during a colic or is eliminated immediately after a colic should be collected and immediately brought to a physician.

Supportive Measures

❖ Take a sitz bath, or hip bath, with "hay flowers" or horsetails twice a week.

❖ Take a footbath of increasing temperature.

❖ Get plenty of bed rest.

❖ Avoid having cold feet.

TROUBLED BY FREQUENT URINATION?
Medicinal Herbs for a Nervous Bladder and Prostate Problems

$\mathcal{M}$any people suffer from a weak bladder or incontinence, although these are subjects rarely discussed. An irritable (or nervous) bladder and prostate problems have a number of causes, some of which are psychovegetative and/or hormonal. Aside from organic factors, an inflammation (for instance, from a cold) can play a role in triggering such conditions.

Before initiating a therapy with medicinal herbs, it's important for the condition to first be diagnosed by a physician. A mildly increased desire to urinate could indicate a benign prostate enlargement, for example. Should this condition be identified, a cure with **stinging nettle** (120) tea or capsules containing stinging nettle extracts can be recommended with good conscience. Replacing a glass of beer with a "medicinal" glass of wine is also suggested. In the event of prostate infections, a physician's treatment can be supplemented by wearing warm clothes, especially below the waist, taking footbaths of increasing temperatures, taking full or sitz baths using **horsetail** extracts or **English lavender** (107) oil, and applying "hay sacks" filled with **"hay flowers"** (221).

For the treatment of a nervous bladder, which entails a frequent desire to urinate without any inflammatory or organic changes, in addition to very warm herbal baths, calming teas and plant capsules containing **garden valerian** (89), **hops** (216), **common,** or **lemon, balm** (242), or **common Saint-John's-wort** (110) are known to help. Saint-John's-wort, together with special attention, is also recommended for bed-wetting in children.

More Helpful Herbs

When the problem becomes more severe, there is a continuous desire and strong stimulus to urinate. An irritable bladder, however, is only a symptom and not an illness in itself. In addition to **sabal,** or **saw, palmetto** (*Sabal serrulata*) extracts, **pumpkin,** or **summer squash** (298), seeds have been proven to be effective for a symptomatic therapy. These seeds are either chewed whole or taken as a granular powder in fluids. Another form that is used is the oil from pumpkin seeds, which is highly concentrated, is neutral in taste, and can be taken in capsules as well.

Pumpkin seeds are helpful for both an irritable bladder in women and the complaints associated with psychoneuroses of the prostate seen in men at a young age or during middle age. The use of pumpkin seeds from a special strain from Asia has been supported by the observation that prostate enlargement is hardly observed at all in some of the Balkan countries, where these seeds are chewed frequently.

Pumpkin seeds contain a fatty oil. Its effect is attributed as coming from beta-sitosterol (the vegetable cholesterol), tocopherols (vitamin E), and the trace elements selenium and magnesium, which are claimed to have a positive effect on the metabolism of the bladder muscles. The strong diuretic effects seen with phytosterol, as well as its indicated antimicrobial properties, help to further corroborate the use of these seeds.

A medicinal plant increasingly being used for a tea to relieve complaints associated with the prostate is **fireweed,** or **small-flowered willow herb** (273). This effect was previously attributed only to hoary willow herb, which contains a substance called sitosterol that has long been used to treat prostate problems. When the sitosterols are resorbed by the gastrointestinal tract, they demonstrate an effect on the inflammatory processes in the prostatic tissues. However, sitosterol has been discovered in the more economical, small-leafed fireweed as well.

Some of the other "antiprostin" teas contain primarily diuretic drugs, as the desire to urinate at night can be reduced by emptying the bladder as much as possible beforehand.

A direct influence on the development of a prostate adenoma (a benign enlargement of the glandular tissues of the prostate) cannot be verified to date, at least not before the sixtieth year of life. In addition, the use of herbal agents has unfortunately not eliminated the need for an operative excision of the adenoma in order to alleviate the disturbed flow of urine. It is also important to point out the need for regular medical checkups in order to rule out the possibility of prostate cancer.

Specific Remedies

In cases of irritation or functional disturbances of the bladder, prostate complaints, or simply to maintain the normal function of the bladder, the following remedies have shown to be helpful:

❖ Pumpkin seeds chewed whole or in the form of a granular powder: Adults take 3 heaping tablespoons daily (approximately 40 grams, or 1½ ounces), with a lot of fluids over a number of weeks.

❖ Pumpkin-seed oil: Three to four capsules of the oil a day (approximately 3 to 4 grams of pumpkin-seed oil per day)

❖ Dry extract from the stinging nettle root: A daily dose of approximately 500 milligrams (½ gram)

❖ Saw palmetto (*Sabal serrulata*) fruit extract: A daily dose of 320 milligrams, usually in the form of one tablet to be taken daily at the same time every day

❖ Combinations from the three herbs above

❖ Beta-sitosterol capsules (derived from the root tuber of the African medicinal plant *Hypoxis rooperi*): A daily dose of 60 milligrams initially, with a long-term therapy of 30 milligrams of beta-sitosterol daily

❖ Capsules with rye-pollen extract: One to two capsules three times a day

❖ Diuretic tea mixtures made from stinging nettle leaves, dandelion herbage and roots, aspen buds, and European white birch leaves are suitable for emptying the bladder fully

before going to bed at night.

In addition, the following two teas are proven palliative agents:

❖ Stinging nettle tea: Add 2 teaspoons of the dry extract from the root to 1 cup of cold water, slowly bring to a simmer, cook for about a minute, and then leave to steep for about 10 minutes. After straining, 3 to 4 cups should be taken daily.

❖ Small-flowered willow herb tea: Brew 2 to 3 teaspoons of the herbage in approximately 150 milliliters (about 5 fluid ounces) of hot water, leave to steep for 10 minutes, and then strain. One cup should be drunk while warm two or three times a day.

The following remedies are useful for *psychoneuroses of the prostate, a nervous bladder, and bed-wetting:*

❖ Tea mixtures from medicinal plants that strengthen the autonomic nervous system: Garden valerian root, common balm (or lemon balm) leaves, hops strobiles, and common Saint-John's-wort (chamomile blossoms and centaury can be added)

❖ Capsules containing a combination of pumpkin-seed oil with dry extracts of the fragrant-sumac bark, leaves from the bearberry, hops strobiles, and the kava-kava root: One to two capsules taken three times a day

Supportive Measures

❖ Partial and full baths with extracts from the horsetail or the milfoil (or yarrow) or with bath oils made from lavender or "hay flowers"

❖ A "hay sack" laid on the lower abdomen

❖ Avoiding drinking liquids in the evening

❖ Keeping sufficiently warm

SELF-TREATMENT FOR "TIRED LEGS"
Medicinal Herbs for Venous Disorders

With venous complaints, a weakness in the walls of the veins that is either inherited or acquired becomes visible after some time as a node- or sack-like dilation of the veins. The walls of the veins lose their elasticity, become overly stretched, and form small tears. The venous valves, whose purpose is to regulate the pressure, can no longer close properly. Metabolic waste products are transported inadequately, and the circulation to the leg as a whole becomes poorer. The small tears heal with the formation of fibrous growths, resulting in the development of varicose veins. Due to this process, which initially is only cosmetically disturbing, the increased pressure in the finer ramifications of the veins can lead to a sensation of tired legs, tingling, itchiness, painful tension, congestion (edema), and, during the last phase, poorly healing ulcers of the leg. Aside from being genetically inherited, varicose veins occur from standing or sitting for long periods of time and through the normal aging processes of the vessels. Characteristic of venous complaints of the leg are overly distended veins as well as congestion and a reduction in the velocity of blood flow.

Prophylactic Measures

It's wise to undertake prophylactic measures at least as soon as the first complaints develop with an increased size of the varicose veins or an inflammation of these structures:

❖ Refrain from standing or sitting for too long, walk or lie down as much as possible, lose weight if necessary, and get enough exercise so that your leg muscles are brought into shape as "venous pumps."

❖ Put your legs up whenever possible—for example, when reading or watching television. Place a rubber-sponge wedge in your bed under your calves.

❖ Take a shower instead of a hot bath, followed by cold affusions over the calves.

❖ Avoid saunas and hot sun.

❖ Help your veins by wearing light, fashionable support stockings. Wear well-fitted compression stockings only after consulting a physician. During the day, these help to hinder the obstruction of blood in the dilated, atonic veins.

❖ Make use of the prophylactic and symptom-relieving effects of medicinal plants.

Herbs for Prevention and Relief

The primary ingredient of nearly all vegetable agents for the veins is an extract from the **horse chestnut** (*Aesculus hippocastanum*) (289). Its main active component, the saponin escin, reduces the number and diameter of the pores in the veins, which inhibits the permeability for fluids and thus hinders the development of edemas. It also has an anti-inflammatory effect and, at the same time, strengthens the walls of the veins. Saponins reduce the surface tension of water, and a froth develops as with soap. This effect is also made use of by the vascular walls. Their ability to become wet is increased, making the drainage of the tissue fluids easier. Extracts from horse chestnut are used in the form of tablets, capsules, and injections. Externally, they are applied in the form of ointments or gels.

Ointments for the veins should not be rubbed in, as this could irritate the unhealthy tissues or even loosen a blood clot. A thin layer applied twice a day is sufficient. Gels have the advantage of having a cooling effect, especially in the summer, and are ideal during an acute stage.

The herbage of **buckwheat** (*Fagopyrum esculentum*), when brewed as a tea, is said to have a favorable effect on venous complaints. Its primary component is rutin, a substance that serves to reduce vascular permeability. An excellent agent against venous obstruction is the blood-flow-promoting and anti-inflammatory component in **mountain arnica** (227) blossom. Sebastian Kneipp regarded this plant highly, saying "Arnica has a reputation as an excellent medicinal plant throughout the world." This claim has since been substantiated in scientific studies.

Used externally, arnica is the agent of choice for strains, contusions, sprains, tired legs, and muscle and joint pains, as well as for the rapid alleviation of hemorrhages (bruises) and for healing wounds. In acute cases, especially in the event of sports injuries, arnica in the form of a tincture is best. Arnica ointment has proven to be most effective for chronic circulatory disturbances, tired legs, and muscle and joint pains.

In the past, arnica was employed internally for cardiac and stomach complaints. However, large amounts taken internally have since been found to result in stomach irritation, diarrhea, and dangerous cardiac conditions.

Remedies

The following remedies are recommended for *venous complaints, swelling, obstructions, and tired and heavy legs:*

❖ Arnica oil mixed with heparin to make an ointment

❖ Arnica tincture diluted with five times as much water for moist wraps or with camphor to make an arnica gel

❖ Extracts from arnica blossoms combined with essential oils, camphor, and menthol to make a cooling fluid to be used in the form of a spray

Arnica ointment is best suited for the long-term therapy of painful venous complaints; arnica gel, because of its cooling effect, is especially effective for hemorrhages, contusions, and sprains, particularly during the warmer times of the year. Both are rubbed in lightly in the morning and during the evening. Arnica fluid is ideal while travelling or during work involving long periods of standing or sitting.

These means of self-treatment are similarly effective:

❖ Ten-minute baths using the extracts of arnica and marigold blossoms in lukewarm water (about 36°C, or 96.8°F), along with a stroking massage: During the bath, the legs are massaged lightly; afterward, cold water is briefly poured over them.

❖ Dry extracts from horse chestnuts in the form of an ointment or a gel, or taken internally in the form of capsules or tablets (a daily dose of about 100 milligrams of escin)

❖ A watery extract from a red domestic grape vine (*Vitis vinifera*) in the form of an ointment or taken internally as capsules or drops (in combination with esculin)

❖ Buckwheat herbage brewed as a tea (1 cup taken three times a day) or in the form of tablets (two tablets taken three times a day)

❖ A mixture of arnica tincture, rosemary oil, and thyme oil combined with alum, citric acid, and tartaric acid used as a compress or a cold wrap (in equal amounts or with five times as much of the latter)

Supportive Measures

❖ Cold affusions of the knees, also including the soles of the feet

❖ Water treading in the bathtub

❖ Elevation of the legs

❖ Supportive stockings, or compressive bandages after consulting a physician

❖ Walking, bicycling, and swimming

❖ Wearing wet socks: This method was developed by Sebastian Kneipp, and it involves putting on a pair of cotton socks moistened with cold water and then putting a pair of woolen socks over them. The socks should be changed when the cotton socks no longer feel cool.

❖ Losing weight

IMPROVING THE QUALITY OF YOUR "SUNSET YEARS"
Medicinal Herbs for Geriatric Complaints

In order to eliminate any false hopes you may have, let me say from the start that there are no plant or chemical agents that can make us younger. More pertinent than the question "How old do you want to get?" is the question "How do you want to get old?" The purpose of this section is to present you with medicinal plants that will help you make the "sunset years" of your life more worth living, more meaningful, and more enjoyable. Getting old is not enough—only if you are in good health and intellectually agile is this stage of life worth striving for.

In line with the motto "Prevention is better than a cure," prophylactic medical measures have become increasingly important components of health care. Many infectious diseases are kept at bay through the use of hygienic measures and as a result of the enormous advances made in medicine. But the application of health education also plays a role. Through health education, we learn about proper nutrition, various forms of exercise, the avoidance of risk factors, balancing the physical and mental aspects of ourselves, and maintaining a positive outlook on life.

Important Geriatric Agents

The average life expectancy is substantially longer today, so there are more older people in the population who are in need of health care. In this time of explosive health costs, it is thus surprising to see that the application of economical plant remedies and prophylactic agents continues to be regarded with some skepticism. But a number of herbal agents from previous sections are well worth remembering:

❖ **Whitethorn** (109, 297) and **rosemary** (44) offer mild support for the heart and the circulatory system.

❖ Bitter drugs such as **absinth sagewort,** or **common wormwood** (293), **yellow gentian** (238), and **centaury** (295) stimulate the secretion of the gastric juices.

❖ **Common peppermint** (257) and **dandelion** (55) increase the flow of bile and alleviate biliary obstructions.

❖ The **purple coneflower** (249) as well as plants containing thuja and bitter principles serve to stimulate the defense mechanisms.

❖ Dietary fibers and swelling substances stimulate the action of the intestines.

❖ Mucilaginous, disinfectant, and expectorant agents—for example, **hollow mallow** (84), **thyme** (259), and **cowslip** (6)—are important for the respiratory system.

❖ **Garlic** (225) and fish oil reduce the blood-lipid levels, providing protection against the development of arteriosclerosis and myocardial infarction.

❖ Aloe, **pot marigold,** or **calendula** (196), witch hazel, and **common Saint-John's-wort** (110) provide care for aging skin and give the skin moisture.

❖ **Pumpkin** (298) seeds, **stinging nettle** (120), and the sabal, or saw, palmetto relieve initial prostate complaints.

❖ **Mountain arnica** (227) and **horse chestnuts** (289) tone damaged and endangered veins.

❖ **Bearberry** (37) leaves, **stinging nettle** (120), and leaves from the **European white birch** (294) disinfect and wash out the kidneys and bladder, which may be in danger of developing stones.

❖ **Garden valerian** (89), **hops** (216), and **common balm,** or **lemon balm** (242), counteract stress factors and allow for a natural, restful sleep.

All of these medicinal plants are "geriatric agents" in the broadest sense of the term, as they alleviate complaints often associated with growing older and are preventive as well. They are not agents against aging but rather agents against common illnesses that occur while aging, as are sensible vitamin and mineral supplements.

It's very important that measures for the maintenance of physical health and mental alertness be initiated on a healthy organism. Therefore, they are best begun before reaching sixty years of age.

More Herbs for Aging

Aside from the medicinal plants already mentioned, some other herbs are known to be especially good for us as we advance in age, including **ginseng.** Native to China, ginseng is one of the oldest medicinal plants of Asia and is primarily cultivated in Korea today. Holding a place in many legends, it has long been linked with increased longevity. The roots in particular, with their humanlike form, were praised as a wonder drug against everyday ailments. These roots have also been associated with having luck and sexual stamina. Because of all these attributes, ginseng has been in great demand and in some places was even more valuable than gold. But all of the active components haven't been isolated yet, nor have all the effects been studied. However, we do know that with ginseng, as with many medicinal plants, all of the components taken as a whole appear to offer more than the sum of the individual parts.

The scientific studies conducted thus far have shown that ginseng

❖ improves the defensive powers of the body against a multitude of new environmental factors,

❖ normalizes altered bodily functions (for example, the lipid metabolism),

❖ strengthens and tones the body,

❖ elevates the function of the brain,

❖ helps the organism handle stress better, and

❖ has a mood-elevating effect.

In order for these verified effects to manifest, 1 to 2 grams of the root or 200 to 400 milligrams of the extract need to be taken. There are as many different products of ginseng as there are various levels of its quality. What is recommended is the quality-controlled, medicinal *Panax Ginseng Meyer,* taken in the form of a tincture, extract, capsules, or tablets.

Similar effects are ascribed to what is known as **Siberian ginseng** (*Eleutherococcus senticosus*). Also called the "taiga root," it has been used by the Russians since the Second World War as a substitute for the real ginseng root that was not available in adequate quantities at that time.

Headaches, ringing in the ears, poor concentration, and other complaints may be the result of diminished blood flow to the brain. In this instance, the active components of the Asian **maidenhair tree,** or **ginkgo** (232), have proven to be effective. The contents of the ginkgo leaf extract (ginkgo flavone glycosides and diterpenes, called "ginkgolides"), known as GBE (Ginkgo biloba extract), dilate and relax the blood vessels, protect their cell membranes, and improve the flow characteristics of the blood. GBE thus results in improved circulation and oxygen supply in the tissues and the brain, as well as a slight reduction in blood pressure. As this extract is beneficial for general cardiovascular health, it enhances overall health and well-being. What's more, GBE has been found to counteract memory loss and depression. The scientifically verified effects and harmlessness of the standardized monoextract from ginkgo leaves, however, is dependent on this pharmacological quality and its unchanging composition.

Remedies

Although exaggerated claims have been made for some geriatric agents, a number of their effects have been verified scientifically. However, increased longevity is not among them, not even for ginseng, despite its reputation for prolonging life. The maximum life expectancy for humans, which is approximately 100 years, cannot at present be extended further. Nevertheless, hygiene, nutrition, exercise, occupation, and social situation, as well as medications, do have a bearing on reducing the rate of aging and on making the age reached more worth living.

The recommendations *for illnesses that occur with aging* can be taken from previous sections. In addition to them, various herbal remedies are presented here that serve to prevent or alleviate *conditions associated with old age.* Before using them in the course of self-treatment, however, it's important to consult your physician to be sure that the symptoms you are experiencing are not the result of a particular illness that may require a specific therapy.

In cases of impaired memory, poor concentration, dizziness, ringing in the ears, or circulatory problems, ginkgo leaves have been found to be effective. The suggested daily dose is 120 to 240 milligrams of dry extract (or one or two tablets or 20 to 40 drops) taken three times a day for at least eight weeks.

In cases of lethargy and a feeling of weakness, for reduced physical powers and powers of concentration, and during recuperative phases, a number of remedies are recommended:

❖ Ginseng root in the form of capsules, a tonic, or a tea: Take 1 to 2 tablespoons (200 to 400 milligrams) of the extract twice a day or two capsules three times a day. As a cure, ginseng needs to be taken for at least three months. But it should not be used in cases of hypertension or arteriosclerosis.

❖ Siberian ginseng ("taiga root") as a tonic or in capsules: Take 1 tablespoon or one capsule three times a day for two to five weeks (the daily dose is approximately 200 milligrams of the extract). During a cure of five weeks, there should be one break after two to three weeks. This remedy should not be used in cases of hypertension, following myocardial infarctions, or during infectious illnesses.

❖ Bitter drugs for strengthening the defense system in the form of a tea or a tonic: Use yellow gentian root, herbage from the absinth sagewort, the centaury, the bark of the condurango, or the peel of the Seville, or bitter, orange.

❖ Plant juice from the sea buckthorn or red-beet juice

For anxiety, mild depression, and restlessness, these two herbs have proven to be helpful:

❖ Saint-John's-wort, taken as a plant juice, a brewed tea, or in capsules

❖ Kava-kava (*Piper methysticum*), the dry extract from the root taken in tablets or capsules (a daily dose of 60 to 120 milligrams of kavapyrones)

The following are *preventive measures you can use against the development of arteriosclerosis, to reduce the blood-lipid level:*

❖ Cultivated garlic in the form of tablets, oil capsules, and plant juice

❖ Lecithin from soybeans or corn in the form of a granular powder, chewable tablets, or a tonic

Supportive Measures

❖ Partial baths with contrasting temperatures, sunbathing, and dry-brush massages

❖ Aromatherapy to combat tiredness and restore vitality, increase powers of concentration, and lift the spirits (rosemary, lavender, thyme, and sweet basil oils, for example)

❖ Gymnastics, breathing exercises, climbing stairs, and swimming

❖ Adequate fluid intake: a minimum of 2 liters, or quarts, a day

❖ Sufficient vitamins, trace elements, and minerals (especially calcium, magnesium, and potassium)

❖ Proper nutrition that takes any metabolic disturbances into account, such as diabetes, gout, or high-blood-lipid levels

❖ Staying involved in life and taking on intellectually challenging pursuits

CHILDREN ARE NOT "LITTLE ADULTS"
Medicinal Herbs for Babies and Children

*S*ebastian Kneipp had a special feeling for children. In 1893, with a large donation, he helped to erect a hospital for poor, sick children in Bad Wörishofen. This remained his favorite endowment, and he took a walk to this institution daily. Playing and talking with the children was his form of relaxation. Today, mothers and their children still recuperate there with the aid of a bathing department equipped with both large and small bathtubs. Of course, a Kneipp cure is no longer used to treat children suffering from tuberculosis. The emphasis these days is to teach people at an early age the importance of a health-conscious way of living. This has also been recognized by the Kneipp Society. As a large health organization, it has successfully initiated the Kneipp health agenda in many kindergarten programs under the motto of making "the children of today into the health-conscious adults of tomorrow."

Children follow many of the principles of the Kneipp philosophy instinctively. They are in constant movement and love to play with water. What is more difficult, however, is getting them to have a breakfast consisting of fruit, whole-grain cereal, and herbal tea instead of the sweet baked goods and soft drinks many of them favor.

In the past, the mother in the family sometimes took on the role of the "therapist," administering many old home remedies—for example, cold, wet compress wrapped around the calves in the event of a fever or a hot-lard cloth placed on the chest during a cold. Unfortunately, many adults today have forgotten these natural methods. But they should be brought back into use, primarily because they encourage the powers of spontaneous healing, which are especially pronounced in children.

When medication is used to support these powers of spontaneous healing, we must bear in mind that children are not "little adults." Side effects are often quite varied, and the dose must be determined individually. Therefore, milder forms of medication are usually recommended in the form of herbal syrups, bath additives, ointments, and inhalants. In addition,

for children it is especially important for the cause of the symptoms to be determined by a physician.

Recommendations for a Range of Common Childhood Ailments

The comforting effects of medicinal plants are seen foremost in skin care. **Chamomile** (105) applications in the form of ointments, bath additives, powder, washes, or poultices are ideal for the care of the sensitive skin of a child. They have antibacterial, anti-inflammatory, and wound-healing effects when used to treat abrasions, contusions, injuries, or diaper dermatitis. The pot marigold, or calendula, arnica, or witch hazel ointments are similarly effective. The astringent effects of the hamamelis-gallic acid cause the development of a sort of protective layer.

Dry, itchy skin is typical of atopic dermatitis (neurodermatitis), diaper rash, and eczema resulting from clothing, as well as of psoriasis. Baths or showers using soybean oil or almond-blossom oil help to restore the fats in the skin, whereas bran or whey as a bath additive serves to reduce the irritation. Patients suffering from neurodermatitis often demonstrate a lack of polyunsaturated fatty acids. These can be supplied through the administration of **common borage** (252) oil or **evening primrose** (241) oil. Both of these oils contain a high concentration of gamma linolenic acid. The external application of evening primrose oil in the form of bath additives or skin oils has also demonstrated very beneficial effects.

Healthy children like to explore their environment, so it's often impossible to avoid some bruises, contusions, and minor burns. After you've cleaned them with water, the application of a sterile gauze bandage soaked in **Saint-John's-wort** (110) oil can be a helpful follow-up measure. This dressing should be changed after 10 hours.

Occasionally, bacteria, viruses, or fungi cause children some disturbances. A herpes infection of the lips is effectively treated with an ointment containing a dry extract from **com-**

mon balm, or **lemon balm** (242). An oral candidiasis, or thrush of the mouth, improves following rinses with a mixture of chamomile tea together with tinctures of myrrh and ratanhia. Warts are more difficult to combat, as they are sometimes the result of a psychosomatic problem. Tenacious, daily swabbing with a solution of thuja extract, juice from the greater celandine, or castor bean oil often allows warts to fall off with their roots after four to six weeks.

Children bring colds home from school a number of times a year. When it comes to colds, the same agents are effective for children as those used for adults. Cold balms or baths containing menthol, however, should never be used, as they may suppress the breathing in babies and small children. Convulsive attacks of coughing and the accompanying obstruction of respiratory secretions (for example, in the case of whooping cough) can be treated effectively with extracts derived from ivy leaves, the round-leafed sundew, or dew plant (*Drosera rotundifolia*), or the herbage of garden thyme. A warm wrap around the chest pleasantly strengthens the effects of the cold balm. Mustard wraps in children can be applied using only the milder white mustard and only for a maximum of 5 minutes. Hot elderberry juice or hot lemon juice with honey are proven home remedies for the treatment of coughs in children. Cooling wraps with curd help to relieve a sore throat. Because a fever is a natural defense mechanism of the body, it should not be reduced with medications unless it goes above 39°C (102.2°F). A temperature can be lowered very reliably with cold, wet compresses wrapped around the calves that are changed every 10 minutes. Plant immunostimulants should not be administered for longer than four days in children (twice a day).

Eating too much (especially when it comes to French fries, soft drinks, and sweets) and too quickly often cause children to have a stomachache. Other likely culprits are infections and stress. What's usually best for children in such cases are chamomile blossoms, peppermint leaves, and leaves from the common balm, or lemon balm. The cause of the stomachache, however, should always be clarified by a physician. Griping pains in babies' stomachs frequently turn their parents' night into a martyrdom. Fennel tea in the bottle and a light massage of the stomach with the application of "wind ointments" containing anise, caraway, true marjoram, and

sweet basil oils are known to help. When a nursing mother drinks caraway tea, this often proves to be indirectly soothing for the infant.

Diarrhea can become a life-threatening situation in babies and small children because of the high loss of fluids and minerals. The best advice is therefore to drink large quantities of fluids. A black tea, which has steeped for at least 15 minutes in order to release the binding tannins, is very suitable for this purpose. It also helps if a small amount of dextrose or a pinch of table salt is added to the tea. In addition, the child can be given a banana (with its high concentration of potassium) or a freshly grated apple. If the opposite effect is desired (meaning in cases of constipation), lactose is added to the bottle. In older children, the gastrointestinal system can be brought back into shape naturally with the aid of figs, soaked plums, or sauerkraut.

Swimming, wet clothes, drinking fluids that are too cold, or sweating may easily cause children to acquire urinary tract infections. In order to avoid the development of chronic renal damage, urinary tract infections should be treated by a physician. However, in cases of bed-wetting, **pumpkin** (257) seeds have been proven to strengthen the bladder. Because this condition may have a psychological basis, as with conflicts at home or in school, the elimination of overstimulation and the reduction of stress can help, along with a tea mixture made from the root of the garden valerian, hops strobiles, and Saint-John's-wort.

Nature is not always harmless. Children have been known to inadvertently swallow all kinds of dangerous substances, from a liquid dish-washing detergent with a lemon aroma to berries from the deadly nightshade plant. Clarifying what should not be put in the mouth is always the best preventive measure. But in cases when it's too late or the child has ignored your warning, it is important that you, first of all, remain calm. Take the suspected bottle or plant with you to a physician immediately. Unsuitable and even possibly dangerous emergency measures include the administration of a saline solution or milk. The ingestion of large amounts of water or activated charcoal tablets, on the other hand, may prove to be advisable. In addition, it's a good idea to have the phone number of the nearest poison information center, although it is hoped you will never need it.

BATHE YOURSELF TO HEALTH
Medicinal Herbs as Bath Additives

Of course, baths are initially for the purpose of cleaning. This is carried out with clear water, with the addition of soap or lathering aids. The next step is more cosmetic. Pleasant aromas and lovely colors achieve a sense of well-being and relaxation, whereas oil-restoring bath additives take care of the skin. A medicinal bath, finally, entails the age-old tradition of using herbs and their extracts for curative purposes.

The use of medicinal plants as bath additives became popular through Sebastian Kneipp. In *My Water Cure* (1897), he said, "I almost never use warm water alone in baths. I always mix in extracts from various medicinal plants." Although some people espouse bathing in cold water, Kneipp emphasized the use of warm water, together with herbal bath additives. "I can only praise the virtues of herbs in a bath," he said in *My Testament*. Herbs not only make for a relaxing bath but, when selected properly and applied correctly, are also an effective aid against everyday complaints.

The aroma of the herbs during the bath may alone bring about a substantial change in one's state of mind. This is primarily why aromatherapy has become so popular. A person's psychological state is a crucial factor during a cure. As colors can also influence our frame of mind, a spruce needle bath, which is initially colorless, is colored green, a rosemary bath is red in color, and a lavender bath is blue. All these colors are brought about through the use of harmless food-coloring agents.

Inhaling the volatile oils from such herbs as thyme, linden (or lime) blossoms, or chamomile, which are transported along with the steam during a bath, has similar disinfectant and anti-inflammatory effects to those from head steam baths (in which herbs are inhaled with the steam with a towel draped over the head).

During the bath, the essential oils penetrate directly through the skin and become a part of the organism.

The bath additives used today are the result of a series of developments that were begun by Father Kneipp, who said, "I have cured more with herbs than with water." These are Kneipp's instructions for a **hay-flower** (221–224) bath from *My Water Cure:* "A small sachet filled with hay flowers is placed into a kettle of boiling water and remains in this extraction for at least a half hour. The entire decoction is poured into a prepared bath." However, these decoctions were not only complicated and difficult to preserve but also discolored the skin and the bathtub, so wooden bathtubs began to be used for such purposes.

During the 1940s, already-prepared, viscous, full extracts were developed in liquid form. But their standardization, preservation, solubility, syrupy consistency, and cloudy appearance in the bathwater made their use problematic.

Bath additives containing tannins and salicylic acids, like oak bark, oat-straw, horsetail, and calamus (or sweet flag), and clay baths are still available in this form. The development of modern cleaning agents and high-grade steel bathtubs, however, has provided a solution to the problems of hygiene and cleaning.

Realizing that "clean" essential oils are responsible for the function of many of these herbal agents, bath additives are produced without any inert materials. Such bath additives demonstrate the following advantages:

❖ They are pure and highly concentrated.
❖ Accurate dosages can be made.
❖ Being germicidal in themselves, they are nonperishable without the aid of any preservatives.

Kinds of Bath Additive

There are basically two skin types: greasy, usually seen in younger people, and dry, observed more as we grow older. As a result, different kinds of modern bath additives have been developed that can be categorized as either bath oils or bath salts.

Bath oils are naturally most suitable for individuals with dry skin. Containing 40 percent aromatic essential oils (for example, common, or lemon, balm, rosemary, chamomile, and spruce needle oils) as their effective agent, bath oils are bound to emulsifying agents that don't irritate the skin. As a result of these agents, the mixtures are distributed throughout the bathwater and even penetrate through the skin more easily. Oil-restoring additives and natural oils (such as soybean, avocado, peanut, jojoba, and almond oil) provide skin care and help to restore the oils of the skin that may be removed as a result of the bath. For very dry skin, there are bath additives that contain only fatty oils and emulsifiers.

Another option for very dry, scaly, or chapped skin are bath oils that don't become distributed throughout the bathwater. These oils form a very thin film on the water surface as well as on the skin, and can be massaged into the skin after the bath.

If you tend to have greasy skin, **bath salts** are probably your best alternative. Natural mineral salts come prepared today and are easily dissolved in the bathwater. They relieve the discomfort of minor aches and pains, relax tired muscles, and refresh the body. In addition, a bath with natural mineral salts taken before you go to bed promotes a restful, sound sleep.

Adding salt to baths has been a common practice since the advent of Kneipp cures. The basic salt is a readily soluble, coarse-grained table salt of food quality. This salt is distinguished through its lovely crystallization and large surface area—a feature that permits the binding of essential oils. The effects of the saline, which serve to mildly swell the skin, are supported by the essential oils, as they are also made water-soluble through the emulsifiers. About 100 grams of salt (about 3½ ounces) are added to each full bath, so that the bathwater has about a third the saline concentration of the sea. Saline baths with increasing salt concentration have demonstrated remarkable effects on the skin when used as a therapy for allergic reactions or as a supportive measure in the treatment of psoriasis.

Bathing Correctly

For a bath cure performed at home to be effective, it's important to note the following points:

❖ You should bathe for a maximum of 10 to 15 minutes.

❖ The water temperature should generally be between 37 and 40°C (98.6 and 104°F).

❖ Sleep-inducing, relaxing baths should be a little cooler (36 to 37°C, or 96.8 to 98.6°F), whereas baths for rheumatic disorders and colds should be slightly warmer (39 to 40°C, or 102.2 to 104°F).

❖ Baths that are too hot put a strain on the circulatory system. In the event of cardiac insufficiency, only partial baths or sitz baths are recommended. Be careful in cases of afflictions involving the veins, and don't bathe if you have a fever!

❖ The temperature in the bathroom should be comfortable. The circulatory system can be stimulated by taking a cold shower after the bath. But don't go into a cool room immediately afterward. Allow your skin, which is "tired" after a bath, to regenerate with the aid of an oil-restoring and moisturizing skin cream. See to it that the skin, which may have become alkaline as a result of soap, regains its protective acidic layer by applying the appropriate lotion or cream. It's not uncommon for people to think they have an itchy allergy when their skin is merely too dry.

If you follow these recommendations, you will feel revived from a cure in your own "home spa"!

HERBAL BATH ADDITIVES

Extracts or essential or fatty oils from:	Effects	Indications
Bran	Anti-inflammatory, antipruritic (relieving itching)	Allergies, skin care, eczema, wound treatment
Chamomile	Anti-inflammatory, skin care, wound healing	Wound treatment, eczema, skin care, inflammation of the mucous membranes
Clay	Anti-inflammatory, blood-flow stimulating	Rheumatism, gout, sports injuries
Common balm, or lemon balm	Calming, relaxing	Nervousness, stress, insomnia
Common juniper	Blood-flow stimulating	Rheumatism, muscular tension, sports injuries
Common valerian	Calming	Insomnia, nervousness
Eucalyptus	Disinfectant, secretolytic	Colds, coughs, runny nose
Evening primrose	Fat-restoring, skin care	Dry eczema, neurodermatitis
Hay flowers	Metabolically stimulating	Rheumatism, damaged intervertebral disks, sciatica, physical exhaustion
Hops	Calming, blood-flow stimulating	Insomnia, nervousness
Horsetail	Astringent, wound healing	Wound treatment, burns, decubitus (pressure sores)
Lavender	Relaxing, tonicizing, refreshing	Fatigue, nervousness, itching, rheumatism
Oak bark	Astringent	Eczema, cold injuries, hemorrhoids
Oat straw	Anti-inflammatory	Skin ailments
Orange/linden blossoms	Compensatory, harmonizing	Nervousness, stress, fatigue
Rosemary	Invigorating, blood-flow stimulating, increase in blood pressure	Low blood pressure, weakness of the heart or circulatory system
Soybean	Fat-restoring, skin care	Dry eczema, neurodermatitis
Spruce needles/mountain pine	Invigorating, disinfectant, blood-flow stimulating, respiratory tract relief	Colds, fatigue
Thyme	Disinfectant, expectorant, spasmolytic	Colds, coughs, bronchitis

GUIDE TO APPROXIMATE EQUIVALENTS

CUSTOMARY				METRIC
Ounces/Pounds	**Cups**	**Tablespoons**	**Teaspoons**	**Grams/Kilograms**
			¼ t.	1.25 g
			½ t.	2.5 g
			1 t.	5 g
			2 t.	10 g
½ oz.		1 T.	3 t.	15 g
1 oz.		2 T.	6 t.	30 g
2 oz.	¼ c.	4 T.	12 t.	60 g
4 oz.	½ c.	8 T.	24 t.	120 g
8 oz.	1 c.	16 T.	48 t.	240 g
1 lb.	2 c.			480 g
2 lb.	4 c.			
2.2 lb.				1 kg

Please keep in mind that these are not precise conversions, but generally may be used in measuring herbs.